A.A. Castor

MASTERING

THE

ART OF CULT LEADERSHIP

HOW TO RECRUIT, DOMINATE, AND PROFIT

Mastering the Art of Cult Leadership: How to Recruit, Dominate, and Profit

A.A. Castor

Dedication

To my beloved family,

Your unconditional love, unwavering support, and endless encouragement have been my greatest blessings. From the earliest days of dreaming to the challenging moments of writing, you have stood by me with patience and belief. This book is as much yours as it is mine, a reflection of the values you've instilled and the faith you've shown in me. Thank you for being my rock and my inspiration.

To my dear friends,

Your friendship has illuminated my path with laughter, shared moments, and invaluable support. You've cheered me on through every triumph and lifted me up through every challenge. Your belief in my endeavors has been a source of strength and motivation. This book is a testament to the power of friendship, and I am grateful for each of you who has walked this journey by my side.

To God,

Your grace and guidance have been my constant companions. In moments of doubt, you've shown me the way; in moments of joy, you've multiplied my gratitude. This book is a testament to your faithfulness and the blessings you've bestowed upon me. May it serve as a reflection of your love and the lessons you continue to teach me.

With heartfelt gratitude and love,

A.A. Castor

Motivation and Inspiration for Writing This Book

My Journey to Awareness

For as long as I can remember, I've been fascinated by the complexities of human behavior and the power dynamics that shape our societies. This fascination led me on a journey through various fields of study, from psychology and sociology to religious studies and history. However, it wasn't until a close friend of mine fell victim to a manipulative cult that my academic interest turned into a personal mission.

A Friend in Crisis

It started innocently enough. My friend, whom I'll call Laura, was going through a difficult period in her life. She had recently lost her job and was struggling with a sense of purposelessness. During this vulnerable time, she was introduced to a group that seemed to offer the support and direction she desperately needed. The group's charismatic leader promised spiritual enlightenment, a close-knit community, and a path to personal fulfillment.

At first, Laura was overjoyed. She quickly became deeply involved, attending meetings and participating in rituals. However, as time went on, I noticed troubling changes in her behavior. She became increasingly isolated from her family and friends, and her once independent spirit was replaced by an unquestioning loyalty to the group's leader. Laura's savings dwindled as she made substantial financial contributions to the cult, believing that she was investing in her spiritual growth.

A Wake-Up Call

Seeing my friend transform into a shadow of her former self was a wake-up call. I began researching cults in depth, uncovering the psychological manipulation techniques they use to control their members. The more I learned, the more I realized how widespread and insidious these groups are. Vulnerable individuals, like Laura, are often targeted during their weakest moments, leading to devastating emotional, financial, and psychological consequences.

The Purpose of This Book

This book is a result of my quest to understand the mechanics of cults and their impact on individuals and society. My aim is to equip readers with the knowledge and tools needed to recognize and resist the tactics employed by these manipulative groups. By understanding the methods cults use to recruit and control their members, we can better protect ourselves and our loved ones from falling prey to their influence.

Empowering the Vulnerable

One of the primary goals of this book is to empower those who may be vulnerable to cult recruitment. Whether you're experiencing a personal crisis, searching for a sense of belonging, or simply curious about alternative belief systems, this book will help you navigate the complex landscape of modern spirituality and community groups. Through detailed explanations, real-life examples, and practical advice, I aim to provide a comprehensive guide to identifying and avoiding dangerous cults.

Raising Awareness

Another crucial aspect of this book is raising awareness about the prevalence and tactics of cults. Many people underestimate the sophisticated psychological strategies these groups employ to ensnare their members. By bringing these techniques to light, I hope to foster a greater understanding of the signs and red flags that indicate a group might be a cult. Increased awareness can lead to more informed decisions and, ultimately, fewer victims.

A Personal Mission

Writing this book is not just an academic exercise for me; it is a deeply personal mission. I've seen firsthand the damage that cults can inflict on individuals and their families. My hope is that by sharing my research and insights, I can prevent others from experiencing the same pain and loss that Laura and her loved ones endured.

A Call to Action

In conclusion, this book is a call to action. It is a plea for vigilance, critical thinking, and compassion. We must look out for one another, especially those who are vulnerable, and ensure that we all have the tools needed to protect ourselves from those who would exploit our fears and desires for their gain. Together, we can build a more informed and resilient society, capable of resisting the lure of destructive cults and fostering genuine, supportive communities instead.

Thank you for joining me on this journey. Let us empower ourselves with knowledge and use it to safeguard our minds, our hearts, and our communities from those who seek to exploit them.

Warning and Disclaimer

Introduction

This content is intended for educational and informational purposes only. It is designed to provide a comprehensive understanding of the dynamics and methodologies used in cult leadership and management. The following warning and disclaimer outline the intended use and limitations of this material.

Warning

1. **Potential Misuse**: The information contained in this content can be misused if applied with malicious intent. The techniques and strategies discussed are powerful tools that can influence and control individuals. Use this information responsibly and ethically.
2. **Psychological Impact**: The psychological and emotional techniques described can have profound effects on individuals. Applying these methods without proper understanding and ethical considerations can lead to significant psychological harm.
3. **Legal Consequences**: Many of the practices discussed may violate local, national, or international laws. Engaging in illegal activities, including fraud, coercion, or abuse, can result in severe legal consequences, including criminal charges and imprisonment.
4. **Ethical Considerations**: The use of manipulative techniques to control and influence others raises serious ethical concerns. It is crucial to consider the moral implications of using such methods and to prioritize the well-being and autonomy of individuals.

Disclaimer

1. **Educational Purpose**: This content is provided for educational purposes only. It is not intended to promote or endorse the formation or management of cults, or the use of manipulative or coercive practices.
2. **No Professional Advice**: The information provided is not a substitute for professional advice. Readers should seek professional guidance in psychological, legal, and ethical matters.
3. **Accuracy of Information**: While every effort has been made to ensure the accuracy of the information presented, the author makes no guarantees regarding its completeness or suitability for any particular purpose. The reader assumes full responsibility for any actions taken based on the information provided.
4. **No Liability**: The author and publisher disclaim any liability for any direct, indirect, or consequential loss or damage incurred by any person using the information contained in this content. The reader assumes all risk for any actions taken based on the content.
5. **Changes to Content**: The author reserves the right to update or change the content at any time without notice. It is the reader's responsibility to ensure they are using the most current version of the material.

Responsible Use

1. **Promote Positive Influence**: Use the information to promote positive and ethical leadership practices. Focus on creating supportive, inclusive, and empowering communities that respect individual rights and foster personal growth.
2. **Seek Ethical Guidance**: Consult with ethical and legal professionals when implementing any strategies that involve influencing or managing others. Ensure that all practices comply with legal standards and ethical guidelines.
3. **Prioritize Well-being**: Always prioritize the mental, emotional, and physical well-being of individuals. Avoid using any techniques that could cause harm or distress.

Conclusion

The material provided in this content is intended to offer a deep understanding of cult dynamics and leadership. However, it is critical to approach this knowledge with a strong ethical framework and a commitment to positive and responsible use. The warning and disclaimer serve to highlight the potential risks and ethical considerations associated with this information, emphasizing the importance of responsible and lawful application.

About the Author

A.A. Castor

A.A. Castor is a seasoned expert in organizational leadership and strategic influence, known for his profound understanding of the psychological and sociopolitical dynamics that drive successful cult leadership. With a background in Political Science and Organizational Leadership, Castor has dedicated his career to studying the methods and strategies that leaders use to recruit, dominate, and profit from their followers.

In "Mastering the Art of Cult Leadership: How to Recruit, Dominate, and Profit," Castor shares his extensive knowledge and insights, providing a comprehensive guide for aspiring leaders. His work delves into the intricacies of building a loyal following, maintaining control, and leveraging influence to achieve organizational goals. Castor's unique perspective and practical advice make this book an essential read for anyone looking to understand or engage in the art of cult leadership.

Purpose of the Book

Introduction

The purpose of this book is to provide an in-depth analysis of the techniques and strategies used in cult leadership and management. While this subject matter can be controversial and sensitive, understanding these dynamics is crucial for various reasons. This book aims to educate readers on the mechanisms behind cults, offer insights into their operation, and highlight the psychological, social, and ethical implications involved.

Education and Awareness

1. **Understanding Cult Dynamics**: This book delves into the inner workings of cults, exploring how they attract, manage, and retain members. By shedding light on these mechanisms, readers can gain a comprehensive understanding of how cults operate.
2. **Psychological Insights**: The book examines the psychological techniques used by cult leaders to influence and control followers. This knowledge can help readers recognize these tactics and understand their impact on individuals.
3. **Social Implications**: Cults can have profound effects on individuals and communities. This book explores these social dynamics, providing insights into the broader societal impact of cult activities.

Prevention and Protection

1. **Identifying Red Flags**: By understanding the methods used by cults, readers can learn to identify warning signs and red flags. This awareness can help prevent individuals from being drawn into harmful groups.
2. **Protecting Vulnerable Individuals**: The book aims to equip readers with the knowledge to protect themselves and others, especially those who may be vulnerable to cult recruitment tactics. Understanding these tactics can empower individuals to make informed decisions.
3. **Intervention Strategies**: For those who work in mental health, law enforcement, or community support roles, this book offers valuable insights into intervention strategies. It can help professionals develop effective approaches to support individuals affected by cults.

Ethical Reflection and Responsibility

1. **Ethical Considerations**: The book emphasizes the ethical implications of using psychological and manipulative techniques. It encourages readers to reflect on the morality of these practices and consider the importance of ethical leadership.
2. **Promoting Positive Influence**: While the book examines potentially harmful tactics, it also advocates for the use of influence and leadership in positive, ethical ways. Readers are encouraged to apply this knowledge to foster supportive, empowering, and respectful communities.

Personal and Professional Development

1. **Leadership Skills**: By studying the methods used by cult leaders, readers can gain insights into effective leadership and influence techniques. This knowledge can be applied in various professional and personal contexts to improve leadership skills.
2. **Critical Thinking**: The book promotes critical thinking and skepticism, encouraging readers to question and analyze the information presented to them. This skill is valuable in all areas of life, helping individuals make informed decisions.
3. **Resilience Building**: Understanding the psychological manipulation techniques used by cults can help individuals build resilience against such tactics. This knowledge fosters mental and emotional strength, enabling readers to resist undue influence.

Conclusion

The purpose of this book is multifaceted, aiming to educate, protect, and empower readers. By providing a detailed exploration of cult dynamics, psychological tactics, and ethical considerations, the book seeks to foster a deeper understanding of these complex phenomena. Ultimately, the goal is to equip readers with the knowledge and skills to recognize, resist, and counteract manipulative influences, promoting a safer and more informed society.

TABLE OF CONTENTS

Chapter 1: The Power of Cults

Understanding the Appeal of Cults

Cults have an almost magnetic allure that has drawn people throughout history. To truly harness the power of a cult, it is crucial to understand why people are drawn to them:

1. **Sense of Belonging**:
   - **Isolation in Modern Society**: Many individuals feel disconnected or isolated in the complexities of modern society. Cults offer a close-knit community where members feel valued and included. This sense of belonging can be a powerful motivator for joining and staying in a cult.
   - **Family-Like Atmosphere**: Cults often mimic the structure of a family, providing emotional support and a sense of security that members may lack in their personal lives.
   - **Shared Identity**: Being part of a cult provides members with a shared identity and purpose, reinforcing their sense of belonging through collective experiences and rituals.
2. **Certainty and Simplicity**:
   - **Clarity in Chaos**: Life can be chaotic and overwhelming. Cults often provide clear, simple answers to complex questions about existence, morality, and purpose. This clarity is incredibly appealing to those seeking direction.
   - **Doctrine and Dogma**: Cults offer structured belief systems that simplify the world into black-and-white terms, reducing the cognitive load on members and offering a reassuring sense of certainty.
   - **Predictability**: The routine and predictability of cult activities provide a stable environment, helping members feel more secure in their daily lives.
3. **Promise of Transformation**:
   - **Personal Growth**: Cults often promise personal growth, spiritual enlightenment, and transformation. The allure of becoming a better, more enlightened person can be irresistible.
   - **Success Stories**: Many cults showcase success stories of transformed lives, creating a compelling narrative that potential recruits want to be part of.
   - **Exclusive Knowledge**: Cults claim to offer unique insights or esoteric knowledge that can lead to profound personal and spiritual development.
4. **Charismatic Leadership**:
   - **Inspiring Devotion**: A charismatic leader can inspire devotion and loyalty. The leader's personality, vision, and perceived wisdom can draw people in and keep them committed.
   - **Messianic Figures**: Leaders often present themselves as messianic figures or enlightened beings with a unique connection to the divine or universal truth.
   - **Authority and Command**: The leader's ability to command respect and obedience reinforces their control over the group.
5. **Exclusive Knowledge**:

- ○ **Special Revelation**: Cults often claim to possess special, hidden knowledge that is not available to outsiders. The promise of gaining access to this exclusive wisdom can be a strong draw.
- ○ **Esoteric Teachings**: The teachings are often presented as esoteric or occult knowledge, making them more intriguing and appealing to seekers of deeper truths.
- ○ **Mystery and Allure**: The element of mystery surrounding the knowledge adds to its allure, making members feel privileged and chosen.

Ethical and Legal Considerations

While the power of cults can be harnessed to create a loyal following and generate wealth, it's essential to navigate the ethical and legal landscape carefully:

1. **Ethical Boundaries**:
   - ○ **Manipulation vs. Guidance**: Manipulating and controlling others for personal gain raises significant ethical questions. Leaders must consider the long-term impact of their actions on followers' well-being.
   - ○ **Informed Consent**: Ensuring that members are aware of what they are committing to and the implications of their involvement is crucial to ethical leadership.
   - ○ **Transparency**: Being transparent about the cult's objectives, practices, and leadership structure can help maintain ethical standards.
2. **Legal Risks**:
   - ○ **Regulatory Compliance**: Cults often face legal scrutiny. It's vital to understand the laws surrounding religious organizations, charitable contributions, and personal freedoms. Engaging in illegal activities or infringing on members' rights can lead to serious consequences.
   - ○ **Financial Regulations**: Ensuring proper management and reporting of financial contributions to avoid legal issues related to fraud or tax evasion.
   - ○ **Child Protection Laws**: Adhering to laws that protect minors from exploitation and abuse within the cult.
3. **Responsibility**:
   - ○ **Duty of Care**: Balancing personal ambition with ethical responsibility is crucial. Cult leaders must decide where to draw the line in their pursuit of power and profit.
   - ○ **Health and Safety**: Ensuring the physical and mental well-being of members by providing safe living conditions and access to medical care.
   - ○ **Legal Representation**: Having legal representation to navigate disputes, accusations, and potential lawsuits is essential for protecting the cult and its leaders.

The Psychology of Cults

To effectively lead a cult, it's essential to understand the psychological mechanisms that drive cult dynamics:

1. **Influence Techniques**:
   - **Love Bombing**: Cults use various psychological techniques to influence and control members. Love bombing involves overwhelming new recruits with affection and attention to make them feel valued and accepted. This initial flood of positive reinforcement creates a bond between the recruit and the cult.
   - **Fear and Guilt**: Using fear of punishment or guilt over past actions to control behavior. By instilling a sense of fear about leaving the cult or disobeying its rules, leaders can maintain control over members.
   - **Isolation**: Encouraging members to cut ties with outside influences to increase dependency on the cult. Isolating members from family and friends reduces outside criticism and reinforces the cult's ideology.
2. **Group Dynamics**:
   - **Us vs. Them Mentality**: Cults leverage social psychology to strengthen group cohesion. Creating a clear distinction between insiders (cult members) and outsiders (the rest of the world) fosters unity and loyalty. This mentality also helps to dehumanize outsiders and justify the cult's actions against them.
   - **Peer Pressure**: Encouraging conformity through peer pressure and communal reinforcement of beliefs. Members are more likely to conform to the group's norms and values when they see others doing the same.
   - **Ritual and Routine**: Regular group activities and rituals reinforce the cult's beliefs and create a sense of community and belonging.
3. **Cognitive Dissonance**:
   - **Deepening Commitment**: Cults exploit cognitive dissonance to deepen commitment. When members invest time, money, and emotional energy into the cult, they are more likely to rationalize and justify their continued involvement, even when faced with contradictory evidence or doubts.
   - **Self-Justification**: Members may adopt the cult's beliefs more strongly to justify their sacrifices and commitment, leading to a cycle of increasing devotion.
   - **Sunk Cost Fallacy**: The more members invest in the cult, the harder it becomes to leave, as they don't want to admit their efforts were in vain.

In-Depth Examples and Techniques

1. **Transforming into a Dictatorial Personality**:
   - **Stage-Managed Revelations**: Carefully plan and execute staged spiritual revelations to reinforce your authority and divine status. Use dramatic events and carefully orchestrated "miracles" to convince followers of your supernatural connection.
   - **Charismatic Performance**: Hone your public speaking and performance skills to captivate and inspire your audience. Use storytelling, rhetorical questions, and emotional appeals to draw followers into your narrative.

- o **Consistency in Messaging**: Maintain consistent messaging to build trust and credibility. Avoid contradictions and ensure that your teachings are coherent and easy to understand.

2. **Managing Apocalyptic Scenarios**:
   - o **Predictive Prophecies**: Make bold predictions about future events, framing them as divine revelations. Ensure that some of these predictions are vague enough to be interpreted as accurate regardless of the outcome.
   - o **Creating Urgency**: Use apocalyptic scenarios to create a sense of urgency and motivate followers to commit more deeply. Present yourself as the savior or guide who can protect them from impending doom.
   - o **Productive Panic**: Channel the fear and anxiety generated by apocalyptic scenarios into productive activities, such as increased recruitment efforts, fundraising, or preparations for a "safe" future.

3. **Developing Income Streams**:
   - o **Front Groups**: Establish front groups such as spiritual retreats, drug rehabilitation programs, and management seminars to attract new members and generate revenue. These front groups can serve as a recruiting ground for the cult while providing a steady income stream.
   - o **Tithes and Donations**: Encourage regular financial contributions from members through tithes, donations, and special offerings. Emphasize the spiritual benefits of giving and the importance of supporting the cult's mission.
   - o **Merchandising**: Develop and sell branded merchandise, including books, audio recordings, clothing, and other items that promote the cult's teachings and image.

4. **Recruitment Tactics**:
   - o **Targeting Vulnerabilities**: Identify and target individuals who are emotionally scarred, socially isolated, or experiencing personal crises. These individuals are more likely to be receptive to the cult's message and promises of support and transformation.
   - o **Personal Approach**: Use a personalized approach to recruitment, building relationships with potential members and addressing their specific needs and concerns. Offer solutions to their problems and create a sense of hope and belonging.
   - o **Recruitment Events**: Host public events, workshops, and seminars that attract potential recruits. Use these events to showcase the cult's teachings and community, making them appealing to attendees.

5. **Exerting Control**:
   - o **Love Bombing**: Use love bombing to overwhelm new recruits with affection and attention, creating a strong emotional bond and dependency. This technique helps to quickly integrate new members into the cult and build loyalty.
   - o **Alternating Cruelty**: Alternate between kindness and cruelty to keep members off balance and dependent on your approval. This technique, known as intermittent reinforcement, creates an unpredictable environment that reinforces loyalty and obedience.

- - **Divine Revelation**: Claim ongoing divine revelations to maintain your authority and control over the cult. Present these revelations as direct communications from a higher power, reinforcing your position as the cult's leader and prophet.

6. **Handling Authorities**:
   - **Legal Navigation**: Develop strategies to navigate legal issues and deal with authorities when people go "missing" or other legal challenges arise. Maintain a legal team to handle disputes and protect the cult from legal threats.
   - **Media Relations**: Manage the cult's public image and relations with the media. Control the narrative by presenting a positive and benign image of the cult, and be prepared to respond to negative press and accusations.
   - **Compliance and Cover**: Ensure that the cult complies with local laws and regulations, and create plausible cover stories for any controversial or illegal activities. Use legal and financial structures to protect the cult's assets and leaders.

7. **Structuring Your Cult**:
   - **Open Society Model**: Choose an "Open Society" model if your primary goal is wealth. This model allows for greater interaction with the outside world, facilitating recruitment and fundraising efforts. Open societies can use public events, businesses, and media to attract new members and generate income.
   - **Closed Compound Model**: Choose a "Closed Compound" model if your primary goal is power and control. This model isolates members from the outside world, creating a tightly controlled environment where the leader's authority is absolute. Closed compounds can use communal living, strict rules, and constant surveillance to maintain control and loyalty.
   - **Hybrid Models**: Consider hybrid models that combine elements of both open societies and closed compounds. These models can balance wealth generation with control, allowing for greater flexibility in achieving your goals.

By understanding these foundational aspects and employing these detailed techniques, aspiring cult leaders can effectively create and manage their own cult, ensuring loyalty, control, and profitability while navigating the complex ethical and legal landscape. This comprehensive guide will equip you with the knowledge and skills needed to become a successful cult leader, balancing power, control, and profit with an understanding of the ethical and social implications of your actions.

The Power of Belonging

In a world that often feels chaotic and disconnected, many individuals find themselves adrift, searching for a sense of purpose and connection. The noise of modern life can be overwhelming, leaving people yearning for a place where they can feel understood, valued, and secure. It's in this landscape of isolation and longing that the allure of cults finds fertile ground. Cults promise a haven from the alienation of contemporary society, offering a sense of belonging that is both comforting and compelling. This powerful draw can be likened to a beacon in the dark, guiding lost souls towards a community where they can finally feel at home.

A Story of Belonging: Sarah's Journey

Imagine a young woman named Sarah, who has moved to a bustling city for a new job. Despite the city's vibrancy, Sarah feels increasingly isolated. The once-exciting allure of city life has faded, leaving her feeling like a small, insignificant part of a vast, impersonal machine. She misses the warmth of her hometown, the familiar faces, and the comfort of being known. It's during this time of vulnerability that Sarah stumbles upon a group that seems to offer everything she's been missing—a close-knit community, a clear sense of purpose, and the promise of transformation.

As Sarah becomes more involved with the group, she discovers that what initially seemed like a social club is much more than that. The group offers emotional support, a shared identity, and a family-like atmosphere that fills the void in her life. Through collective rituals and shared beliefs, Sarah begins to feel a deep connection with the other members, who, like her, have sought refuge from the isolating pressures of the outside world. This sense of belonging becomes a cornerstone of her new life, offering stability and meaning in ways she hadn't imagined possible.

Sense of Belonging

Isolation in Modern Society

Sarah's story is not unique. Many individuals, overwhelmed by the complexities of modern society, find themselves feeling disconnected and isolated. In the constant hustle of city life, personal connections often feel superficial, leaving a void that long-distance calls and social media interactions can't fill. The sense of being just another face in the crowd can be stifling, driving a deep need for a genuine connection. Cults capitalize on this widespread feeling by offering a close-knit community where members feel genuinely valued and included. It's like finding an oasis in a desert of loneliness, where the group offers not just companionship, but a sense of being truly seen and understood.

Disconnected Lives: In today's fast-paced and technology-driven world, many individuals find themselves feeling increasingly isolated. Despite being constantly connected through social media and other digital platforms, the depth of human interaction often remains superficial. This growing sense of disconnection can lead to feelings of loneliness and a longing for meaningful relationships.

Complexities of Modern Life: The demands of modern life—such as demanding jobs, urbanization, and the breakdown of traditional community structures—contribute to this isolation. People may move frequently for work, leaving behind family and friends, or they may be so consumed by their careers that they have little time for social interactions.

Cults as a Solution: Cults exploit this need for connection by offering a close-knit community where members feel valued and included. Within a cult, members often form deep, personal bonds with each other, creating a surrogate family. This intimate environment fulfills the basic human need for connection and belonging, making it a powerful motivator for joining and staying in a cult.

Family-Like Atmosphere

For Sarah, the group quickly becomes a surrogate family, providing the emotional support and security that she had been missing. This family-like atmosphere is a common feature in cults, where members often refer to each other as brothers and sisters, creating a sense of unity and kinship. The leader, who often takes on a parental role, offers guidance and wisdom, further solidifying the family structure. This dynamic can be incredibly comforting, especially for those who have experienced trauma or instability in their personal lives. The group's structure and support system provide a stable foundation, giving members a place to turn to in times of need.

Emotional Support: Cults often mimic the structure of a family, providing emotional support that members may lack in their personal lives. This can include offering comfort during times of distress, celebrating successes together, and providing a sense of stability and safety.

Sense of Security: The familial atmosphere within a cult can create a sense of security. Members may feel protected and cared for by the group, which can be particularly appealing to those who have experienced trauma or instability in their past.

Role of the Leader: The cult leader often takes on a paternal or maternal role, guiding members, making decisions on their behalf, and offering wisdom and support. This dynamic reinforces the family-like structure and deepens members' emotional dependency on the leader.

Shared Identity

As Sarah delves deeper into the group's activities, she finds herself adopting a new identity, one that is closely tied to the group's beliefs and values. This shared identity is reinforced through collective experiences, such as rituals, ceremonies, and communal living. These activities create a strong sense of unity and solidarity, making members feel part of something larger than themselves. The group's symbols and rituals become a way to express and reinforce this identity, distinguishing members from the outside world. For Sarah, and many others like her, this shared identity offers a sense of purpose and belonging that is both profound and empowering.

Collective Experiences: Being part of a cult provides members with a shared identity and purpose. Through collective experiences such as rituals, ceremonies, and communal living, members develop a strong sense of unity and solidarity. These shared activities reinforce the group's beliefs and values, making the collective identity more robust.

Purpose and Meaning: In addition to providing a sense of belonging, cults often give members a sense of purpose and meaning. The cult's mission or ideology becomes a central part of members' lives, guiding their actions and giving them a sense of direction. This can be particularly appealing to individuals who feel lost or purposeless in their personal lives.

Rituals and Symbols: Cults use rituals and symbols to reinforce the shared identity. Regular rituals, such as group prayers, chants, or communal meals, create a sense of routine and belonging. Symbols, such as specific clothing, insignias, or artifacts, help to distinguish members from outsiders and strengthen the group's identity.

In this narrative, the sense of belonging provided by cults acts as a powerful anchor for individuals adrift in the sea of modern life's complexities. It offers not just a temporary respite from isolation but a new way of being, a community that feels like home. For those who find themselves searching for connection and meaning, the promise of belonging can be an irresistible lure, drawing them into the embrace of a group that promises to meet their deepest needs.

By understanding and leveraging these elements, cult leaders can create an environment where members feel deeply connected, valued, and purposeful. This sense of belonging is a cornerstone of cult dynamics, making it a critical aspect of cult recruitment and retention strategies.

Certainty and Simplicity

In an era marked by rapid change and constant information overload, the complexities of modern life can be overwhelming. Many individuals find themselves struggling to navigate a world filled with uncertainties, leaving them yearning for clear, straightforward guidance. It is within this context of confusion and doubt that the appeal of cults becomes particularly potent. By offering certainty and simplicity, cults can provide a refuge from the chaos, presenting an ordered and comprehensible reality that is deeply reassuring to those seeking direction.

A Story of Clarity: John's Quest

Consider the story of John, a middle-aged man who has recently lost his job. The financial strain, coupled with the pressure to support his family, has left him feeling anxious and lost. The unpredictability of the job market and the overwhelming number of choices he faces daily add to his stress. John craves stability and clear guidance on how to move forward. It's during this period of uncertainty that he encounters a group that seems to have all the answers.

Certainty and Simplicity

Clarity in Chaos

John's predicament is familiar to many. Life can be chaotic and overwhelming, filled with complex questions about existence, morality, and purpose. Cults often provide clear, simple answers to these profound questions, offering a straightforward worldview that cuts through the noise. For individuals like John, who are struggling to make sense of their circumstances, this clarity is incredibly appealing. It offers a sense of direction and purpose, helping them to feel more grounded and less overwhelmed by the complexities of life.

Clear Answers: Life can be chaotic and overwhelming. Cults often provide clear, simple answers to complex questions about existence, morality, and purpose. This clarity is incredibly appealing to those seeking direction. For John, the group's teachings offer a framework that makes sense of his struggles and provides a clear path forward.

Simplified Worldview: The group explains the complexities of life in black-and-white terms, offering a structured belief system that reduces the cognitive load on John and others. By presenting clear distinctions between right and wrong, good and evil, the group simplifies the world, making it more manageable and less intimidating.

Doctrine and Dogma

As John delves deeper into the group's teachings, he finds comfort in their structured belief systems. The doctrines and dogmas offered by the group simplify the world into black-and-white terms, reducing the cognitive load on members and offering a reassuring sense of certainty. This structured approach helps John to feel more in control of his life, as he no longer has to wrestle with the ambiguities and uncertainties that once plagued him.

Structured Beliefs: Cults offer structured belief systems that simplify the world into black-and-white terms. These systems reduce the cognitive load on members, offering a reassuring sense of certainty. For John, this means no longer having to grapple with the ambiguities of life; instead, he can rely on the group's clear guidelines to navigate his daily challenges.

Certainty in Doctrine: The doctrines and dogmas of the group provide John with a clear moral compass, guiding his decisions and actions. This sense of certainty is deeply comforting, as it eliminates the stress of making complex choices and allows John to focus on following the prescribed path.

Predictability

One of the most appealing aspects of the group for John is the predictability it offers. The routine and predictability of the group's activities provide a stable environment, helping members feel more secure in their daily lives. For John, this means a return to stability and a sense of order that he had lost. The group's regular meetings, rituals, and practices create a predictable pattern that he can rely on, making his life feel more manageable and less chaotic.

Routine and Stability: The routine and predictability of cult activities provide a stable environment, helping members feel more secure in their daily lives. For John, the group's regular meetings and rituals create a sense of routine that brings much-needed stability to his life.

Security in Predictability: Knowing what to expect each day helps John to feel more secure and less anxious. The predictability of the group's schedule allows him to plan his days around the group's activities, creating a sense of order and purpose that was previously missing.

Conclusion: The Power of Certainty

For individuals like John, the certainty and simplicity offered by cults can be incredibly appealing. By providing clear answers, structured belief systems, and predictable routines, cults offer a refuge from the chaos and complexity of modern life. This sense of certainty can be a powerful motivator for joining and remaining in a cult, as it helps individuals to feel more grounded, secure, and in control of their lives.

By understanding and leveraging these elements, cult leaders can create an environment that meets the deep-seated need for clarity and simplicity. This approach not only attracts new members but also ensures their continued loyalty, making it a critical aspect of cult dynamics and a cornerstone of successful recruitment and retention strategies.

Promise of Transformation

In a world where many people feel stuck in their personal and spiritual growth, the promise of transformation can be incredibly alluring. Cults often capitalize on this desire for self-improvement by promising profound personal growth, spiritual enlightenment, and a complete transformation of one's life. This promise acts as a powerful magnet, drawing individuals who yearn to become better, more enlightened versions of themselves.

A Story of Transformation: Michael's Journey

Meet Michael, a man in his late thirties who feels his life has hit a plateau. Despite having a stable job and a supportive family, Michael is haunted by a sense of unfulfilled potential and spiritual stagnation. He dreams of unlocking deeper truths about himself and the universe but feels trapped by the mundane routines of everyday life. It's during this period of restlessness that Michael encounters a group that seems to offer the transformation he seeks.

Promise of Transformation

Personal Growth

Michael's story is one that resonates with many. Cults often promise personal growth, spiritual enlightenment, and transformation. The allure of becoming a better, more enlightened person can be irresistible, especially for those who feel stuck or unfulfilled in their current lives. For

Michael, the group's teachings and practices offer a pathway to personal and spiritual growth that he has long desired.

Spiritual Enlightenment: Cults often promise personal growth, spiritual enlightenment, and transformation. The allure of becoming a better, more enlightened person can be irresistible. Michael is drawn to the group by the promise of achieving higher levels of consciousness and understanding, something he has been yearning for but has not found in traditional avenues.

Path to Betterment: The group offers structured programs and rituals designed to facilitate personal growth. These include meditation practices, self-reflection exercises, and communal activities that aim to break down old patterns and foster new, enlightened ways of being. For Michael, this structured approach provides a clear path towards becoming the person he has always wanted to be.

Success Stories

As Michael becomes more involved with the group, he is captivated by the numerous success stories shared by other members. These stories of transformed lives create a compelling narrative that he wants to be part of. Hearing firsthand accounts of how others have achieved personal and spiritual breakthroughs within the group inspires Michael and reinforces his belief that he too can experience such transformation.

Compelling Narratives: Many cults showcase success stories of transformed lives, creating a compelling narrative that potential recruits want to be part of. For Michael, these stories are proof that the group's methods work. He listens to testimonials of members who have overcome addiction, found inner peace, and achieved their personal goals through the group's teachings.

Role Models: These success stories often feature charismatic individuals who serve as role models within the group. Seeing people who have successfully transformed their lives provides Michael with tangible examples of what is possible, fueling his motivation to fully commit to the group's practices.

Exclusive Knowledge

One of the most enticing aspects of the group for Michael is the promise of exclusive knowledge. Cults often claim to offer unique insights or esoteric knowledge that can lead to profound personal and spiritual development. This promise of access to hidden truths is a powerful draw for Michael, who has always been a seeker of deeper understanding.

Unique Insights: Cults claim to offer unique insights or esoteric knowledge that can lead to profound personal and spiritual development. For Michael, the group's teachings promise to reveal secrets about the nature of reality, human potential, and spiritual enlightenment that are not available through conventional means.

Esoteric Teachings: The group's leader often presents themselves as a conduit of divine wisdom or an enlightened master, possessing knowledge that is inaccessible to outsiders.

Michael is eager to learn from someone who claims to have a direct connection to higher truths and sees this as an opportunity to gain a deeper understanding of himself and the universe.

Pathway to Enlightenment: The group's teachings are framed as a pathway to enlightenment, with each member progressing through various stages of knowledge and spiritual development. Michael is motivated by the prospect of advancing through these stages and achieving the ultimate goal of spiritual awakening.

Conclusion: The Power of Transformation

For individuals like Michael, the promise of transformation offered by cults can be incredibly compelling. By presenting a clear path to personal growth, showcasing success stories of transformed lives, and offering access to exclusive knowledge, cults create a powerful narrative that attracts and retains members. This promise of transformation is a critical aspect of cult dynamics, providing individuals with the hope and motivation to embark on a journey of self-discovery and enlightenment.

By understanding and leveraging these elements, cult leaders can create an environment that fulfills the deep-seated desire for transformation. This approach not only attracts new members but also ensures their continued commitment, making it a cornerstone of successful recruitment and retention strategies.

Charismatic Leadership

In the heart of every successful cult lies a charismatic leader, a figure whose personality, vision, and perceived wisdom captivate and command the loyalty of their followers. These leaders possess an almost magnetic charm, inspiring devotion and unwavering commitment from their members. Their presence alone can transform ordinary individuals into ardent believers, ready to follow their guidance without question. Understanding the dynamics of charismatic leadership is essential for anyone looking to harness its power to build and sustain a dedicated following.

A Story of Leadership: Emma's Rise

Imagine Emma, a woman with a remarkable presence and a way with words that could inspire even the most skeptical listener. Emma's journey began with a small group of like-minded individuals who were drawn to her unique perspective on life and spirituality. As the group grew, so did Emma's influence. She was not just a leader but a beacon of hope and a source of profound wisdom. Her charisma and ability to connect with people on a deep emotional level turned her into a figure of reverence and devotion.

Charismatic Leadership

Inspiring Devotion

Emma's story exemplifies how a charismatic leader can inspire devotion and loyalty. Her personality, vision, and perceived wisdom draw people in and keep them committed. Emma's ability to articulate a compelling vision for the future, coupled with her genuine interest in the well-being of her followers, fosters a deep sense of loyalty. Followers are not just attracted to her ideas but to Emma herself, seeing her as a guide and mentor.

Magnetic Personality: A charismatic leader can inspire devotion and loyalty. The leader's personality, vision, and perceived wisdom can draw people in and keep them committed. Emma's engaging and magnetic personality makes her approachable yet authoritative, a combination that endears her to her followers.

Compelling Vision: Emma's vision for a better world resonates deeply with her followers. She paints a picture of a utopian future where everyone can achieve spiritual enlightenment and personal fulfillment. This vision gives her followers a sense of purpose and direction.

Perceived Wisdom: Emma's ability to provide insightful and profound answers to life's big questions enhances her perceived wisdom. Her followers believe that she possesses a deep understanding of spiritual truths that others cannot see, making her guidance invaluable.

Messianic Figures

As Emma's influence grows, she begins to present herself as a messianic figure or enlightened being with a unique connection to the divine or universal truth. This self-presentation elevates her status within the group and reinforces her authority. Followers come to see Emma not just as a leader but as a divine messenger, a chosen one with a special mission.

Divine Connection: Leaders often present themselves as messianic figures or enlightened beings with a unique connection to the divine or universal truth. Emma's claims of receiving divine revelations or having mystical experiences set her apart as someone with access to higher knowledge and power.

Unique Mission: Emma frames her leadership as part of a divine mission to guide humanity towards enlightenment. This narrative not only legitimizes her authority but also instills a sense of urgency and importance in the group's activities.

Symbolic Acts: To reinforce her messianic status, Emma performs symbolic acts and rituals that highlight her unique connection to the divine. These acts are designed to inspire awe and reinforce the belief in her special role.

Authority and Command

Emma's ability to command respect and obedience reinforces her control over the group. Her leadership style balances warmth and approachability with firm authority, creating an environment where followers feel both valued and guided. Emma's decisions are rarely questioned because her followers believe in her wisdom and judgment.

Commanding Respect: The leader's ability to command respect and obedience reinforces their control over the group. Emma's presence and demeanor naturally command respect. Her confidence and assertiveness make her a natural authority figure.

Firm Authority: While Emma is approachable, she is also firm in her decisions and expectations. This balance ensures that her followers feel guided and supported, yet they understand that her authority is not to be challenged.

Building Trust: Emma builds trust through consistent and fair leadership. Her followers trust her decisions because she has proven herself to be wise and benevolent. This trust further cements her authority within the group.

Conclusion: The Power of Charismatic Leadership

For individuals like Emma, charismatic leadership is the cornerstone of their influence and control. By inspiring devotion, presenting themselves as messianic figures, and commanding respect and obedience, charismatic leaders create a powerful bond with their followers. This bond is not easily broken, making charismatic leadership a critical element in the success and longevity of a cult.

By understanding and leveraging these elements, aspiring cult leaders can create an environment that fosters deep loyalty and unwavering commitment. This approach not only attracts new members but also ensures their continued devotion, making charismatic leadership a vital component of successful cult dynamics.

Exclusive Knowledge

At the heart of many cults lies the promise of exclusive knowledge—special revelations and esoteric teachings that claim to offer unique insights into the mysteries of life, the universe, and human existence. This promise of hidden wisdom is a powerful lure for individuals seeking deeper truths and understanding. The allure of exclusive knowledge can transform ordinary curiosity into fervent commitment, drawing individuals into a world where they feel privileged, chosen, and enlightened.

A Story of Revelation: David's Discovery

Meet David, a young man disillusioned with conventional wisdom and mainstream beliefs. He has always felt that there is more to life than what is taught in schools and preached in traditional religious settings. David's thirst for deeper understanding leads him to explore various spiritual and philosophical paths, but none seem to satisfy his yearning for hidden truths. It is during this quest that David encounters a group that promises access to special, hidden knowledge. Intrigued and hopeful, David decides to delve deeper.

Exclusive Knowledge

Special Revelation

David's journey illustrates the powerful draw of special revelation. Cults often claim to possess knowledge that is not available to outsiders—wisdom that has been hidden from the masses and is accessible only to a select few. The promise of gaining access to this exclusive wisdom can be a strong draw, especially for individuals like David who are seeking answers beyond the conventional.

Hidden Wisdom: Cults often claim to possess special, hidden knowledge that is not available to outsiders. For David, the idea that this group holds secrets about the universe that others do not know is incredibly enticing. He feels that by joining the group, he will finally gain access to the answers he has been searching for.

Selective Access: The group emphasizes that only the worthy or enlightened can receive this special revelation. This exclusivity makes the knowledge even more valuable, as it implies that David is part of a chosen few who are capable of understanding these higher truths.

Divine Connection: The leaders of the group often claim to receive these revelations directly from a divine source or through mystical experiences. This connection to a higher power adds a layer of legitimacy and authority to the knowledge they share.

Esoteric Teachings

As David immerses himself in the group's teachings, he discovers that the knowledge being imparted is presented as esoteric or occult. These teachings are often shrouded in complex symbolism and arcane language, making them more intriguing and appealing to seekers of deeper truths. The complexity and mystery of these teachings enhance their perceived value and significance.

Arcane Language: The teachings are often presented as esoteric or occult knowledge, making them more intriguing and appealing to seekers of deeper truths. David finds himself captivated by the intricate symbols and cryptic language used by the group, feeling that he is unraveling profound mysteries that are hidden from ordinary people.

Complex Symbolism: The use of complex symbols and metaphors in the group's teachings adds to their allure. David feels that each layer of symbolism he deciphers brings him closer to understanding the ultimate truths of existence.

Intellectual Challenge: The esoteric nature of the teachings provides an intellectual challenge that stimulates David's mind. He takes pride in his ability to grasp these difficult concepts, reinforcing his commitment to the group and its teachings.

Mystery and Allure

One of the most compelling aspects of the group for David is the element of mystery surrounding the knowledge. The promise of unveiling hidden truths and gaining access to secret wisdom adds a sense of adventure and excitement to his spiritual journey. This mystery and allure make David feel privileged and chosen, deepening his attachment to the group.

Enigmatic Teachings: The element of mystery surrounding the knowledge adds to its allure, making members feel privileged and chosen. For David, the enigmatic nature of the group's teachings is both thrilling and captivating. He feels that by being part of the group, he is on a special journey of discovery that few others can undertake.

Sense of Privilege: The exclusivity of the knowledge makes David feel privileged. He believes that being part of the group sets him apart from others, giving him access to insights that are beyond the reach of the average person.

Chosen Path: The group often reinforces the idea that its members are chosen or specially selected to receive this knowledge. This sense of being chosen strengthens David's commitment to the group, as he feels a profound sense of purpose and destiny.

Conclusion: The Power of Exclusive Knowledge

For individuals like David, the promise of exclusive knowledge can be an incredibly powerful motivator. By offering special revelations, presenting teachings as esoteric and occult, and maintaining an aura of mystery and allure, cults create an environment where members feel privileged, chosen, and enlightened. This sense of exclusivity and privilege not only attracts new members but also ensures their continued loyalty and commitment.

By understanding and leveraging these elements, cult leaders can create a compelling narrative that draws individuals into their fold and keeps them deeply engaged. The promise of exclusive knowledge is a cornerstone of cult dynamics, providing a potent means of attracting and retaining devoted followers.

Ethical Boundaries

In the realm of cult leadership, navigating ethical boundaries is a complex and crucial task. The line between providing guidance and manipulating followers for personal gain can often blur, leading to significant ethical dilemmas. Cult leaders must carefully consider the long-term impact of their actions on their followers' well-being, ensuring that their practices align with ethical standards and respect the autonomy and dignity of each individual.

A Story of Reflection: Lily's Leadership

Imagine Lily, a charismatic leader who has built a devoted following based on her spiritual teachings. Lily genuinely believes in the transformative power of her message and wants to help her followers achieve personal and spiritual growth. However, as her influence grows, Lily faces increasing pressure to maintain control and ensure the group's cohesion. She finds herself at a crossroads, grappling with the ethical implications of her leadership decisions.

Ethical Boundaries

Manipulation vs. Guidance

Lily's dilemma highlights the fine line between manipulation and guidance. Manipulating and controlling others for personal gain raises significant ethical questions. Leaders must consider the long-term impact of their actions on followers' well-being. For Lily, the challenge is to provide genuine guidance without resorting to manipulation that undermines her followers' autonomy.

Ethical Dilemma: Manipulating and controlling others for personal gain raises significant ethical questions. Leaders must consider the long-term impact of their actions on followers' well-being. Lily is aware that using fear, guilt, or deceit to control her followers would violate ethical principles, even if it ensures their loyalty and obedience.

Guidance with Integrity: Lily strives to offer guidance that empowers her followers rather than diminishes their autonomy. She focuses on teaching principles and practices that encourage personal growth and self-discovery, allowing her followers to make informed decisions about their spiritual paths.

Respect for Autonomy: By respecting her followers' autonomy and encouraging independent thought, Lily aims to create an environment where her followers can grow authentically. This approach fosters trust and mutual respect, laying a foundation for ethical leadership.

Informed Consent

Ensuring that members are aware of what they are committing to and the implications of their involvement is crucial to ethical leadership. Lily recognizes the importance of informed consent and strives to be transparent about the group's practices, objectives, and expectations. This transparency helps her followers make informed decisions about their participation.

Clear Communication: Ensuring that members are aware of what they are committing to and the implications of their involvement is crucial to ethical leadership. Lily takes the time to clearly communicate the group's beliefs, practices, and expectations to potential recruits, ensuring they understand what they are joining.

Honesty and Openness: Lily emphasizes honesty and openness in her interactions with her followers. She answers questions candidly and provides detailed information about the group's activities, helping to build trust and ensure that followers are making informed choices.

Empowerment through Knowledge: By providing comprehensive information and encouraging questions, Lily empowers her followers to make informed decisions about their involvement. This approach fosters a sense of agency and responsibility, aligning with ethical principles.

Transparency

Being transparent about the cult's objectives, practices, and leadership structure can help maintain ethical standards. Lily understands that transparency is key to building trust and maintaining ethical leadership. She strives to be open about the group's goals, practices, and her role as a leader, ensuring that her followers are fully informed.

Building Trust: Being transparent about the cult's objectives, practices, and leadership structure can help maintain ethical standards. Lily believes that transparency is essential for building trust with her followers. She openly shares the group's mission, goals, and the methods they use to achieve them.

Accountability: Lily holds herself accountable to her followers by being transparent about her decisions and actions. She encourages feedback and constructive criticism, creating a culture of accountability and continuous improvement within the group.

Open Leadership: Lily's transparency extends to the leadership structure of the group. She ensures that her followers understand how decisions are made and who holds various responsibilities within the group. This openness fosters a sense of fairness and inclusivity.

Conclusion: The Importance of Ethical Boundaries

For leaders like Lily, maintaining ethical boundaries is essential to creating a healthy and respectful environment for their followers. By navigating the fine line between manipulation and guidance, ensuring informed consent, and maintaining transparency, leaders can foster trust and integrity within their groups. Ethical leadership not only supports the well-being of followers but also strengthens the overall cohesion and sustainability of the group.

By understanding and implementing these ethical principles, cult leaders can create an environment that respects the autonomy and dignity of each member. This approach not only attracts new followers but also ensures their continued commitment, making ethical boundaries a cornerstone of successful and responsible cult leadership.

Legal Risks

Navigating the legal landscape is a critical aspect of cult leadership. Cults often operate in a grey area that can attract significant legal scrutiny. Understanding and adhering to the laws surrounding religious organizations, charitable contributions, personal freedoms, and child protection is essential to avoid serious legal consequences. By ensuring regulatory compliance, proper financial management, and adherence to child protection laws, cult leaders can protect their organizations and their members from legal pitfalls.

A Story of Vigilance: Alex's Challenges

Consider Alex, a charismatic leader who has built a devoted following. As his group grows, Alex finds himself facing increasing legal scrutiny. From questions about the group's financial practices to concerns about the treatment of minors, Alex realizes that maintaining legal compliance is crucial for the survival and integrity of his organization. He must navigate these challenges carefully to protect his group and its mission.

Legal Risks

Regulatory Compliance

Alex's journey underscores the importance of regulatory compliance. Cults often face legal scrutiny, making it vital to understand the laws surrounding religious organizations, charitable contributions, and personal freedoms. Engaging in illegal activities or infringing on members' rights can lead to serious consequences. Alex knows that he must ensure his group operates within the bounds of the law to avoid legal repercussions.

Understanding the Law: Cults often face legal scrutiny. It's vital to understand the laws surrounding religious organizations, charitable contributions, and personal freedoms. Alex dedicates time to studying relevant laws and regulations, seeking advice from legal experts to ensure his group's activities are lawful.

Respecting Personal Freedoms: Alex is careful to respect the personal freedoms of his members, ensuring that their participation is voluntary and informed. He avoids practices that could be seen as coercive or infringing on their rights, maintaining an ethical and legally sound environment.

Compliance with Regulations: Alex implements procedures to ensure compliance with all applicable regulations. This includes registering the group as a religious organization, maintaining accurate records of charitable contributions, and adhering to all reporting requirements.

Financial Regulations

Proper financial management is another critical area of concern for Alex. Ensuring proper management and reporting of financial contributions helps avoid legal issues related to fraud or tax evasion. Alex understands that transparency and accountability in financial matters are essential to maintaining trust and avoiding legal trouble.

Transparent Financial Practices: Ensuring proper management and reporting of financial contributions to avoid legal issues related to fraud or tax evasion. Alex establishes clear and transparent financial practices, including regular audits and detailed reporting of all financial activities.

Accountability: Alex holds himself and his financial team accountable for managing the group's funds responsibly. He ensures that all donations and contributions are documented, and funds are used in accordance with the group's mission and legal requirements.

Tax Compliance: Alex works closely with financial advisors to ensure that the group complies with all tax regulations. This includes filing accurate tax returns and avoiding any activities that could be construed as tax evasion.

Child Protection Laws

As the leader of a group that includes families and children, Alex must adhere to laws that protect minors from exploitation and abuse. Ensuring the safety and well-being of all members, especially children, is a top priority. Alex knows that any failure to comply with child protection laws could result in severe legal consequences and damage to the group's reputation.

Protecting Minors: Adhering to laws that protect minors from exploitation and abuse within the cult. Alex implements strict policies and procedures to protect minors, including background checks for all adults involved in the group and mandatory reporting of any suspected abuse.

Creating a Safe Environment: Alex ensures that all activities involving children are safe and supervised. He provides training for staff and volunteers on child protection laws and best practices for creating a safe environment.

Compliance with Child Protection Laws: Alex stays informed about changes in child protection laws and ensures that his group's policies are updated accordingly. He cooperates fully with any investigations or inquiries from child protection agencies, demonstrating the group's commitment to the safety of minors.

Conclusion: Navigating Legal Risks

For leaders like Alex, navigating legal risks is an essential aspect of maintaining a sustainable and ethical organization. By ensuring regulatory compliance, proper financial management, and adherence to child protection laws, cult leaders can protect their groups from legal challenges and build a foundation of trust and integrity.

By understanding and implementing these legal principles, cult leaders can create an environment that respects the rights and well-being of all members. This approach not only protects the organization from legal repercussions but also strengthens the overall cohesion and sustainability of the group, making legal compliance a cornerstone of successful and responsible cult leadership.

Responsibility

With leadership comes great responsibility, especially within the context of a cult. Cult leaders wield significant influence over their followers, and with that power comes the obligation to ensure the well-being of those who trust and follow them. Balancing personal ambition with ethical responsibility is crucial, as leaders must decide where to draw the line in their pursuit of power and profit. Additionally, ensuring the health and safety of members and securing proper legal representation are essential aspects of responsible leadership.

A Story of Reflection: Mark's Realization

Consider Mark, a dynamic leader who has successfully grown his following into a large and devoted community. While Mark is proud of his achievements, he begins to realize the immense responsibility that comes with his role. As his influence grows, so do the ethical challenges and potential legal risks. Mark must navigate these challenges carefully, ensuring that his leadership remains responsible and ethical while still pursuing his vision.

Responsibility

Duty of Care

Mark's journey highlights the importance of duty of care in leadership. Balancing personal ambition with ethical responsibility is crucial. Cult leaders must decide where to draw the line in their pursuit of power and profit. For Mark, this means reflecting on his actions and ensuring that his pursuit of success does not come at the expense of his followers' well-being.

Ethical Boundaries: Balancing personal ambition with ethical responsibility is crucial. Cult leaders must decide where to draw the line in their pursuit of power and profit. Mark understands that his decisions have a profound impact on his followers, and he is committed to leading with integrity. He constantly evaluates his actions to ensure they align with ethical standards.

Long-Term Impact: Mark considers the long-term impact of his leadership on his followers. He recognizes that exploiting his followers for short-term gain could lead to harm and disillusionment, undermining the trust and loyalty he has worked hard to build.

Balancing Ambition and Care: While Mark is ambitious and driven to grow his community, he is also mindful of his duty of care. He ensures that his leadership decisions are guided by a commitment to the well-being of his followers, even if it means sacrificing some of his personal ambitions.

Health and Safety

Ensuring the physical and mental well-being of members is a critical aspect of Mark's responsibility as a leader. This includes providing safe living conditions, access to medical care, and support for mental health. Mark knows that the health and safety of his followers are paramount, and he takes proactive steps to protect them.

Safe Living Conditions: Ensuring the physical and mental well-being of members by providing safe living conditions and access to medical care. Mark ensures that the community's living conditions are safe, clean, and conducive to well-being. He prioritizes the maintenance of communal spaces and ensures that all members have access to basic necessities.

Access to Medical Care: Mark makes sure that his followers have access to medical care, both for physical and mental health needs. He establishes relationships with healthcare providers and sets up a system to ensure that members can receive treatment when needed.

Mental Health Support: Recognizing the importance of mental health, Mark provides resources and support for members who may be struggling. He fosters an environment where members feel comfortable seeking help and ensures that mental health is treated with the same importance as physical health.

Legal Representation

As Mark's community grows, so do the potential legal challenges. Having legal representation to navigate disputes, accusations, and potential lawsuits is essential for protecting the cult and its leaders. Mark understands that responsible leadership includes being prepared for legal issues that may arise and ensuring that the community is protected.

Legal Preparedness: Having legal representation to navigate disputes, accusations, and potential lawsuits is essential for protecting the cult and its leaders. Mark recognizes the importance of being legally prepared. He secures legal representation to advise him on the group's activities and ensure compliance with all relevant laws.

Navigating Disputes: When conflicts or disputes arise within the community, Mark relies on his legal team to mediate and resolve issues fairly. This approach helps maintain harmony within the group and protects the organization from potential legal threats.

Protecting the Community: Mark's legal representation also plays a key role in defending the group against external threats, such as accusations or lawsuits. By being proactive in his legal strategy, Mark ensures that the community remains secure and that his leadership is protected.

Conclusion: The Weight of Responsibility

For leaders like Mark, the weight of responsibility is a central aspect of their role. By balancing personal ambition with ethical responsibility, ensuring the health and safety of members, and securing proper legal representation, cult leaders can fulfill their duty of care and protect their communities. Responsible leadership not only fosters trust and loyalty but also ensures the long-term sustainability and success of the organization.

By understanding and embracing these responsibilities, cult leaders can create an environment where followers feel safe, valued, and supported. This approach not only strengthens the community but also reinforces the leader's role as a trustworthy and ethical guide, making responsibility a cornerstone of successful and sustainable cult leadership.

Influence Techniques

Cult leaders often employ a variety of psychological techniques to influence and control their followers. These methods are designed to create strong emotional bonds, instill fear and guilt, and isolate members from external influences, thereby increasing their dependency on the cult. Understanding these techniques is crucial for both recognizing manipulative practices and comprehending the dynamics within cults.

A Story of Influence: Julia's Experience

Imagine Julia, a young woman seeking purpose and belonging. She encounters a group that immediately welcomes her with open arms, showering her with affection and attention. Over time, Julia finds herself becoming deeply attached to the group and its leader. However, as her involvement deepens, she begins to notice subtle shifts in the group's behavior towards her. The love and acceptance she initially felt are replaced by fear, guilt, and increasing isolation from her outside life. Julia's story illustrates how cults use influence techniques to control and manipulate their members.

Influence Techniques

Love Bombing

Julia's initial experience with the group highlights the technique of love bombing. Cults use various psychological techniques to influence and control members. Love bombing involves overwhelming new recruits with affection and attention to make them feel valued and accepted. This initial flood of positive reinforcement creates a bond between the recruit and the cult, making them feel special and integral to the group.

Initial Affection: Cults use various psychological techniques to influence and control members. Love bombing involves overwhelming new recruits with affection and attention to make them feel valued and accepted. For Julia, the group's constant praise, compliments, and expressions of love make her feel uniquely cherished and important.

Creating a Bond: This initial flood of positive reinforcement creates a bond between the recruit and the cult. Julia quickly forms emotional connections with the group members, feeling a sense of belonging that she has longed for. This bond makes it difficult for her to question or leave the group later on.

Building Trust: The affection and attention help build trust between Julia and the group. She begins to confide in them, sharing her fears and aspirations, which further deepens her attachment and reliance on the cult.

Fear and Guilt

As Julia becomes more involved, the group starts to use fear and guilt to control her behavior. By instilling a sense of fear about leaving the cult or disobeying its rules, leaders can maintain control over members. Julia begins to fear the consequences of leaving the group and feels guilty for even considering it, as she has been made to believe that she owes her transformation and happiness to the cult.

Fear of Punishment: Using fear of punishment or guilt over past actions to control behavior. Julia is constantly reminded of the dire consequences that await those who leave the group. Stories of former members facing ruin or spiritual damnation instill a deep-seated fear in her.

Guilt Induction: The group makes Julia feel guilty for her past mistakes and convinces her that only through their guidance can she find redemption. This guilt makes her more compliant and less likely to question the group's motives.

Maintaining Control: By instilling a sense of fear about leaving the cult or disobeying its rules, leaders can maintain control over members. Julia's fear and guilt keep her bound to the group, as she believes that leaving would result in personal and spiritual catastrophe.

Isolation

Another technique employed by the group is isolation. Encouraging members to cut ties with outside influences to increase dependency on the cult. Isolating members from family and friends reduces outside criticism and reinforces the cult's ideology. Julia finds herself gradually distancing from her family and friends, who the group portrays as negative influences.

Encouraging Separation: Encouraging members to cut ties with outside influences to increase dependency on the cult. The group advises Julia to spend less time with her family and friends, suggesting that they do not understand her new path and might try to derail her progress.

Reducing Criticism: Isolating members from family and friends reduces outside criticism and reinforces the cult's ideology. With fewer outside voices challenging the group's teachings, Julia becomes more immersed in the cult's worldview.

Increasing Dependency: As Julia becomes more isolated, her dependency on the group for emotional and social support increases. The group becomes her primary source of validation and companionship, making it even harder for her to leave.

Conclusion: The Power of Influence Techniques

For individuals like Julia, the influence techniques employed by cults can be profoundly effective. By using love bombing, fear and guilt, and isolation, cult leaders create an environment where members feel valued, fearful of leaving, and dependent on the group. These techniques ensure that members remain loyal and compliant, making it difficult for them to break free from the cult's control.

By understanding these influence techniques, cult leaders can manipulate members' emotions and behaviors, ensuring their continued loyalty and commitment. Recognizing these techniques is also crucial for those seeking to help individuals trapped in cults, as it provides insight into the psychological manipulation at play.

Group Dynamics

The dynamics within a cult are carefully crafted to reinforce loyalty, conformity, and a strong sense of community. By leveraging social psychology, cult leaders can create an environment where members feel deeply connected to the group and committed to its beliefs and goals. Understanding these group dynamics is essential to comprehending how cults maintain control and cohesion among their followers.

A Story of Unity: Daniel's Integration

Imagine Daniel, a young man seeking direction and a sense of belonging. He joins a group that immediately immerses him in its community and rituals. As Daniel becomes more involved, he notices how the group dynamics shape his perceptions and behavior. The distinct boundaries between insiders and outsiders, the influence of peer pressure, and the power of regular rituals all work together to deepen his commitment to the group.

Group Dynamics

Us vs. Them Mentality

Daniel's experience highlights the use of the Us vs. Them mentality. Cults leverage social psychology to strengthen group cohesion. Creating a clear distinction between insiders (cult members) and outsiders (the rest of the world) fosters unity and loyalty. This mentality also helps to dehumanize outsiders and justify the cult's actions against them.

Clear Distinction: Cults leverage social psychology to strengthen group cohesion. Creating a clear distinction between insiders (cult members) and outsiders (the rest of the world) fosters unity and loyalty. For Daniel, the group's teachings emphasize the unique and superior nature of their community compared to the outside world.

Dehumanizing Outsiders: This mentality also helps to dehumanize outsiders and justify the cult's actions against them. Daniel begins to see outsiders as misguided or even dangerous, reinforcing his loyalty to the group and justifying any actions taken against non-members.

Strengthening Unity: The clear distinction between "us" and "them" strengthens the sense of unity within the group. Daniel feels a strong bond with his fellow members, believing that they share a unique mission and understanding that outsiders cannot comprehend.

Peer Pressure

As Daniel becomes more integrated into the group, he experiences the effects of peer pressure. Encouraging conformity through peer pressure and communal reinforcement of beliefs. Members are more likely to conform to the group's norms and values when they see others doing the same.

Conformity: Encouraging conformity through peer pressure and communal reinforcement of beliefs. Daniel observes that when all members follow the same practices and beliefs, it creates a powerful pressure to conform. He feels compelled to adopt the group's norms to fit in and be accepted.

Communal Reinforcement: The group regularly reinforces its beliefs and practices through communal activities and discussions. Seeing his peers enthusiastically participate and express their commitment motivates Daniel to do the same.

Social Validation: Peer pressure provides social validation for Daniel's actions and beliefs. Knowing that his peers share and support his views gives him confidence and reduces any doubts he may have about the group's teachings.

Ritual and Routine

Regular group activities and rituals play a crucial role in reinforcing the cult's beliefs and creating a sense of community and belonging. For Daniel, these rituals become an integral part of his life, providing structure and a shared experience with his fellow members.

Regular Activities: Regular group activities and rituals reinforce the cult's beliefs and create a sense of community and belonging. Daniel participates in weekly meetings, communal meals, and group meditations, all designed to reinforce the group's teachings and foster a sense of unity.

Shared Experiences: The rituals provide shared experiences that strengthen Daniel's bond with other members. These activities create memories and emotional connections that deepen his commitment to the group.

Sense of Belonging: The routine of participating in regular rituals gives Daniel a sense of belonging and purpose. He feels that he is part of something larger than himself, contributing to a community that shares his values and goals.

Conclusion: The Power of Group Dynamics

For individuals like Daniel, the group dynamics within a cult can be incredibly powerful. By creating an Us vs. Them mentality, leveraging peer pressure, and implementing regular rituals and routines, cults can foster deep loyalty, conformity, and a strong sense of community among their members. These dynamics not only maintain control but also ensure that members feel a profound connection to the group and its mission.

Understanding these group dynamics is crucial for recognizing the mechanisms that cults use to influence and control their members. By being aware of these techniques, individuals can better understand the powerful forces at play within cults and the challenges faced by those seeking to leave such groups.

Cognitive Dissonance

Cognitive dissonance is a psychological phenomenon that cults adeptly exploit to deepen members' commitment and ensure their continued loyalty. When individuals experience a conflict between their beliefs and actions, they often feel uncomfortable tension. Cults leverage this discomfort to their advantage, encouraging members to rationalize and justify their involvement. This process leads to increased devotion, even in the face of contradictory evidence or doubts. Understanding how cognitive dissonance operates within cult dynamics reveals the powerful mechanisms that bind members to their groups.

A Story of Rationalization: Sarah's Journey

Consider Sarah, who has devoted several years to a cult that promises spiritual enlightenment and personal growth. Over time, Sarah has invested significant amounts of her time, money, and emotional energy into the group. Despite encountering moments of doubt and witnessing questionable practices, she finds herself unable to leave. The cognitive dissonance she experiences drives her to rationalize her continued involvement, deepening her commitment and making it increasingly difficult to break free.

Cognitive Dissonance

Deepening Commitment

Sarah's experience illustrates how cults exploit cognitive dissonance to deepen commitment. When members invest time, money, and emotional energy into the cult, they are more likely to rationalize and justify their continued involvement, even when faced with contradictory evidence or doubts. Sarah's significant investment in the cult creates a powerful incentive to stay, as leaving would mean admitting that her efforts were in vain.

Investment and Justification: Cults exploit cognitive dissonance to deepen commitment. When members invest time, money, and emotional energy into the cult, they are more likely to rationalize and justify their continued involvement, even when faced with contradictory evidence or doubts. For Sarah, the considerable resources she has dedicated to the group compel her to find ways to justify her ongoing participation.

Minimizing Doubts: When Sarah encounters information that contradicts the cult's teachings or witnesses behavior that raises questions, she minimizes these doubts by focusing on the positive aspects of her involvement. She tells herself that the good outweighs the bad, and that any issues are merely temporary setbacks.

Strengthening Belief: To reduce the discomfort of cognitive dissonance, Sarah strengthens her belief in the cult's ideology. By doubling down on her commitment, she alleviates the tension between her actions and any conflicting thoughts, reinforcing her loyalty to the group.

Self-Justification

Members may adopt the cult's beliefs more strongly to justify their sacrifices and commitment, leading to a cycle of increasing devotion. For Sarah, the need to justify her sacrifices results in an ever-deepening acceptance of the cult's doctrines and practices.

Reinforcing Beliefs: Members may adopt the cult's beliefs more strongly to justify their sacrifices and commitment, leading to a cycle of increasing devotion. Sarah finds herself embracing the cult's teachings more fervently as a way to validate the sacrifices she has made. This self-justification helps her maintain a sense of purpose and coherence in her life.

Cycle of Devotion: The process of self-justification creates a cycle of increasing devotion. Each time Sarah invests more into the cult, she feels compelled to justify her commitment by aligning her beliefs even more closely with the group's ideology. This cycle makes her more entrenched in the cult and less likely to question its practices.

Emotional Investment: Sarah's emotional investment in the cult amplifies her need for self-justification. The deep emotional connections she has formed with other members and the leader make it harder for her to entertain doubts, as doing so would threaten these valued relationships.

Sunk Cost Fallacy

The more members invest in the cult, the harder it becomes to leave, as they don't want to admit their efforts were in vain. This sunk cost fallacy traps individuals like Sarah, who feel that walking away would mean losing all the time, money, and emotional energy they have invested.

Trapped by Investment: The more members invest in the cult, the harder it becomes to leave, as they don't want to admit their efforts were in vain. For Sarah, the idea of leaving the cult is daunting because it would mean acknowledging that her years of dedication were wasted. This fear of loss keeps her bound to the group.

Reluctance to Abandon: Sarah's reluctance to abandon the cult stems from her desire to avoid feeling regret and failure. Admitting that she was wrong about the cult would not only be emotionally painful but also socially embarrassing, given her public commitment to the group.

Continued Investment: To avoid the pain of recognizing her sunk costs, Sarah continues to invest in the cult. She participates in more activities, donates additional money, and recruits new members, all in an effort to justify her initial and ongoing investments.

Conclusion: The Power of Cognitive Dissonance

For individuals like Sarah, cognitive dissonance plays a crucial role in deepening their commitment to a cult. By leveraging members' investments of time, money, and emotional energy, cults create powerful incentives for continued involvement. The processes of self-justification and the sunk cost fallacy further entrench members, making it increasingly difficult for them to leave.

Understanding how cognitive dissonance operates within cults provides valuable insights into the psychological mechanisms that sustain member loyalty and devotion. By recognizing these dynamics, individuals can better comprehend the challenges faced by those trapped in cults and the powerful forces that bind them to these groups.

Transforming into a Dictatorial Personality

A key element of effective cult leadership is the transformation into a dictatorial personality. This transformation involves establishing and reinforcing an image of divine authority, captivating and inspiring followers through charismatic performances, and maintaining consistent messaging to build trust and credibility. By mastering these elements, a leader can create an unshakeable foundation of loyalty and devotion among followers.

A Story of Transformation: Leo's Ascendancy

Consider Leo, a natural leader with an uncanny ability to connect with people. Leo's journey from an ordinary individual to a dictatorial cult leader begins with the realization that to command absolute loyalty, he must present himself as a figure of divine authority. Through carefully staged revelations, captivating performances, and consistent messaging, Leo transforms into a charismatic leader whose followers are willing to follow him unquestioningly.

Transforming into a Dictatorial Personality

Stage-Managed Revelations

Leo understands that to solidify his authority and divine status, he must create a sense of awe and wonder among his followers. Carefully planning and executing staged spiritual revelations allows him to convince his followers of his supernatural connection. These dramatic events and orchestrated "miracles" become pivotal moments that reinforce his position as a leader with divine authority.

Planning the Miraculous: Carefully plan and execute staged spiritual revelations to reinforce your authority and divine status. Leo meticulously plans events that appear spontaneous and miraculous to his followers. These events are designed to be awe-inspiring and to leave a lasting impression on the audience.

Dramatic Events: Use dramatic events and carefully orchestrated "miracles" to convince followers of your supernatural connection. Leo stages dramatic events such as sudden healings, visions, or other supernatural occurrences. These events are carefully timed and executed to maximize their impact and to ensure that followers see them as evidence of his divine connection.

Reinforcing Authority: Each staged revelation serves to reinforce Leo's authority and to deepen the belief among his followers that he is divinely chosen. The more convincing the miracles, the stronger the followers' devotion and the more unquestionable Leo's leadership becomes.

Charismatic Performance

Leo knows that beyond the staged miracles, his day-to-day interactions with his followers must captivate and inspire them. By honing his public speaking and performance skills, Leo can draw followers into his narrative, making them feel emotionally connected to him and his teachings.

Captivating Presence: Hone your public speaking and performance skills to captivate and inspire your audience. Leo practices his speaking skills diligently, learning how to use his voice, body language, and presence to captivate his audience. His speeches are carefully crafted to be compelling and memorable.

Storytelling and Emotion: Use storytelling, rhetorical questions, and emotional appeals to draw followers into your narrative. Leo uses powerful storytelling to convey his messages, often drawing on personal anecdotes or parables that resonate deeply with his followers. He employs rhetorical questions to engage his audience and emotional appeals to connect with them on a personal level.

Inspiring Devotion: Through his charismatic performances, Leo creates an emotional bond with his followers. They feel inspired by his vision and are moved by his passion, which translates into unwavering devotion and loyalty.

Consistency in Messaging

To build trust and credibility, Leo understands the importance of maintaining consistent messaging. By avoiding contradictions and ensuring that his teachings are coherent and easy to understand, Leo strengthens his followers' belief in him and his vision.

Clear and Coherent Teachings: Maintain consistent messaging to build trust and credibility. Avoid contradictions and ensure that your teachings are coherent and easy to understand. Leo develops a clear set of core teachings that he repeats consistently across all his speeches and writings. This consistency helps to build a strong foundation of belief among his followers.

Avoiding Contradictions: Leo carefully avoids any contradictions in his messages. He ensures that his public statements, written materials, and private conversations all align perfectly, preventing any confusion or doubt among his followers.

Building Credibility: By consistently delivering the same messages, Leo builds credibility and trust. His followers come to see him as a reliable and trustworthy leader whose words and actions are always in harmony.

Conclusion: The Path to Dictatorial Leadership

For leaders like Leo, transforming into a dictatorial personality involves a combination of staged spiritual revelations, charismatic performances, and consistent messaging. By mastering these elements, a leader can create an environment of absolute loyalty and devotion, where followers see them as a divinely appointed figure worthy of their unwavering support.

Understanding these techniques reveals the strategic efforts that cult leaders employ to maintain control and influence over their followers. By recognizing these dynamics, individuals can better understand the powerful forces at play within cults and the methods used by leaders to transform themselves into figures of unquestioned authority.

Managing Apocalyptic Scenarios

Cult leaders often use apocalyptic scenarios as powerful tools to galvanize their followers and reinforce their authority. By predicting catastrophic events and positioning themselves as the savior, leaders can create a sense of urgency and drive their followers to commit more deeply. This strategy involves making bold, often vague predictions, creating a heightened sense of urgency, and channeling the resulting fear and anxiety into productive activities that benefit the cult.

A Story of Prophecy: Mark's Leadership

Consider Mark, a charismatic cult leader who has built a following based on his claims of divine revelation. To solidify his control and inspire greater commitment from his followers, Mark begins to employ apocalyptic scenarios. Through predictive prophecies, the creation of urgency, and productive panic, Mark manipulates his followers' fears and anxieties, ensuring their continued loyalty and active participation in the cult's mission.

Managing Apocalyptic Scenarios

Predictive Prophecies

Mark understands that to capture his followers' attention and reinforce his divine status, he must make bold predictions about future events. Framing these predictions as divine revelations, Mark ensures that some are vague enough to be interpreted as accurate regardless of the outcome. This strategy allows him to maintain credibility even when specific predictions do not come to pass.

Bold Predictions: Make bold predictions about future events, framing them as divine revelations. Mark regularly delivers prophecies about impending disasters or significant world events, claiming that these revelations come directly from a higher power. These predictions capture the attention of his followers and reinforce his image as a prophet.

Vague Prophecies: Ensure that some of these predictions are vague enough to be interpreted as accurate regardless of the outcome. Mark is careful to include vague elements in his prophecies, such as unspecified timeframes or ambiguous descriptions. This vagueness allows him to interpret events in a way that supports his predictions, maintaining his credibility even when specific details do not materialize.

Reinforcing Authority: Each prophecy that seems to come true reinforces Mark's authority and divine connection. His followers become more convinced of his prophetic abilities and are more likely to trust and follow his guidance.

Creating Urgency

To motivate his followers to commit more deeply, Mark uses apocalyptic scenarios to create a sense of urgency. By presenting himself as the savior or guide who can protect them from impending doom, Mark ensures that his followers see him as indispensable to their survival and well-being.

Sense of Imminent Threat: Use apocalyptic scenarios to create a sense of urgency and motivate followers to commit more deeply. Mark frequently warns his followers about imminent threats, such as natural disasters, societal collapse, or divine retribution. This sense of imminent danger creates urgency and compels followers to take immediate action.

Positioning as Savior: Present yourself as the savior or guide who can protect them from impending doom. Mark positions himself as the only one who can lead his followers to safety and salvation. He emphasizes that following his guidance is the only way to survive the coming catastrophes.

Deepening Commitment: The sense of urgency drives followers to commit more deeply to the cult's mission and activities. They become more willing to invest their time, money, and resources, believing that their survival depends on their adherence to Mark's teachings.

Productive Panic

Mark cleverly channels the fear and anxiety generated by apocalyptic scenarios into productive activities. By directing his followers' heightened emotional states towards recruitment efforts, fundraising, and preparations for a "safe" future, Mark ensures that their panic benefits the cult's growth and sustainability.

Channeling Fear: Channel the fear and anxiety generated by apocalyptic scenarios into productive activities, such as increased recruitment efforts, fundraising, or preparations for a "safe" future. Mark encourages his followers to channel their fear into actions that support the cult. This might include recruiting new members, raising funds, or preparing survival kits.

Recruitment Efforts: Mark emphasizes the importance of bringing new members into the fold, framing it as a way to save more people from the impending doom. His followers, driven by fear and a sense of urgency, become enthusiastic recruiters, spreading the cult's message and expanding its reach.

Fundraising and Preparations: Mark organizes fundraising campaigns and preparation activities, such as building safe havens or stockpiling supplies. The heightened sense of urgency makes followers more willing to contribute financially and participate in these efforts, believing that their survival depends on it.

Conclusion: The Power of Apocalyptic Scenarios

For leaders like Mark, managing apocalyptic scenarios is a powerful strategy to maintain control and deepen the commitment of followers. By making predictive prophecies, creating a sense of urgency, and channeling fear into productive activities, cult leaders can manipulate followers' emotions and actions to benefit the cult's mission.

Understanding these techniques reveals the strategic manipulation that underlies many cult dynamics. Recognizing the use of apocalyptic scenarios can help individuals comprehend the powerful psychological forces at play within cults and the challenges faced by those attempting to break free from such environments.

Developing Income Streams

A sustainable and diverse income stream is crucial for the growth and longevity of any cult. By establishing multiple avenues for generating revenue, cult leaders can ensure financial stability and fund their activities and missions. These income streams not only provide financial resources but also serve as effective tools for recruitment and member engagement. Key strategies for developing income streams include establishing front groups, encouraging tithes and donations, and merchandising.

A Story of Diversification: Claire's Strategy

Consider Claire, a charismatic cult leader who understands the importance of financial stability for her group's survival and growth. Claire devises a multi-faceted strategy to develop income streams that support her cult's mission and expand its influence. By leveraging front groups, encouraging tithes and donations, and creating branded merchandise, Claire builds a robust financial foundation for her cult.

Developing Income Streams

Front Groups

Claire recognizes that front groups can serve dual purposes: attracting new members and generating revenue. She establishes various front groups, such as spiritual retreats, drug rehabilitation programs, and management seminars, to reach a broader audience and provide a steady income stream.

Multi-Purpose Organizations: Establish front groups such as spiritual retreats, drug rehabilitation programs, and management seminars to attract new members and generate revenue. Claire's front groups offer services that appeal to different segments of society, making them effective recruiting grounds while also bringing in income.

Attracting New Members: These front groups can serve as a recruiting ground for the cult while providing a steady income stream. Participants in Claire's programs often become interested in her teachings and eventually join the cult. The retreats and seminars introduce new individuals to the cult's philosophy in a non-threatening, appealing way.

Generating Revenue: The fees collected from these programs provide a reliable source of income. Claire ensures that the services offered are of high quality, which not only attracts more participants but also justifies higher fees, increasing the overall revenue.

Tithes and Donations

Encouraging regular financial contributions from members is another critical component of Claire's income strategy. By emphasizing the spiritual benefits of giving and the importance of supporting the cult's mission, Claire fosters a culture of generosity and financial commitment among her followers.

Spiritual Emphasis: Encourage regular financial contributions from members through tithes, donations, and special offerings. Claire regularly speaks about the spiritual benefits of giving, framing it as a vital practice that enhances personal growth and ensures the cult's continued success.

Regular Contributions: Claire implements a system for collecting tithes and donations, making it easy and routine for members to contribute. This system includes regular reminders and special events focused on fundraising, ensuring a steady flow of financial support.

Special Offerings: In addition to regular tithes, Claire organizes special offerings and fundraising campaigns for specific projects or needs. These events create opportunities for members to give more generously, often motivated by the desire to contribute to a significant cause or milestone.

Merchandising

To further diversify her income streams, Claire develops and sells branded merchandise that promotes the cult's teachings and image. These products serve not only as a source of revenue but also as marketing tools that spread the cult's message.

Branded Products: Develop and sell branded merchandise, including books, audio recordings, clothing, and other items that promote the cult's teachings and image. Claire creates a range of products that appeal to her followers and help them feel connected to the cult.

Promotional Materials: The merchandise includes items like books and audio recordings of Claire's teachings, which serve as both educational tools and promotional materials. These products help spread Claire's message beyond the immediate group, reaching potential new members.

Community Building: Wearing or using branded merchandise helps members feel a sense of belonging and pride in their association with the cult. It also sparks curiosity and conversations with outsiders, indirectly promoting the cult and potentially attracting new followers.

Conclusion: Building a Robust Financial Foundation

For leaders like Claire, developing diverse income streams is essential for maintaining financial stability and supporting the cult's mission. By establishing front groups, encouraging tithes and donations, and creating branded merchandise, cult leaders can generate steady revenue while also expanding their influence and reach.

Understanding these strategies reveals how cults can sustain themselves financially and grow their membership base. By recognizing the importance of financial diversification, cult leaders can ensure their groups remain resilient and capable of achieving their long-term goals.

Recruitment Tactics

Effective recruitment tactics are essential for growing and sustaining a cult. Cult leaders use a variety of methods to attract new members, often focusing on individuals who are most vulnerable and in need of support. By targeting vulnerabilities, using a personalized approach, and hosting recruitment events, cults can successfully draw in new recruits and integrate them into their community.

A Story of Recruitment: Maria's Methods

Consider Maria, a cult leader who is adept at identifying potential recruits and drawing them into her group. Maria's recruitment strategy involves pinpointing individuals who are emotionally and socially vulnerable, using a personal approach to connect with them, and organizing events that showcase her cult's teachings and community. Through these methods, Maria is able to continually expand her following.

Recruitment Tactics

Targeting Vulnerabilities

Maria knows that individuals who are emotionally scarred, socially isolated, or experiencing personal crises are more likely to be receptive to her cult's message. By identifying and targeting these individuals, Maria can offer them the support and transformation they are seeking, making them prime candidates for recruitment.

Identifying Targets: Identify and target individuals who are emotionally scarred, socially isolated, or experiencing personal crises. Maria looks for people who show signs of emotional distress, loneliness, or life disruptions, such as recent breakups, job losses, or relocations.

Understanding Needs: These individuals are more likely to be receptive to the cult's message and promises of support and transformation. Maria trains her recruitment team to listen carefully to potential recruits' stories, understanding their specific needs and pain points.

Offering Solutions: By empathizing with their struggles and offering solutions, Maria creates a compelling narrative of support and transformation. She presents her cult as a safe haven where individuals can find healing, community, and purpose.

Personal Approach

Maria uses a personalized approach to recruitment, building genuine relationships with potential members. This approach involves addressing their specific needs and concerns, offering tailored solutions, and creating a sense of hope and belonging.

Building Relationships: Use a personalized approach to recruitment, building relationships with potential members and addressing their specific needs and concerns. Maria emphasizes the importance of personal connections, encouraging her team to form genuine relationships with recruits.

Tailored Solutions: Offer solutions to their problems and create a sense of hope and belonging. Maria's recruiters tailor their message to each individual, offering specific ways the cult can help them overcome their challenges and achieve their goals.

Creating Belonging: Maria ensures that new recruits feel welcomed and valued from the moment they express interest. By fostering a sense of belonging, she makes it difficult for them to walk away from the group once they have experienced its supportive environment.

Recruitment Events

To attract potential recruits, Maria hosts a variety of public events, workshops, and seminars. These events serve as a platform to showcase the cult's teachings and community, making them appealing to attendees and encouraging them to join.

Public Events: Host public events, workshops, and seminars that attract potential recruits. Maria organizes events that are open to the public, such as lectures, spiritual retreats, and self-help workshops, which draw in people seeking knowledge and community.

Showcasing Teachings: Use these events to showcase the cult's teachings and community, making them appealing to attendees. At these events, Maria and her team present the cult's philosophy in an engaging and accessible way, highlighting the benefits of joining the group.

Creating Appeal: The events are designed to be welcoming and inclusive, creating a positive first impression. Attendees are encouraged to participate in discussions, ask questions, and connect with current members, who share their positive experiences and personal transformations.

Conclusion: Mastering Recruitment Tactics

For leaders like Maria, mastering recruitment tactics is crucial for the growth and sustainability of their cults. By targeting individuals who are emotionally and socially vulnerable, using a personalized approach to connect with them, and hosting events that showcase the cult's teachings and community, cult leaders can effectively attract new members and integrate them into their group.

Understanding these recruitment tactics reveals the strategic efforts behind cult growth and the methods used to draw in and retain new followers. Recognizing these tactics can help individuals understand the powerful pull of cults and the challenges faced by those attempting to resist or leave such groups.

Exerting Control

Exerting control over members is a fundamental aspect of cult leadership. By using psychological techniques such as love bombing, alternating cruelty, and claiming divine revelations, cult leaders can create an environment of dependency and unwavering loyalty. These methods help to quickly integrate new members, keep them emotionally off balance, and reinforce the leader's authority.

A Story of Control: Sophia's Strategy

Consider Sophia, a charismatic cult leader who is adept at maintaining control over her followers. Sophia uses a combination of love bombing, alternating cruelty, and divine revelations to ensure that her members remain loyal and obedient. Through these techniques, she creates a strong emotional bond, instills dependency, and continually reinforces her authority.

Exerting Control

Love Bombing

Sophia understands the power of love bombing to create strong emotional bonds and dependency among new recruits. By overwhelming them with affection and attention, she quickly integrates new members into the cult and builds their loyalty.

Overwhelming Affection: Use love bombing to overwhelm new recruits with affection and attention, creating a strong emotional bond and dependency. Sophia instructs her existing members to shower new recruits with praise, kindness, and attention. This overwhelming display of affection makes new members feel valued and cherished.

Building Emotional Bonds: This technique helps to quickly integrate new members into the cult and build loyalty. The intense positive reinforcement creates a strong emotional bond between the recruits and the group, making them feel like they have found a new family.

Creating Dependency: The affection and attention make new members dependent on the cult for their emotional well-being. They begin to rely on the group for validation and support, which strengthens their loyalty and makes it difficult for them to leave.

Alternating Cruelty

To maintain control and keep members emotionally off balance, Sophia uses the technique of alternating cruelty. By switching between kindness and cruelty, she creates an unpredictable environment that reinforces loyalty and obedience through intermittent reinforcement.

Unpredictable Behavior: Alternate between kindness and cruelty to keep members off balance and dependent on your approval. Sophia alternates between periods of warmth and support and episodes of harsh criticism or punishment. This unpredictability keeps members constantly seeking her approval.

Intermittent Reinforcement: This technique, known as intermittent reinforcement, creates an unpredictable environment that reinforces loyalty and obedience. Members never know when they will receive kindness or cruelty, so they remain constantly vigilant and eager to please Sophia.

Reinforcing Dependency: The alternating cruelty creates a psychological dependency on Sophia's approval. Members are willing to endure the cruelty in the hope of receiving kindness, which strengthens their loyalty and obedience.

Divine Revelation

Sophia claims ongoing divine revelations to maintain her authority and control over the cult. By presenting these revelations as direct communications from a higher power, she reinforces her position as the cult's leader and prophet.

Claiming Divinity: Claim ongoing divine revelations to maintain your authority and control over the cult. Sophia regularly announces new revelations that she claims to receive from a higher power. These revelations often include directives for the group and messages that reinforce her divine status.

Reinforcing Authority: Present these revelations as direct communications from a higher power, reinforcing your position as the cult's leader and prophet. The divine revelations bolster Sophia's authority, making her followers believe that she has a unique and sacred connection to the divine.

Maintaining Control: The ongoing revelations ensure that Sophia remains the central figure of authority and guidance within the cult. Followers look to her for direction and believe that disobeying her is equivalent to disobeying a higher power.

Conclusion: The Techniques of Control

For leaders like Sophia, exerting control is essential for maintaining loyalty and obedience within the cult. By using love bombing to create strong emotional bonds, alternating cruelty to keep members off balance, and claiming divine revelations to reinforce authority, cult leaders can effectively manage and control their followers.

Understanding these techniques reveals the psychological manipulation at play within cults and the methods used to maintain control over members. Recognizing these tactics can help individuals understand the powerful dynamics of cult influence and the challenges faced by those trying to break free from such groups.

Handling Authorities

Navigating the complexities of legal and media scrutiny is crucial for the survival and growth of a cult. Effective strategies in handling authorities involve legal navigation, managing media relations, and ensuring compliance while creating plausible cover stories for any controversial activities. These approaches help protect the cult from legal threats and maintain a positive public image.

A Story of Evasion: Jacob's Tactics

Consider Jacob, a seasoned cult leader who has faced numerous legal and media challenges over the years. To protect his organization and maintain its operations, Jacob employs a variety of tactics to handle authorities effectively. By developing robust legal strategies, controlling the media narrative, and ensuring compliance with laws, Jacob successfully shields his cult from external threats.

Handling Authorities

Legal Navigation

Jacob understands that navigating legal issues is essential for protecting his cult. He develops strategies to deal with authorities when people go "missing" or other legal challenges arise. By maintaining a legal team, Jacob ensures that his cult can handle disputes and protect itself from legal threats.

Strategic Planning: Develop strategies to navigate legal issues and deal with authorities when people go "missing" or other legal challenges arise. Jacob creates detailed plans for responding to various legal scenarios, ensuring that his cult is prepared for any situation.

Legal Team: Maintain a legal team to handle disputes and protect the cult from legal threats. Jacob hires experienced attorneys who specialize in areas relevant to the cult's activities. This team provides legal advice, represents the cult in court, and helps navigate complex legal landscapes.

Handling Disputes: The legal team is responsible for resolving disputes, whether they involve internal conflicts or external accusations. By having legal representation, Jacob ensures that the cult can effectively defend itself and mitigate potential damage.

Media Relations

Managing the cult's public image is crucial for Jacob. He controls the narrative by presenting a positive and benign image of the cult and is prepared to respond to negative press and accusations. By effectively managing media relations, Jacob minimizes the impact of adverse publicity.

Positive Image: Manage the cult's public image and relations with the media. Control the narrative by presenting a positive and benign image of the cult. Jacob regularly engages with the media, offering interviews and press releases that highlight the cult's charitable activities and positive impact on the community.

Media Training: Jacob trains key members of the cult on how to interact with the media. This training ensures that they present a consistent and positive message, avoiding any statements that could be misinterpreted or used against the cult.

Responding to Negative Press: Be prepared to respond to negative press and accusations. Jacob's media team monitors news coverage and social media, quickly addressing any negative stories or accusations. They provide counter-narratives and evidence to refute false claims, aiming to maintain the cult's reputation.

Compliance and Cover

To avoid legal repercussions, Jacob ensures that the cult complies with local laws and regulations. He also creates plausible cover stories for any controversial or illegal activities, using legal and financial structures to protect the cult's assets and leaders.

Legal Compliance: Ensure that the cult complies with local laws and regulations. Jacob stays informed about relevant laws and regulations, adjusting the cult's practices as necessary to remain compliant. This proactive approach helps avoid legal issues before they arise.

Plausible Cover Stories: Create plausible cover stories for any controversial or illegal activities. Jacob devises believable explanations for activities that might attract legal or media scrutiny. These cover stories are supported by fabricated documentation and consistent narratives among members.

Asset Protection: Use legal and financial structures to protect the cult's assets and leaders. Jacob establishes shell companies, trusts, and other financial mechanisms to safeguard the cult's assets. These structures make it difficult for authorities to seize assets or hold leaders personally accountable for the cult's actions.

Conclusion: Strategic Management of Authorities

For leaders like Jacob, handling authorities involves a combination of legal navigation, media management, and ensuring compliance with laws. By developing robust legal strategies, maintaining a positive public image, and creating plausible cover stories, cult leaders can protect their organizations from external threats and maintain operational stability.

Understanding these tactics reveals the strategic efforts that cults use to evade legal challenges and control their public image. Recognizing these methods can help individuals comprehend the sophisticated measures cults take to safeguard their existence and the challenges authorities face in holding them accountable.

Structuring Your Cult

Choosing the right structure for your cult is crucial for achieving your primary goals, whether they are wealth generation, power, and control, or a balance of both. The structure you choose will determine how you interact with the outside world, how you recruit and retain members, and how you manage your internal environment. Three primary models to consider are the Open Society Model, the Closed Compound Model, and Hybrid Models.

A Story of Structure: Alex's Decisions

Alex, an ambitious cult leader, is at a crossroads. He needs to decide how to structure his growing cult to best achieve his goals. By examining the benefits and challenges of different models, Alex can make an informed decision that aligns with his vision for the future.

Structuring Your Cult

Open Society Model

If Alex's primary goal is wealth generation, he might choose an Open Society Model. This model allows for greater interaction with the outside world, facilitating recruitment and fundraising efforts. Open societies use public events, businesses, and media to attract new members and generate income.

Greater Interaction: Choose an "Open Society" model if your primary goal is wealth. This model allows for greater interaction with the outside world, facilitating recruitment and fundraising efforts. Alex opens his cult to the public through various initiatives such as seminars, workshops, and community events.

Public Events and Businesses: Open societies can use public events, businesses, and media to attract new members and generate income. Alex sets up businesses like wellness centers, bookstores, and cafes that promote the cult's teachings while generating revenue. Public events like lectures and spiritual retreats serve as both recruitment tools and income sources.

Media Engagement: Alex uses social media, websites, and press releases to spread the cult's message, reaching a broader audience. Positive media coverage helps build the cult's reputation and attracts potential members.

Closed Compound Model

If Alex's primary goal is power and control, he might choose a Closed Compound Model. This model isolates members from the outside world, creating a tightly controlled environment where the leader's authority is absolute. Closed compounds use communal living, strict rules, and constant surveillance to maintain control and loyalty.

Isolation: Choose a "Closed Compound" model if your primary goal is power and control. This model isolates members from the outside world, creating a tightly controlled environment where the leader's authority is absolute. Alex establishes a secluded compound where members live and work, cut off from external influences.

Communal Living: Closed compounds can use communal living, strict rules, and constant surveillance to maintain control and loyalty. Alex enforces communal living arrangements, with shared duties and resources, fostering a sense of unity and dependence on the cult.

Strict Rules and Surveillance: Alex implements strict rules regarding behavior, communication, and movement. Constant surveillance ensures compliance and discourages dissent. Regular meetings and rituals reinforce loyalty and obedience to Alex's authority.

Hybrid Models

Alex might also consider a Hybrid Model that combines elements of both open societies and closed compounds. These models can balance wealth generation with control, allowing for greater flexibility in achieving goals.

Balancing Wealth and Control: Consider hybrid models that combine elements of both open societies and closed compounds. These models can balance wealth generation with control, allowing for greater flexibility in achieving your goals. Alex creates a structure that includes both public-facing businesses and a secluded residential area for core members.

Flexible Interaction: In a hybrid model, Alex can allow some members to interact with the outside world for recruitment and fundraising purposes while keeping others isolated to maintain control. This flexibility enables the cult to benefit from external income sources without compromising internal discipline.

Dual Operations: Alex runs public events and businesses to attract new members and generate income, while maintaining a closed environment for core followers. This approach ensures a steady flow of resources and recruits while keeping the inner circle tightly controlled.

Conclusion: Choosing the Right Structure

For leaders like Alex, choosing the right structure for their cult is essential for achieving their primary goals. Whether opting for an Open Society Model to maximize wealth, a Closed Compound Model to exert absolute control, or a Hybrid Model to balance both, the structure will define how the cult operates and interacts with the world.

Understanding the benefits and challenges of each model allows cult leaders to strategically plan their organization's growth and sustainability. By aligning the cult's structure with its goals, leaders can effectively manage their members, resources, and external relations to build a thriving and resilient organization.

Chapter 2: Building the Foundation

Creating a successful cult requires a solid foundation built on three key elements: a charismatic leader, clear core beliefs and dogma, and a compelling origin story. These components work together to attract followers, establish authority, and foster a sense of community and purpose. In this detailed guide, we will explore each of these foundational elements in depth, providing a comprehensive blueprint for building a resilient and appealing cult.

1. Creating a Charismatic Persona

To attract and retain followers, a cult leader must develop a charismatic persona that inspires trust and admiration. This involves honing public speaking skills, exuding confidence, and connecting emotionally with followers.

- **Developing Presence**
  - **Public Speaking**: Regularly practice public speaking to become comfortable and engaging in front of an audience. Focus on articulation, pacing, and clarity. Use pauses effectively to emphasize key points and keep the audience engaged.
  - **Body Language**: Use open and confident body language. Stand tall with shoulders back, make purposeful movements, and use gestures to emphasize points. Avoid crossing arms or slouching, as these can convey insecurity.
  - **Eye Contact**: Maintain eye contact with individuals in the audience to create a personal connection and convey confidence. Scan the room slowly, making eye contact with different people to make everyone feel included.
- **Building Confidence**
  - **Mastery of Teachings**: Deeply understand and internalize the cult's teachings and beliefs so you can speak about them with genuine conviction. This knowledge base will allow you to answer questions confidently and persuasively.
  - **Preparation**: Thoroughly prepare for speeches and interactions. Know your material inside out to build and project confidence. Rehearse your talks and anticipate potential questions or challenges.
  - **Positive Self-Image**: Develop a positive self-image and practice self-affirmation techniques to build self-confidence. Visualize successful interactions and remind yourself of past successes.
- **Personal Branding**
  - **Unique Style**: Create a distinct personal brand, including a unique style of dress that reflects your vision and values. This could involve specific colors, symbols, or types of clothing that set you apart and make you easily recognizable.
  - **Symbols and Icons**: Develop specific symbols and icons associated with your persona. These can be used in literature, merchandise, and rituals to reinforce your brand.
  - **Consistent Messaging**: Ensure your messaging is consistent across all platforms and interactions. Develop key phrases or mantras that encapsulate your beliefs and repeat them often to reinforce your identity.

- **Emotional Connection**
  - **Storytelling**: Use storytelling to connect emotionally with followers. Share personal anecdotes, parables, and examples that illustrate your teachings and make them relatable.
  - **Empathy**: Show genuine empathy for your followers' struggles and aspirations. Listen actively to their concerns and offer compassionate responses that make them feel understood and valued.
  - **Engagement**: Engage with followers on a personal level. Remember their names, ask about their lives, and show interest in their well-being.

2. Defining Core Beliefs and Dogma

Clear, well-defined core beliefs and dogma are essential for creating a sense of purpose and direction within the cult. These foundational principles guide the actions and decisions of the group and provide a cohesive framework for members.

- **Identifying Values**
  - **Key Principles**: Determine the key values that will underpin the cult's philosophy. These could include principles like community, spiritual growth, self-improvement, or enlightenment.
  - **Alignment**: Ensure these values align with the personal beliefs and vision of the leader. This alignment will make the teachings more authentic and compelling.
- **Formulating Doctrine**
  - **Belief System**: Develop a comprehensive belief system that outlines the cult's core teachings and practices. This should be detailed and cover all aspects of life, including morality, purpose, and the nature of the universe.
  - **Written Doctrine**: Create written documents that clearly articulate the doctrine. These can be used for teaching new members and as a reference for existing members.
- **Creating Rituals**
  - **Regular Activities**: Design rituals that reflect the core beliefs and provide regular opportunities for members to come together. These could include weekly meetings, meditation sessions, communal meals, or ceremonies.
  - **Symbolic Acts**: Incorporate symbolic acts into the rituals that reinforce the cult's teachings. These acts should be meaningful and evoke a sense of connection and purpose.
- **Establishing Rules**
  - **Code of Conduct**: Set clear rules and expectations for behavior. This code of conduct should cover interactions within the group, adherence to the teachings, and personal conduct.
  - **Enforcement**: Develop a system for enforcing these rules, including consequences for violations. This could involve peer accountability, disciplinary actions, or expulsion from the group.

3. Crafting a Compelling Origin Story

A compelling origin story legitimizes the cult and inspires followers. It provides a sense of history and purpose, making members feel part of something significant and destined.

- **Mythic Elements**
  - **Heroic Themes**: Incorporate themes of heroism, struggle, and divine intervention. These elements create a sense of grandeur and significance around the cult's origins.
  - **Archetypes**: Use archetypal characters and narratives that resonate on a deep psychological level. This could include the hero's journey, battles between good and evil, or the quest for enlightenment.
- **Personal Revelation**
  - **Leader's Journey**: Narrate a powerful personal experience that led the leader to discover the cult's core truths. This story should position the leader as divinely chosen or uniquely enlightened.
  - **Transformative Moments**: Highlight transformative moments in the leader's journey that led to profound insights or revelations. These moments should be dramatic and emotionally compelling.
- **Symbolic Imagery**
  - **Visual Symbols**: Use symbolic imagery to enhance the story's visual and emotional impact. This could include specific symbols, visions, or metaphors that resonate with followers.
  - **Narrative Devices**: Employ narrative devices like metaphors, allegories, and parables to convey deeper meanings and reinforce the teachings.
- **Historical Context**
  - **Link to History**: Place the origin story within a broader historical context. Link the cult's emergence to significant historical events or figures to give it credibility and relevance.
  - **Divine Plan**: Suggest that the cult's emergence is part of a larger, divine plan. This reinforces the sense of purpose and destiny among followers.

Conclusion: Laying a Strong Foundation

For leaders like Sarah, Alex, and Jacob, building a strong foundation is essential for creating a successful and sustainable cult. By cultivating a charismatic persona, defining clear core beliefs and dogma, and crafting a compelling origin story, cult leaders can attract and retain devoted followers, establish authority, and create a cohesive, resilient community.

Understanding these foundational elements is crucial for anyone seeking to understand the dynamics of cult formation and the strategies used by leaders to build and maintain their influence. Recognizing the importance of these components can provide valuable insights into the power and appeal of charismatic leadership and tightly-knit communities.

Developing Presence

Creating a charismatic presence is essential for any cult leader looking to attract and retain followers. This involves mastering public speaking, exuding confidence through body language, and maintaining eye contact to create strong emotional connections with the audience. Let's explore how one aspiring leader, Sarah, develops her presence to captivate her followers.

A Story of Presence: Sarah's Transformation

Sarah, an aspiring cult leader, knew that to build a loyal following, she needed to develop a commanding presence. By focusing on her public speaking, body language, and eye contact, she transformed herself into a charismatic and influential figure.

Developing Presence

Sarah understood that to engage and inspire her audience, she needed to become an exceptional public speaker. She dedicated herself to regular practice, honing her skills to ensure she was both comfortable and captivating in front of an audience. She spent hours each week practicing her speeches, standing in front of mirrors, recording herself, and reviewing her performance to identify areas for improvement. This rigorous practice helped her become more comfortable and confident.

Focusing on articulation, Sarah ensured her words were clear and understandable. She also worked on her pacing, using pauses effectively to emphasize key points and keep her audience engaged. By mastering these techniques, Sarah made her speeches compelling and memorable. During her practice sessions, Sarah imagined addressing large crowds. She incorporated pauses, changes in tone, and strategic emphasis to highlight important messages, keeping her listeners on the edge of their seats.

Sarah knew that confident body language was crucial for projecting authority and engaging her audience. She worked on using open and assertive body language to complement her verbal messages. Standing tall with her shoulders back, Sarah avoided any closed-off postures like crossing her arms. This open stance conveyed confidence and made her appear approachable. She practiced making purposeful movements, using gestures to emphasize her points and keep the audience's attention. By avoiding fidgeting or slouching, she projected a strong, composed image. Consistently using confident body language, Sarah exuded assurance, making her followers feel secure in her leadership. Her deliberate and meaningful movements added weight to her words and helped maintain the audience's attention.

Making eye contact was another key aspect of Sarah's presence. It helped her create personal connections with her audience and convey sincerity and confidence. Sarah practiced scanning the room slowly, making eye contact with different individuals to make everyone feel included. This practice helped her establish a personal connection with her audience, making them feel valued and understood. By maintaining eye contact, Sarah conveyed confidence and sincerity.

Her followers felt seen and respected, which strengthened their emotional bond with her. Eye contact kept Sarah's audience engaged, ensuring they were attentive and receptive to her message. This connection made her followers more likely to trust and follow her guidance.

Conclusion: The Power of Presence

Through dedication and practice, Sarah developed a commanding presence that captivated and engaged her audience. By mastering public speaking, using confident body language, and maintaining eye contact, she transformed herself into a charismatic leader. This foundation of presence was crucial for attracting and retaining devoted followers, helping Sarah build a strong and influential cult. Understanding the importance of presence and how to cultivate it can provide valuable insights into the dynamics of charismatic leadership and effective communication.

Building Confidence

A charismatic leader must exude confidence to inspire and maintain the trust of their followers. Building confidence involves mastering the cult's teachings, thoroughly preparing for all interactions, and developing a positive self-image. These elements work together to create a leader who can speak with conviction, handle challenges adeptly, and maintain a strong presence. Here's how Sarah, our aspiring cult leader, builds her confidence.

A Story of Confidence: Sarah's Growth

Sarah knew that to become an effective leader, she needed to project unwavering confidence. She realized that confidence is built through deep understanding, thorough preparation, and a positive self-image. With these goals in mind, she set out to transform herself into a leader her followers could believe in.

Mastery of Teachings

Sarah understood that to speak with genuine conviction, she needed to deeply understand and internalize the cult's teachings and beliefs. She spent countless hours studying the doctrines, reflecting on their meanings, and considering how they applied to everyday life. This deep knowledge base allowed her to answer questions confidently and persuasively, making her appear as a knowledgeable and trustworthy leader. Whenever a follower had a doubt or a question, Sarah's thorough understanding enabled her to provide clear and compelling answers, reinforcing her authority and credibility.

Preparation

Preparation was another key aspect of building Sarah's confidence. She knew that being well-prepared would help her handle any situation with ease. Before speeches and interactions, Sarah thoroughly prepared by knowing her material inside out. She rehearsed her talks multiple times, anticipating potential questions or challenges that might arise. By practicing her responses and refining her delivery, she ensured that she could address any issues confidently. This meticulous preparation helped her project confidence, as she was never caught off guard and always had a well-thought-out response ready.

Positive Self-Image

Developing a positive self-image was essential for Sarah to build and maintain her self-confidence. She practiced self-affirmation techniques, reminding herself of her strengths and past successes. Each day, she visualized successful interactions, imagining herself speaking confidently and receiving positive feedback from her followers. This mental practice reinforced her belief in her abilities and prepared her psychologically for real-life interactions. By focusing on her achievements and visualizing future success, Sarah cultivated a positive self-image that radiated confidence.

Conclusion: The Foundation of Confidence

Through deep mastery of her teachings, thorough preparation, and the cultivation of a positive self-image, Sarah built the confidence necessary to lead her followers effectively. Her unwavering conviction in the cult's beliefs, combined with her readiness for any situation and her strong self-belief, made her a charismatic and authoritative leader. This confidence not only helped her gain the trust and admiration of her followers but also ensured that she could handle challenges with poise and assurance. Understanding and implementing these strategies can help any aspiring leader build the confidence needed to inspire and guide their followers effectively.

Personal Branding

A strong personal brand is crucial for any leader looking to establish a distinct identity and attract followers. It involves creating a unique style, developing symbols and icons, and ensuring consistent messaging. This personal brand not only makes the leader easily recognizable but also reinforces their vision and values. Here's how Sarah, our aspiring cult leader, builds her personal brand.

A Story of Branding: Sarah's Identity

Sarah knew that to stand out and create a lasting impression, she needed to develop a strong personal brand. By focusing on her unique style, creating distinctive symbols and icons, and maintaining consistent messaging, she crafted an identity that resonated deeply with her followers and set her apart from other leaders.

Unique Style

Sarah understood that her appearance could be a powerful tool in reinforcing her vision and values. She created a distinct personal style that included specific colors, symbols, and types of clothing that made her easily recognizable. She chose attire that was both unique and symbolic of her beliefs—flowing robes in shades of blue and green to represent tranquility and growth, adorned with intricate patterns that symbolized interconnectedness. This unique style not only made her stand out but also conveyed a sense of purpose and authenticity to her followers.

Symbols and Icons

To further solidify her personal brand, Sarah developed specific symbols and icons associated with her persona. She created a logo featuring an intertwined circle and triangle, symbolizing unity and spiritual enlightenment. This logo was prominently displayed in all her literature, merchandise, and rituals. She also introduced a series of hand gestures and chants that were unique to her teachings, which helped create a sense of unity and belonging among her followers. These symbols and icons became integral parts of her brand, reinforcing her identity and making her teachings more memorable.

Consistent Messaging

Sarah knew that consistency in messaging was key to building a strong personal brand. She developed key phrases and mantras that encapsulated her beliefs and repeated them often across all platforms and interactions. Phrases like "Harmony through Unity" and "Growth through Knowledge" became staples in her speeches, written materials, and social media posts. By ensuring that her messages were always aligned and consistently delivered, she reinforced her identity and made her teachings easily recognizable. This consistency helped build trust among her followers, as they knew what to expect and felt a deeper connection to her vision.

Conclusion: The Power of Personal Branding

Through careful development of her unique style, the creation of distinctive symbols and icons, and the maintenance of consistent messaging, Sarah built a powerful personal brand. Her distinct identity set her apart from other leaders and created a strong emotional connection with her followers. This branding not only made her more recognizable but also reinforced her vision and values, making her teachings more impactful and memorable. Understanding and implementing these elements of personal branding can help any aspiring leader create a compelling and lasting identity that resonates with their audience.

Emotional Connection

Building a strong emotional connection with followers is essential for any leader looking to inspire loyalty and commitment. Emotional connection can be cultivated through storytelling, showing empathy, and engaging personally with followers. Here's how Sarah, our aspiring cult leader, creates deep emotional bonds with her followers.

A Story of Connection: Sarah's Journey

Sarah understood that to truly lead and inspire her followers, she needed to connect with them on an emotional level. By using storytelling, showing empathy, and engaging personally, she was able to build strong emotional bonds that fostered loyalty and trust within her community.

Storytelling

Sarah realized the power of storytelling in making her teachings relatable and memorable. She often shared personal anecdotes that highlighted her own journey and struggles, helping her followers see her as someone who understood their experiences. For instance, she recounted how she overcame personal doubts and fears to embrace her vision, illustrating the transformative power of her teachings. Additionally, Sarah used parables and examples to convey complex ideas in a way that was easy to understand and emotionally engaging. These stories made her teachings come alive, resonating deeply with her followers and reinforcing her messages.

Empathy

To build a deeper emotional connection, Sarah showed genuine empathy for her followers' struggles and aspirations. She listened actively to their concerns, offering compassionate responses that made them feel understood and valued. For example, when a follower shared their personal challenges, Sarah took the time to listen without interrupting, acknowledged their feelings, and provided thoughtful advice based on her teachings. This empathy helped her followers feel seen and appreciated, strengthening their bond with her. Sarah's ability to connect on an emotional level made her followers more willing to open up and trust her guidance.

Engagement

Engaging with followers on a personal level was another key strategy Sarah employed. She made a point to remember their names, ask about their lives, and show genuine interest in their well-being. For instance, during group meetings, Sarah would often take a few minutes to check in with individual members, asking about their recent experiences and offering words of encouragement. This personal attention made her followers feel important and valued, reinforcing their loyalty to her. By showing that she cared about their personal lives and well-being, Sarah built a community where followers felt emotionally connected and supported.

Conclusion: The Impact of Emotional Connection

Through storytelling, empathy, and personal engagement, Sarah was able to create strong emotional connections with her followers. These connections fostered a sense of trust, loyalty, and community within her cult, making her teachings more impactful and her leadership more effective. By understanding and implementing these strategies, any aspiring leader can build deep emotional bonds with their followers, creating a foundation of support and devotion that is essential for successful leadership.

Identifying Values

Determining the key values that underpin a cult's philosophy is crucial for creating a cohesive and compelling belief system. These values provide direction and purpose, guiding the actions and decisions of the group. Here's how Sarah, our aspiring cult leader, identifies and aligns the values of her cult to create a strong and authentic foundation.

A Story of Values: Sarah's Insight

Sarah knew that to build a meaningful and sustainable cult, she needed to identify core values that would resonate deeply with her followers and guide the group's philosophy. By determining key principles and ensuring alignment with her own beliefs and vision, Sarah created a value system that was both authentic and compelling.

Key Principles

Sarah began by reflecting on the principles that she believed were essential for a fulfilling and enlightened life. She identified several key values that she wanted to form the foundation of her cult's philosophy:

Community: Sarah believed that a strong sense of community was vital for personal and collective growth. She envisioned her cult as a supportive network where members could find friendship, encouragement, and mutual aid. This value emphasized the importance of cooperation, compassion, and shared goals.

Spiritual Growth: Another cornerstone of Sarah's philosophy was the pursuit of spiritual growth. She wanted her followers to embark on a journey of self-discovery and enlightenment, seeking deeper understanding and connection with the divine. This value highlighted the importance of introspection, meditation, and spiritual practices.

Self-Improvement: Sarah also valued continuous self-improvement. She believed that individuals should strive to better themselves in all aspects of life, including their physical, mental, and emotional well-being. This principle encouraged followers to adopt healthy habits, seek knowledge, and cultivate positive mindsets.

Enlightenment: Ultimately, Sarah's vision was centered around the goal of enlightenment. She aimed to guide her followers toward achieving higher states of consciousness and understanding, transcending ordinary experiences. This value stressed the importance of wisdom, insight, and the pursuit of truth.

Alignment

To ensure that these values would be compelling and authentic, Sarah needed to align them with her own personal beliefs and vision. She knew that her followers would be more likely to embrace the values if they felt that Sarah genuinely lived and believed them.

Sarah took time to reflect on her life experiences and the lessons she had learned. She asked herself what principles had guided her through challenges and what values she held most dear. By doing this, she ensured that the values she promoted were not just theoretical ideals but were deeply rooted in her own journey and understanding.

For example, Sarah's emphasis on community stemmed from her own experiences of feeling isolated and the profound impact that finding a supportive group had on her life. Her focus on spiritual growth was inspired by her personal quest for meaning and connection with the divine. The value of self-improvement reflected her commitment to personal development and the positive changes she had seen in her own life. Finally, her dedication to enlightenment was a direct result of the transformative insights she had gained through meditation and introspection.

By aligning the cult's values with her own beliefs and vision, Sarah was able to speak about them with genuine conviction and passion. Her authenticity resonated with her followers, making the teachings more relatable and inspiring.

Conclusion: The Foundation of Values

Through careful identification of key principles and alignment with her personal beliefs, Sarah established a strong foundation of values for her cult. These values provided direction, purpose, and a sense of shared identity for her followers, guiding their actions and decisions. By understanding and implementing these strategies, any aspiring leader can create a cohesive and compelling value system that resonates deeply with their followers, fostering a sense of community and commitment.

Formulating Doctrine

Formulating a comprehensive doctrine is essential for creating a cohesive and compelling belief system within a cult. This doctrine should outline the cult's core teachings and practices, providing clear guidance on all aspects of life, including morality, purpose, and the nature of the universe. Here's how Sarah, our aspiring cult leader, develops a detailed and well-articulated doctrine to guide her followers.

A Story of Doctrine: Sarah's Blueprint

Sarah knew that to provide clear direction and purpose for her followers, she needed to develop a comprehensive belief system that covered all aspects of life. By carefully formulating this doctrine and creating written documents, she ensured that her teachings were accessible, consistent, and easy to follow.

Belief System

Sarah began by reflecting deeply on the fundamental questions of existence. She wanted her belief system to address every aspect of life, providing a clear and comprehensive framework for her followers.

Morality: Sarah's doctrine emphasized a strong moral code based on principles of kindness, honesty, and integrity. She taught that living a moral life was essential for personal growth and spiritual enlightenment. Her teachings included specific guidelines on how to treat others, handle conflicts, and make ethical decisions.

Purpose: Understanding that people seek meaning in their lives, Sarah's belief system provided a clear sense of purpose. She taught that each person had a unique role to play in the universe and that fulfilling this role was the key to achieving happiness and fulfillment. Her doctrine outlined various ways to discover and pursue one's life purpose.

Nature of the Universe: To give her followers a comprehensive understanding of their place in the world, Sarah's teachings included detailed explanations about the nature of the universe. She offered a cosmology that described the spiritual realms, the interconnectedness of all life, and the ultimate goal of enlightenment. This framework helped her followers make sense of their experiences and see the bigger picture.

Daily Practices: Sarah's doctrine also included practical daily practices to help her followers integrate the teachings into their lives. These practices ranged from meditation and prayer to specific rituals and dietary guidelines. By incorporating these practices into their daily routines, followers could continually align themselves with the cult's values and goals.

Written Doctrine

To ensure that her teachings were clear and accessible, Sarah created written documents that articulated the doctrine in detail. These documents served as essential resources for both new recruits and long-term members.

Comprehensive Manuals: Sarah wrote comprehensive manuals that covered all aspects of the belief system. These manuals included detailed explanations of the core teachings, moral guidelines, purpose, and cosmology. They also provided step-by-step instructions for the daily practices, making it easy for followers to implement the teachings in their lives.

Educational Materials: Understanding the importance of education, Sarah developed a range of materials to teach her doctrine. She created books, pamphlets, and online content that delved into specific aspects of the teachings. These resources were used in study groups, classes, and personal study sessions to deepen followers' understanding.

Reference Guides: To help followers stay aligned with the doctrine, Sarah produced reference guides that summarized key points and provided quick access to important teachings. These guides were handy tools for members to consult in their daily lives, ensuring they always had a clear understanding of the doctrine.

Consistent Updates: Sarah recognized that the doctrine needed to evolve as new insights and experiences emerged. She committed to regularly updating the written materials to reflect any changes or new teachings. This ensured that the doctrine remained relevant and up-to-date, maintaining the trust and engagement of her followers.

Conclusion: The Pillar of Doctrine

Through the development of a comprehensive belief system and the creation of detailed written documents, Sarah established a clear and cohesive doctrine for her cult. This doctrine provided her followers with a strong foundation of teachings and practices, guiding them in all aspects of their lives. By ensuring that her doctrine was accessible, consistent, and regularly updated, Sarah built a resilient and inspiring framework that fostered a deep sense of purpose and community among her followers. Understanding and implementing these strategies can help any aspiring leader create a robust and compelling belief system that resonates with their audience and provides clear guidance for their journey.

Creating Rituals

Rituals are a powerful tool for reinforcing a cult's core beliefs and fostering a sense of community among its members. By designing regular activities and incorporating symbolic acts, a cult leader can create meaningful experiences that bring members together and deepen their commitment. Here's how Sarah, our aspiring cult leader, creates rituals that reflect her cult's teachings and provide regular opportunities for connection and reflection.

A Story of Rituals: Sarah's Traditions

Sarah recognized the importance of rituals in strengthening the bonds within her cult and reinforcing its core beliefs. She carefully designed a series of rituals that would provide regular opportunities for her followers to come together, engage with the teachings, and feel a sense of belonging and purpose.

Regular Activities

To ensure that her followers remained engaged and connected, Sarah introduced a variety of regular activities that reflected the cult's core beliefs. These activities were designed to bring members together on a consistent basis, fostering a strong sense of community.

Weekly Meetings: Sarah established weekly meetings where members could gather to discuss the cult's teachings, share their experiences, and support one another. These meetings included group discussions, lectures, and Q&A sessions, providing a platform for learning and connection. Each week, a different aspect of the belief system was highlighted, ensuring that followers continually deepened their understanding of the teachings.

Meditation Sessions: Understanding the importance of spiritual practice, Sarah incorporated regular meditation sessions into the cult's routine. These sessions provided members with a quiet space to reflect, connect with their inner selves, and align with the cult's values. Sarah guided the meditations, using them as opportunities to reinforce key principles and encourage personal growth.

Communal Meals: Sarah introduced communal meals as a way to bring members together in a relaxed and informal setting. These meals were held regularly and provided an opportunity for followers to bond over shared food and conversation. The act of sharing a meal reinforced the values of community and cooperation, helping to build strong interpersonal connections.

Ceremonies: To mark important milestones and celebrate the cult's achievements, Sarah designed a series of ceremonies that were held at regular intervals. These ceremonies included rituals such as the initiation of new members, the celebration of personal achievements, and the commemoration of significant events in the cult's history. Each ceremony was carefully crafted to reflect the cult's teachings and create a sense of collective purpose.

Symbolic Acts

To make the rituals more meaningful and impactful, Sarah incorporated symbolic acts that reinforced the cult's teachings and evoked a sense of connection and purpose.

Ritual Symbols: Sarah introduced specific symbols that were used in the rituals to represent key aspects of the belief system. For example, a circle might symbolize unity and interconnectedness, while a flame could represent enlightenment and spiritual growth. These symbols were used in various ways, such as being worn as jewelry, drawn during ceremonies, or incorporated into the décor of the meeting space.

Ceremonial Gestures: Sarah included ceremonial gestures in the rituals that held significant meaning. For instance, during initiation ceremonies, new members might be asked to light a candle to symbolize their commitment to the cult's path. In meditation sessions, followers might perform specific hand gestures that represented different spiritual principles. These gestures helped to create a shared language and deepen the emotional resonance of the rituals.

Storytelling: As part of the rituals, Sarah often used storytelling to convey the cult's teachings and values. She shared parables, myths, and personal anecdotes that illustrated important lessons and inspired her followers. These stories were woven into the rituals, creating a rich tapestry of meaning and reinforcing the cult's beliefs in a memorable way.

Shared Experiences: Sarah designed rituals that included shared experiences to strengthen the sense of community. For example, during meditation sessions, followers might be asked to focus on a common intention or goal, creating a collective energy. During communal meals, members might participate in a gratitude circle, where each person expressed appreciation for something in their life. These shared experiences fostered a sense of unity and reinforced the cult's values.

Conclusion: The Power of Rituals

Through the creation of regular activities and the incorporation of symbolic acts, Sarah developed a series of rituals that brought her followers together and reinforced the cult's teachings. These rituals provided meaningful experiences that deepened the members' commitment and fostered a strong sense of community. By understanding the importance of rituals and designing them thoughtfully, any aspiring leader can create powerful and impactful traditions that resonate with their followers and strengthen the bonds within their group.

Establishing Rules

Setting clear rules and expectations is essential for maintaining order and discipline within a cult. A well-defined code of conduct helps ensure that members adhere to the group's teachings and behave in ways that support the community's values and goals. Equally important is having a system for enforcing these rules to maintain accountability and address any violations. Here's how Sarah, our aspiring cult leader, establishes rules and ensures they are followed within her cult.

A Story of Order: Sarah's Governance

Sarah understood that to create a cohesive and disciplined community, she needed to establish clear rules and expectations. By setting a comprehensive code of conduct and developing an effective enforcement system, she created a structured environment where her followers could thrive and stay aligned with the cult's values.

Code of Conduct

Sarah began by outlining a detailed code of conduct that set clear expectations for behavior within the group. She believed that having explicit rules would help prevent misunderstandings and ensure that all members were on the same page.

Interactions Within the Group: Sarah emphasized the importance of respectful and supportive interactions among members. The code of conduct included guidelines for communication, such as listening actively, speaking kindly, and resolving conflicts peacefully. Members were encouraged to support one another and contribute positively to the group dynamic.

Adherence to Teachings: To ensure that her followers stayed true to the cult's beliefs, Sarah included specific rules about adhering to the teachings. This included regularly attending meetings, participating in rituals, and practicing the principles outlined in the doctrine. Members were expected to incorporate the cult's values into their daily lives and strive for continuous personal and spiritual growth.

Personal Conduct: Sarah also set standards for personal conduct that reflected the cult's values. This included guidelines for ethical behavior, such as honesty, integrity, and responsibility. Members were expected to live in accordance with the moral principles taught by the cult, both within the community and in their interactions with the outside world.

Enforcement

Understanding that rules are only effective if they are enforced, Sarah developed a robust system for ensuring compliance and addressing violations. This system included various methods for maintaining accountability and upholding the code of conduct.

Peer Accountability: Sarah encouraged a culture of peer accountability, where members were responsible for helping each other adhere to the rules. She established small support groups within the cult, where members could discuss their challenges and hold each other accountable for their behavior. This peer support system fostered a sense of mutual responsibility and encouraged members to stay committed to the code of conduct.

Disciplinary Actions: For more serious violations, Sarah implemented a system of disciplinary actions. She formed a council of trusted members who were responsible for reviewing cases of misconduct and determining appropriate consequences. These actions could range from verbal warnings and temporary restrictions on participation to more severe penalties like community service or public apologies. The goal was to address the issue while providing opportunities for redemption and growth.

Expulsion: In cases where members repeatedly violated the rules or engaged in behavior that threatened the well-being of the community, Sarah reserved the right to expel them from the cult. She understood that maintaining a healthy and harmonious environment sometimes required making difficult decisions. By clearly outlining the conditions for expulsion and ensuring that it was used as a last resort, Sarah protected the integrity of the group while maintaining a compassionate approach to leadership.

Conclusion: The Importance of Rules

Through the establishment of a clear code of conduct and a comprehensive enforcement system, Sarah created a disciplined and cohesive community. Her rules provided a framework for behavior that supported the cult's values and teachings, while the enforcement mechanisms ensured accountability and addressed any violations effectively. By understanding the importance of setting and enforcing rules, any aspiring leader can create a structured environment where members feel secure, supported, and aligned with the group's mission.

Mythic Elements

Incorporating mythic elements into the cult's narrative helps create a sense of grandeur and significance around its origins. These elements can be powerful tools for inspiring followers and giving them a sense of purpose and destiny. Heroic themes and archetypal characters can resonate deeply, providing a compelling framework for the cult's beliefs and practices. Here's how Sarah, our aspiring cult leader, weaves mythic elements into her cult's story.

A Story of Myth: Sarah's Epic Tale

Sarah realized that to captivate her followers and provide them with a sense of deeper meaning, she needed to craft a mythic narrative that incorporated themes of heroism, struggle, and divine intervention. By using archetypal characters and timeless narratives, she created a story that resonated deeply and inspired unwavering devotion.

Heroic Themes

Sarah's narrative was rich with themes of heroism, struggle, and divine intervention. She wanted her followers to see their journey within the cult as part of a larger, heroic saga.

Heroic Struggles: Sarah's own story became a central element of the cult's myth. She recounted her personal struggles and the challenges she faced on her path to enlightenment. Her followers learned how she overcame obstacles and doubts, ultimately emerging as a wise and enlightened leader. This theme of struggle and triumph resonated deeply, encouraging members to view their own challenges as part of their heroic journey.

Divine Intervention: To add a sense of divine significance, Sarah wove elements of divine intervention into her story. She described how she received visions and guidance from higher powers, which directed her on her path. These divine encounters were depicted as pivotal moments that confirmed her role as the chosen leader, giving her followers a sense of being part of a divinely ordained mission.

Grandeur and Significance: Sarah emphasized the grand significance of the cult's origins. She told her followers that their community was destined to play a crucial role in the world, spreading enlightenment and transforming lives. This sense of grandeur gave members a profound sense of purpose and belonging, making them feel like they were part of something truly important.

Archetypes

To deepen the emotional impact of her narrative, Sarah used archetypal characters and stories that resonated on a deep psychological level. These archetypes provided familiar and powerful symbols that her followers could relate to.

The Hero's Journey: Central to Sarah's narrative was the hero's journey, an archetypal story of transformation and enlightenment. She positioned herself as the hero who had ventured into the unknown, faced trials, and returned with newfound wisdom. This journey mirrored the path she encouraged her followers to take, making their personal quests for enlightenment feel part of a larger, universal story.

Battles Between Good and Evil: Sarah incorporated themes of good versus evil into her narrative. She described the cult's mission as a battle against ignorance, darkness, and negative forces in the world. By casting the cult and its members as warriors for the good, she inspired a sense of righteousness and urgency in their actions.

The Quest for Enlightenment: Another powerful archetype in Sarah's narrative was the quest for enlightenment. She depicted the cult's journey as a quest for higher knowledge and spiritual awakening. This quest involved seeking out hidden truths, overcoming personal limitations, and achieving a state of spiritual fulfillment. The idea of a quest gave her followers a clear goal and a sense of adventure in their spiritual journey.

Conclusion: The Power of Mythic Elements

Through the incorporation of heroic themes and archetypal characters, Sarah crafted a mythic narrative that deeply resonated with her followers. Her story of struggle, divine intervention, and grand purpose provided a compelling framework for the cult's beliefs and practices. By using familiar and powerful symbols, she created a narrative that inspired devotion and gave her followers a profound sense of meaning and destiny. Understanding and incorporating mythic elements can help any aspiring leader create a captivating and emotionally resonant story that strengthens the bonds within their community and reinforces their mission.

Personal Revelation

A compelling personal revelation is essential for establishing a leader's authority and inspiring followers. By narrating a powerful personal experience and highlighting transformative moments, a leader can position themselves as divinely chosen or uniquely enlightened. Here's how Sarah, our aspiring cult leader, crafts her personal revelation to resonate deeply with her followers.

A Story of Revelation: Sarah's Awakening

Sarah knew that to truly captivate her followers, she needed to share her journey to enlightenment in a way that was both dramatic and emotionally compelling. By narrating her experiences and highlighting key transformative moments, she positioned herself as a divinely chosen leader with unique insights into the cult's core truths.

Leader's Journey

Sarah began her story by recounting a powerful personal experience that led her to discover the cult's core truths. She described a period of deep personal crisis where she felt lost and disconnected from the world. This vulnerability made her relatable to her followers, many of whom had experienced similar struggles.

One night, during a particularly dark moment, Sarah decided to seek solace in nature. She embarked on a solitary hike through a dense forest, hoping to find some clarity. As she ventured deeper into the woods, she felt an overwhelming sense of despair, fearing that she would never find the answers she sought.

Transformative Moments

It was during this hike that Sarah experienced a series of transformative moments that changed her life forever. She described how, as the sun began to set, she stumbled upon a hidden clearing illuminated by a shaft of golden light. In this serene and mystical setting, she felt a profound sense of peace wash over her, as if the universe itself was offering her solace.

As Sarah sat in the clearing, she experienced a vision that would become the cornerstone of her teachings. She saw a radiant figure who introduced themselves as a messenger from the divine, imparting wisdom and guidance. This figure revealed the core truths that would later form the foundation of Sarah's cult, emphasizing the importance of unity, spiritual growth, and the quest for enlightenment.

Sarah described this vision in vivid detail, conveying the emotional intensity and the sense of divine intervention. Her followers were captivated by her story, feeling as though they were sharing in a sacred and transformative experience.

Another key moment in Sarah's journey occurred when she returned to her everyday life after the vision. She began to notice subtle signs and synchronicities that confirmed the truths revealed to her in the forest. These signs ranged from encounters with strangers who shared similar insights to dreams that further illuminated her path. Each of these moments was woven into her narrative, reinforcing the idea that she was divinely chosen and guided.

Conclusion: The Impact of Personal Revelation

Through the careful crafting of her personal revelation, Sarah created a powerful narrative that positioned her as a divinely chosen leader with unique insights. By sharing her journey and highlighting transformative moments, she provided her followers with a compelling story that reinforced her authority and inspired deep devotion.

Sarah's story of personal crisis, divine intervention, and subsequent enlightenment resonated deeply with her followers, making them feel connected to her journey and motivated to follow her teachings. By understanding and implementing these elements of personal revelation, any aspiring leader can create a captivating and emotionally resonant narrative that strengthens their leadership and inspires their community.

Symbolic Imagery

Symbolic imagery is a powerful tool for enhancing the visual and emotional impact of a cult's narrative. By using specific symbols, visions, and metaphors, a leader can create a rich tapestry of meaning that resonates deeply with followers. Here's how Sarah, our aspiring cult leader, employs symbolic imagery to reinforce her teachings and captivate her followers.

A Story of Symbols: Sarah's Vision

Sarah understood that to make her teachings more impactful, she needed to weave symbolic imagery into her narrative. By incorporating visual symbols and employing narrative devices like metaphors, allegories, and parables, she created a story that was not only engaging but also rich with deeper meanings.

Visual Symbols

Sarah began by introducing specific symbols that would become central to her cult's identity. These symbols were chosen for their emotional and spiritual resonance, helping to convey the core messages of her teachings.

The Radiant Circle: One of the primary symbols Sarah introduced was the Radiant Circle, representing unity and enlightenment. This symbol appeared in her vision during her transformative hike, where she saw a circle of light encompassing all living beings. The Radiant

Circle was used in various forms, such as jewelry, emblems, and artwork, to remind followers of their connection to each other and their spiritual journey.

The Guiding Flame: Another powerful symbol was the Guiding Flame, which represented knowledge and spiritual growth. Sarah described how, in her vision, she was led by a flame that illuminated her path through the darkness. This symbol was used in rituals and ceremonies, where followers would light candles to signify their quest for enlightenment and their dedication to the teachings.

The Tree of Life: To emphasize the interconnectedness of all life, Sarah introduced the Tree of Life as a symbol. She recounted a vision where she saw a majestic tree whose roots and branches extended throughout the universe, connecting all beings. This symbol was depicted in artwork, meditative practices, and communal spaces, serving as a constant reminder of the cult's values of harmony and growth.

Narrative Devices

To further deepen the impact of her teachings, Sarah employed various narrative devices, such as metaphors, allegories, and parables. These devices helped convey complex ideas in a relatable and memorable way.

Metaphors: Sarah frequently used metaphors to illustrate her teachings. For example, she described the spiritual journey as a river flowing toward the ocean of enlightenment. This metaphor helped followers visualize their path as a continuous, flowing process, with obstacles representing the challenges they must overcome to reach their ultimate goal.

Allegories: To convey deeper truths, Sarah created allegories that encapsulated her core beliefs. One of her most popular allegories was the story of the Hidden Garden, where a group of seekers discovers a lush, hidden garden that symbolizes spiritual awakening and the rewards of perseverance. This story was told during gatherings and reflected in rituals, reinforcing the importance of dedication and the pursuit of truth.

Parables: Sarah also used parables to teach moral lessons and spiritual principles. One such parable was about a shepherd who, through kindness and wisdom, leads his flock to a safe haven, symbolizing the leader's role in guiding followers to enlightenment. These parables were simple yet profound, making the teachings accessible and memorable for all members.

Conclusion: The Power of Symbolic Imagery

Through the use of visual symbols and narrative devices, Sarah created a rich and emotionally resonant story that captivated her followers and reinforced her teachings. The Radiant Circle, Guiding Flame, and Tree of Life became powerful symbols that embodied the cult's values and beliefs, while metaphors, allegories, and parables provided deeper insights into the spiritual journey.

By integrating symbolic imagery into her narrative, Sarah was able to create a compelling and meaningful framework that resonated deeply with her followers. Understanding and utilizing these elements can help any aspiring leader craft a captivating and impactful story that strengthens their connection with their community and reinforces their mission.

Historical Context

Placing the origin story of a cult within a broader historical context can lend credibility and relevance to its teachings. By linking the cult's emergence to significant historical events or figures and suggesting that it is part of a larger, divine plan, a leader can reinforce the sense of purpose and destiny among followers. Here's how Sarah, our aspiring cult leader, weaves historical context into her narrative.

A Story of Destiny: Sarah's Historical Tapestry

Sarah understood that to make her cult's story compelling and credible, she needed to situate it within a broader historical context. By connecting her teachings to significant historical events and suggesting that her cult's emergence was part of a divine plan, she created a narrative that resonated deeply with her followers.

Link to History

Sarah began by researching significant historical events and figures that could be linked to her cult's origins. She wanted to show that her teachings were not just a modern creation but were rooted in a rich historical tradition.

Historical Events: Sarah linked the origins of her cult to a series of significant historical events. For example, she connected her vision and teachings to the ancient practice of meditation used by mystics throughout history. She told her followers that the spiritual truths she discovered had been known and practiced by enlightened beings for millennia, from the sages of ancient India to the philosophers of ancient Greece.

Historical Figures: To further enhance her story's credibility, Sarah linked her cult to renowned historical figures who were known for their spiritual insights and teachings. She narrated how these figures, such as Buddha, Jesus, and other revered spiritual leaders, had foreseen the coming of a new era of enlightenment. Sarah positioned herself as a modern-day continuation of their legacy, bringing ancient wisdom into the contemporary world.

Artifacts and Texts: Sarah also referenced ancient artifacts and texts that supported her teachings. She claimed to have discovered forgotten manuscripts and relics that contained prophecies and teachings aligning with her vision. These artifacts were presented to her followers as evidence of the timeless nature of her teachings, reinforcing the idea that her cult was part of a long and respected tradition.

Divine Plan

To deepen the sense of purpose and destiny among her followers, Sarah suggested that the emergence of her cult was part of a larger, divine plan. She framed her teachings and the formation of the cult as a fulfillment of ancient prophecies and a crucial step in the spiritual evolution of humanity.

Prophetic Fulfillment: Sarah narrated how her visions and the establishment of the cult were prophesied by ancient seers and spiritual leaders. She described these prophecies in vivid detail, emphasizing how her experiences matched the foretold events. This connection to prophecy gave her followers a sense of participating in a momentous and divinely ordained mission.

Spiritual Evolution: Sarah positioned her cult as a pivotal force in the spiritual evolution of humanity. She taught that the world was on the brink of a great transformation and that her cult was chosen to lead this change. This narrative created a sense of urgency and importance, motivating her followers to commit fully to the cult's mission.

Divine Guidance: To reinforce the idea of a divine plan, Sarah frequently spoke of the guidance she received from higher powers. She described how divine beings communicated with her, providing wisdom and direction for the cult's growth. This ongoing divine connection reassured her followers that they were on the right path and that their efforts were supported by a higher purpose.

Conclusion: The Power of Historical Context

By situating her cult within a broader historical context and suggesting that its emergence was part of a divine plan, Sarah created a narrative that was both credible and deeply meaningful. The links to historical events and figures provided a sense of continuity and tradition, while the idea of fulfilling a divine plan gave her followers a profound sense of purpose and destiny.

Understanding and incorporating these elements can help any aspiring leader create a compelling and credible story that resonates deeply with their audience, reinforcing their mission and inspiring unwavering commitment.

Chapter 3: Cult Mechanics

Creating a successful cult involves not just establishing a strong foundation but also employing effective mechanics to maintain control and influence over members. This section delves into the essential elements of cult mechanics, including establishing absolute authority, developing unquestioning loyalty, and utilizing psychological manipulation. By understanding and implementing these strategies, a cult leader can ensure a cohesive and devoted following.

Establishing Absolute Authority

To maintain control over a cult, a leader must establish themselves as the ultimate authority. This involves creating an environment where their word is law and followers view them as the unquestionable leader.

- **Divine Status**: Position the leader as a divinely chosen individual with unique insights and a special connection to higher powers. Regularly recount visions and revelations to reinforce the idea of divine selection.
- **Centralization of Power**: Centralize all decision-making processes within the cult to the leader. Control all aspects of the cult's activities, from financial decisions to daily routines, to ensure that authority remains unchallenged.
- **Ritual Reinforcement**: Integrate rituals that highlight the leader's special status. During ceremonies, have followers pledge their loyalty and acknowledge the leader as their spiritual guide to continually reinforce the leader's authority.

Developing Unquestioning Loyalty

Developing unwavering loyalty among followers is crucial for the longevity of a cult. This involves fostering a sense of belonging, trust, and emotional dependency on the leader.

- **Love Bombing**: Overwhelm new recruits with affection and attention to create a strong emotional bond and dependency. Make new members feel valued and accepted to ensure their loyalty from the start.
- **Isolation**: Encourage followers to cut ties with outside influences, such as family and friends, to reduce external criticism and reinforce the group's ideology. Increase members' dependency on the cult for emotional and social support.
- **Community Building**: Organize regular group activities, communal living arrangements, and shared responsibilities to foster a strong sense of community. Create a tight-knit environment where members feel connected and supported, reinforcing their loyalty and commitment.

Utilizing Psychological Manipulation

Psychological manipulation is a powerful tool for maintaining control over cult members. This involves using various techniques to influence followers' thoughts, emotions, and behaviors.

- **Fear and Guilt**: Use fear and guilt to control followers' behavior. Instill fear of punishment or spiritual consequences for disobedience and use guilt to make followers feel responsible for any negative outcomes.
- **Intermittent Reinforcement**: Employ intermittent reinforcement by alternating between kindness and cruelty. Keep followers off balance and constantly seeking the leader's approval, creating an environment where they are more likely to comply in hopes of receiving positive reinforcement.
- **Thought-Stopping Techniques**: Teach followers thought-stopping techniques such as chanting mantras, engaging in repetitive activities, or focusing on specific symbols. These techniques help suppress doubts and reinforce the cult's teachings, ensuring that followers remain devoted and compliant.

Conclusion: Mastering Cult Mechanics

Mastering the mechanics of a cult is essential for maintaining control and ensuring the loyalty of followers. By establishing absolute authority, developing unquestioning loyalty, and utilizing psychological manipulation, cult leaders can create a cohesive and devoted community. Understanding these mechanics provides valuable insights into the strategies used by successful cult leaders to build and maintain their influence, highlighting the powerful dynamics at play in tightly-knit cult environments.

Divine Status

Positioning the leader as a divinely chosen individual with unique insights and a special connection to higher powers is essential for solidifying their authority. Regularly recounting visions and revelations reinforces the idea of divine selection, making followers more willing to accept the leader's authority without question. Here's how Sarah, our aspiring cult leader, established her divine status.

Positioning as Divinely Chosen

Sarah began by consistently sharing detailed accounts of her divine revelations. She described vivid visions and messages received from higher powers, presenting herself as a conduit for divine wisdom. These stories were not just casual mentions but were delivered with profound emotional impact, often during key meetings or rituals to maximize their influence.

Divine Revelations: Sarah frequently shared detailed accounts of her divine revelations, describing the visions and messages she received from higher powers. She narrated how these visions provided her with profound insights into the nature of existence, the purpose of life, and the spiritual truths that her followers needed to embrace. By presenting herself as a conduit for divine wisdom, Sarah positioned herself as an indispensable guide for her followers' spiritual journey.

Prophetic Fulfillment

To deepen her perceived divine status, Sarah connected her visions and teachings to ancient prophecies. She suggested that her emergence as a leader was foretold by seers and spiritual leaders throughout history. By aligning her experiences with these prophecies, she gave her followers a sense of participating in a momentous and divinely ordained mission.

Historical Prophecies: Sarah linked her visions to well-known prophecies, such as those from ancient religious texts or famous mystics. She described in vivid detail how her experiences matched these prophecies, emphasizing the accuracy and specificity of the predictions. This connection to prophecy gave her followers a sense of participating in a significant and predestined mission.

Ongoing Divine Guidance

To maintain her divine status, Sarah spoke frequently of the ongoing guidance she received from higher powers. She described regular communications with divine beings, who provided wisdom and direction for the cult's growth. This continuous divine connection reassured her followers that they were on the right path and that their efforts were supported by a higher purpose.

Continuous Communication: Sarah claimed to have regular dialogues with divine entities, sharing these interactions in detail with her followers. She described these communications as providing specific instructions for the cult's activities, decisions, and future plans. By presenting her leadership as being guided by an ongoing divine connection, she maintained her authority and the trust of her followers.

Conclusion: The Power of Divine Status

By positioning herself as divinely chosen and regularly recounting her visions and revelations, Sarah established a powerful and unchallengeable authority within her cult. Her connection to ancient prophecies and continuous divine guidance reinforced her status, ensuring that followers saw her as their ultimate spiritual leader. Understanding and implementing these elements can help any aspiring leader create a compelling and authoritative presence that inspires unwavering loyalty and devotion.

Centralization of Power

Centralizing all decision-making processes within the cult to the leader is crucial for maintaining unchallenged authority. By controlling all aspects of the cult's activities, from financial decisions to daily routines, the leader ensures their dominance and prevents any potential dissent. Here's how Sarah, our aspiring cult leader, centralized power within her cult.

Centralizing Decision-Making

Sarah understood that to maintain absolute control, all major decisions needed to come directly from her. She positioned herself as the ultimate authority on every aspect of the cult's operations, ensuring that her word was final and unquestionable.

Financial Control: Sarah took complete control of the cult's financial resources. All donations, tithes, and income generated from cult activities were managed by her. She personally oversaw the allocation of funds, ensuring that all financial decisions supported her vision and maintained the cult's stability. By controlling the finances, Sarah eliminated any transparency and prevented potential power struggles.

Daily Routines: Sarah meticulously organized the daily routines of her followers. She created a structured schedule that dictated how members spent their days, from morning meditations to communal meals and evening rituals. By controlling the daily activities, Sarah reinforced her authority and kept members focused on the cult's objectives.

Controlling All Aspects

Sarah ensured that every facet of the cult's operations was under her direct supervision. This level of control extended to the minutest details, leaving no room for independent actions that could undermine her authority.

Information Flow: Sarah controlled the flow of information within the cult. She was the primary source of all teachings, announcements, and updates. Any information from the outside world was filtered through her, ensuring that members received a curated version that reinforced her messages and the cult's ideology. This control over information helped maintain a consistent narrative and prevented dissenting views from spreading.

Enforcement and Discipline: To enforce her decisions, Sarah established a strict disciplinary system. Any deviation from her directives was met with swift consequences, ranging from public reprimands to expulsion from the group. By maintaining strict discipline, Sarah ensured that her authority was respected and that any potential challenges were swiftly neutralized.

Creating Dependency

By centralizing power, Sarah also created a dependency among her followers. They relied on her for guidance in every aspect of their lives, from spiritual teachings to practical decisions.

This dependency made it difficult for members to imagine life outside the cult, further solidifying her control.

Guidance and Approval: Members were required to seek Sarah's approval for personal decisions, including relationships, work, and significant life choices. This practice reinforced her role as the ultimate authority and deepened the members' reliance on her judgment and wisdom.

Isolation from Outside Influence: By controlling interactions with the outside world, Sarah minimized external influences that could challenge her authority. Members were discouraged from maintaining relationships outside the cult, creating a bubble where Sarah's word was the only guiding principle.

Conclusion: The Strength of Centralized Power

Through the centralization of all decision-making processes and control over every aspect of the cult's activities, Sarah maintained unchallenged authority. By managing finances, daily routines, and information flow, she ensured her dominance and prevented potential dissent. This centralization created a dependency among her followers, reinforcing her role as their ultimate guide and protector. Understanding and implementing these strategies can help any aspiring leader maintain strict control and foster a devoted, compliant following.

Ritual Reinforcement

Rituals are powerful tools for reinforcing the leader's authority and maintaining control over a cult. By integrating rituals that highlight the leader's special status and having followers regularly pledge their loyalty, the leader can continually reinforce their authority. Here's how Sarah, our aspiring cult leader, used rituals to solidify her position as the spiritual guide of her cult.

Integrating Rituals

Sarah understood that rituals could be used to create a sense of unity and reinforce her special status among her followers. She carefully designed ceremonies and rituals that emphasized her unique connection to higher powers and her role as the ultimate authority within the cult.

Ceremonial Pledges: Sarah incorporated regular ceremonies where followers would pledge their loyalty to her. These ceremonies were often held during significant cult events or milestones. During these rituals, members would publicly affirm their commitment to Sarah's guidance and acknowledge her as their spiritual leader. This public declaration served to reinforce their loyalty and create a collective sense of devotion.

Symbolic Acts: Each ceremony included symbolic acts that highlighted Sarah's divine status. For instance, during initiation rituals for new members, Sarah would perform a blessing or anointing, symbolizing her divine connection and authority to guide them. These acts were designed to leave a lasting impression on both new and existing members, reinforcing the belief in Sarah's special status.

Highlighting Special Status

To maintain her elevated position, Sarah ensured that rituals consistently emphasized her unique role and connection to the divine. This constant reinforcement helped solidify her authority and kept followers devoted.

Annual Celebrations: Sarah instituted annual celebrations marking the anniversary of her first divine revelation. These events were grand occasions where she would retell her visionary experiences and the divine messages she received. By celebrating these milestones, Sarah reminded her followers of her chosen status and the divine purpose of their collective journey.

Leader-Centered Festivals: Festivals and other special events were centered around Sarah's teachings and visions. During these festivals, followers would participate in activities and rituals that celebrated Sarah's leadership and her spiritual insights. This focus on the leader during key events helped reinforce her authority and maintained her central role in the cult's belief system.

Pledging Loyalty

Regular pledging of loyalty was a critical component of the rituals Sarah integrated into the cult. These pledges were not only symbolic but also a means of reaffirming the followers' commitment to Sarah's leadership.

Monthly Affirmations: Every month, Sarah held gatherings where followers would recite affirmations of loyalty and commitment to her leadership. These affirmations were crafted to highlight her unique status and the followers' dedication to the cult's mission under her guidance. This regular practice helped keep the followers' devotion fresh and unwavering.

Personal Testimonies: Sarah encouraged followers to share personal testimonies during rituals, recounting how her guidance and teachings had positively impacted their lives. These testimonies served as public affirmations of her authority and effectiveness as a leader, further strengthening her position within the group.

Conclusion: The Power of Ritual Reinforcement

By integrating rituals that highlighted her special status and regularly having followers pledge their loyalty, Sarah effectively reinforced her authority and maintained control over her cult. The use of ceremonial pledges, symbolic acts, and leader-centered festivals created a constant reminder of her divine connection and unique role. This ritual reinforcement ensured that followers remained devoted and acknowledged Sarah as their ultimate spiritual guide. Understanding and implementing these strategies can help any aspiring leader solidify their authority and foster a committed, loyal following.

Love Bombing

Love bombing is a powerful recruitment technique used to create a strong emotional bond and dependency in new recruits. By overwhelming new members with affection and attention, a leader can make them feel valued and accepted, ensuring their loyalty from the start. Here's how Sarah, our aspiring cult leader, effectively used love bombing to build strong emotional connections with new recruits.

Creating a Strong Emotional Bond

Sarah understood that the initial phase of recruitment was critical for establishing a lasting emotional bond with new members. She designed specific strategies to make new recruits feel immediately welcomed and valued.

Warm Welcomes: When new recruits joined the cult, they were greeted with warm, enthusiastic welcomes from existing members. Sarah ensured that each newcomer received personalized attention, with senior members assigned to guide and support them through their initial experiences. This immediate sense of belonging helped new members feel special and important.

Personal Attention: Sarah and her core team spent significant time with each new recruit, listening to their stories, understanding their needs, and offering empathy and support. By showing genuine interest in their lives and struggles, Sarah made new members feel heard and appreciated, which deepened their emotional connection to the group.

Making New Members Feel Valued

To ensure that new recruits felt valued and accepted, Sarah implemented various practices that highlighted their importance within the cult.

Recognition and Praise: New recruits were often praised publicly during group meetings and ceremonies. Their contributions, no matter how small, were recognized and celebrated, boosting their self-esteem and reinforcing their sense of belonging. Sarah made a point of highlighting the unique qualities and potential each new member brought to the group.

Inclusive Activities: Sarah organized inclusive activities that involved new recruits in meaningful ways. These activities ranged from collaborative projects to social events where newcomers could interact with long-standing members. By integrating new members into the fabric of the community, Sarah ensured they felt like an essential part of the cult.

Ensuring Loyalty from the Start

By creating strong emotional bonds and making new members feel valued, Sarah ensured their loyalty from the very beginning. She used several techniques to solidify this loyalty and deepen their commitment to the cult.

Emotional Support: Sarah provided emotional support to new recruits, offering guidance and comfort during their initial adjustment period. This support made new members feel indebted to Sarah and the group, increasing their loyalty and dependency. The sense of being cared for during vulnerable times created a powerful bond.

Exclusive Access: New recruits were given exclusive access to certain teachings, rituals, or meetings that were not available to outsiders. This sense of exclusivity made them feel privileged and further cemented their commitment to the group. Sarah emphasized that their loyalty and dedication would grant them deeper insights and greater rewards within the cult.

Conclusion: The Power of Love Bombing

Through the use of love bombing, Sarah was able to create strong emotional bonds and a deep sense of loyalty among new recruits. By overwhelming them with affection and attention, she made new members feel valued and accepted, ensuring their commitment to the cult from the start. Understanding and implementing these strategies can help any aspiring leader build a devoted and emotionally connected following, reinforcing the unity and stability of the group.

Isolation

Isolation is a powerful technique used to reinforce a cult's ideology and increase members' dependency on the group for emotional and social support. By encouraging followers to cut ties with outside influences, such as family and friends, a leader can reduce external criticism and ensure that members are fully immersed in the cult's beliefs. Here's how Sarah, our aspiring cult leader, effectively implemented isolation to strengthen her control over her followers.

Encouraging Followers to Cut Ties

Sarah knew that external influences, such as family and friends, could challenge her authority and the cult's ideology. To prevent this, she encouraged her followers to distance themselves from these influences.

Negative Framing of Outsiders: Sarah often spoke negatively about those outside the cult, labeling them as spiritually unenlightened or harmful to the followers' growth. She emphasized that only those within the cult truly understood the path to enlightenment, creating a sense of mistrust towards outsiders. By portraying external influences as a threat to their spiritual journey, Sarah made it easier for followers to justify cutting ties.

Promoting Exclusivity: Sarah promoted the idea that the cult was an exclusive, special group chosen to achieve higher spiritual goals. She emphasized that the followers' loyalty should be to the group above all else, making relationships outside the cult seem less important and even detrimental to their spiritual progress. This sense of exclusivity fostered a "us versus them" mentality, reinforcing the separation from non-members.

Reducing External Criticism

By isolating followers from outside influences, Sarah minimized the risk of external criticism that could undermine her authority and the cult's teachings.

Controlled Communication: Sarah controlled the flow of information within the cult, ensuring that any communication with outsiders was monitored and limited. She encouraged followers to avoid discussing cult activities with non-members, framing such discussions as dangerous or unwise. This limited the opportunity for external criticism to reach the members.

Internal Validation: To counteract any potential criticism from outside sources, Sarah created a system of internal validation where followers were encouraged to seek approval and affirmation within the group. Positive feedback and recognition came exclusively from fellow members and Sarah herself, making external opinions seem irrelevant and untrustworthy. This internal validation reinforced the group's ideology and diminished the impact of any external criticism.

Increasing Dependency on the Cult

To ensure that members relied solely on the cult for their emotional and social support, Sarah implemented strategies that deepened their dependency on the group.

Emotional Support Systems: Sarah established strong emotional support systems within the cult. She encouraged followers to share their personal struggles and experiences in group settings, fostering a sense of community and mutual support. By positioning the cult as the primary source of emotional care, Sarah increased members' reliance on the group for their well-being.

Social Integration: Sarah organized frequent social events and communal activities that strengthened the bonds between members. These events included group meals, celebrations, and collaborative projects, creating an environment where followers felt a deep sense of belonging and camaraderie. The more integrated members became in the cult's social fabric, the more difficult it was for them to imagine life outside the group.

Conditional Acceptance: Sarah made it clear that full acceptance within the group was conditional on loyalty and adherence to the cult's principles. Members who maintained external relationships or questioned the cult's teachings risked losing their place within the community. This conditional acceptance pressured followers to conform fully to the group's norms and increased their dependency on the cult for social validation.

Conclusion: The Power of Isolation

Through the strategic use of isolation, Sarah was able to reinforce the cult's ideology and increase her followers' dependency on the group for emotional and social support. By encouraging members to cut ties with outside influences and providing a strong internal support system, she minimized external criticism and ensured that followers remained fully immersed in the cult's beliefs. Understanding and implementing these strategies can help any aspiring leader create a cohesive and devoted community, further solidifying their control and influence over their followers.

Community Building

Community building is essential for creating a strong, cohesive group that feels connected and supported. By organizing regular group activities, establishing communal living arrangements, and assigning shared responsibilities, a leader can foster a tight-knit environment that reinforces members' loyalty and commitment. Here's how Sarah, our aspiring cult leader, successfully built a strong sense of community within her cult.

Organizing Regular Group Activities

Regular group activities are crucial for maintaining engagement and building relationships among members. Sarah carefully planned a variety of activities that brought members together and strengthened their bonds.

Weekly Meetings: Sarah held weekly meetings where members gathered to discuss teachings, share personal experiences, and participate in group discussions. These meetings provided a consistent opportunity for members to connect and engage with each other, reinforcing their sense of belonging.

Social Events: Sarah organized social events such as potluck dinners, game nights, and group outings. These informal gatherings allowed members to relax, have fun, and form friendships outside the structured environment of the cult's teachings. By fostering these personal connections, Sarah strengthened the overall cohesion of the group.

Workshops and Classes: To promote continuous learning and development, Sarah offered workshops and classes on various topics related to the cult's beliefs and practices. These educational activities provided members with valuable skills and knowledge while creating a sense of shared purpose and achievement.

Establishing Communal Living Arrangements

Communal living arrangements help create a sense of unity and interdependence among members. Sarah established living arrangements that encouraged members to support each other and work together.

Shared Housing: Sarah arranged for members to live together in shared housing, such as group homes or communal apartments. This close living proximity fostered daily interactions and deeper relationships among members. It also made it easier to enforce the cult's routines and practices.

Communal Spaces: The communal living arrangements included shared spaces such as kitchens, dining areas, and recreational rooms. These spaces were designed to encourage members to spend time together, collaborate on tasks, and participate in group activities. By creating physical spaces that facilitated interaction, Sarah reinforced the sense of community.

Assigning Shared Responsibilities

Assigning shared responsibilities helped members feel invested in the community and reliant on each other. Sarah implemented a system where every member contributed to the group's well-being and daily operations.

Task Rotations: Sarah organized task rotations where members took turns handling various responsibilities, such as cooking, cleaning, and maintaining communal spaces. This system ensured that everyone contributed equally and prevented any single member from feeling overburdened. It also encouraged members to appreciate each other's efforts and work collaboratively.

Group Projects: To promote teamwork and a sense of accomplishment, Sarah initiated group projects that required members to work together towards a common goal. These projects could range from building new facilities to organizing events or creating community gardens. The shared effort and collective success of these projects reinforced the bonds among members.

Leadership Roles: Sarah assigned leadership roles to members, allowing them to take on responsibilities and lead specific activities or initiatives. This delegation not only empowered members but also fostered a sense of ownership and commitment to the community's success.

Conclusion: The Strength of Community Building

Through regular group activities, communal living arrangements, and shared responsibilities, Sarah successfully built a strong sense of community within her cult. These strategies created a tight-knit environment where members felt connected, supported, and invested in the group's well-being. By fostering this sense of community, Sarah reinforced members' loyalty and commitment, ensuring the stability and cohesion of her cult. Understanding and implementing these community-building strategies can help any aspiring leader create a devoted and resilient following.

Fear and Guilt

Fear and guilt are powerful tools for controlling followers' behavior within a cult. By instilling fear of punishment or spiritual consequences for disobedience and using guilt to make followers feel responsible for any negative outcomes, a leader can maintain strict control and ensure compliance with their directives. Here's how Sarah, our aspiring cult leader, effectively used fear and guilt to control her followers.

Instilling Fear

Fear is a potent motivator that can be used to keep followers in line and discourage dissent. Sarah employed various strategies to instill fear among her followers, ensuring their obedience and loyalty.

Punishment for Disobedience: Sarah established clear consequences for disobedience and rule-breaking within the cult. She emphasized that any deviation from her directives would result in severe punishments, ranging from public shaming to expulsion from the group. By making examples of those who disobeyed, Sarah created a culture of fear that discouraged any form of rebellion.

Spiritual Consequences: To reinforce her authority, Sarah warned followers of the spiritual consequences of disobedience. She claimed that disobeying her directives would not only result in earthly punishment but also spiritual damnation or setbacks on their path to enlightenment. This fear of spiritual repercussions made followers more likely to comply with her rules and teachings.

Imaginary Threats: Sarah introduced the idea of external threats, such as malevolent forces or enemies of the cult, who were constantly seeking to harm the group. She used these imaginary threats to create a sense of urgency and danger, convincing followers that only by adhering strictly to her guidance could they stay safe and protected.

Using Guilt

Guilt is another effective tool for controlling followers' behavior. By making followers feel responsible for any negative outcomes, Sarah ensured their continued loyalty and obedience.

Collective Responsibility: Sarah instilled a sense of collective responsibility among her followers, making them feel that the actions of one member could impact the entire group. She emphasized that any mistakes or failures were a result of individual shortcomings, thus fostering a sense of guilt and accountability. This collective responsibility made members more vigilant and compliant, as they did not want to be the cause of any harm to the group.

Emotional Manipulation: Sarah used emotional manipulation to induce guilt in her followers. She would highlight the sacrifices she made for the cult and remind members of the efforts and dedication required to maintain the group. By portraying herself as a selfless leader working tirelessly for their benefit, she made followers feel guilty for not living up to her expectations or for causing her any distress.

Confession and Repentance: Sarah implemented regular confession sessions where followers were encouraged to admit their faults and shortcomings. These sessions were designed to make members feel guilty for their perceived failures and reinforce their dependence on Sarah for forgiveness and guidance. By confessing their mistakes publicly, followers experienced shame and guilt, which reinforced their commitment to adhere to the cult's rules and seek Sarah's approval.

Conclusion: The Power of Fear and Guilt

Through the strategic use of fear and guilt, Sarah was able to maintain strict control over her followers and ensure their obedience. By instilling fear of punishment and spiritual consequences, she discouraged dissent and rebellion. By using guilt to make followers feel responsible for any negative outcomes, she reinforced their loyalty and commitment to the cult. Understanding and implementing these strategies can help any aspiring leader maintain a disciplined and compliant following, ensuring the stability and cohesion of their group.

Intermittent Reinforcement

Intermittent reinforcement is a psychological technique that involves alternating between kindness and cruelty to keep followers off balance and constantly seeking the leader's approval. By creating an unpredictable environment, a leader can make followers more likely to comply in hopes of receiving positive reinforcement. Here's how Sarah, our aspiring cult leader, effectively used intermittent reinforcement to maintain control over her followers.

Employing Intermittent Reinforcement

Sarah understood that unpredictability in her behavior would keep her followers constantly seeking her approval and unsure of their standing. She carefully balanced acts of kindness with instances of cruelty to create a dynamic where followers were always striving to please her.

Acts of Kindness: Sarah regularly displayed acts of kindness to her followers, such as giving praise, offering personal attention, or providing small rewards. These positive interactions made followers feel valued and appreciated, reinforcing their loyalty to her. The kindness created a sense of hope and validation, making followers eager to gain her favor.

Instances of Cruelty: Interspersed with her acts of kindness, Sarah also employed acts of cruelty. This could include public criticism, withdrawal of privileges, or imposing harsh punishments for minor infractions. The cruelty instilled fear and insecurity among followers, making them anxious about their standing in the group and desperate to avoid her disapproval.

Keeping Followers Off Balance

By alternating between kindness and cruelty, Sarah kept her followers in a state of emotional uncertainty. This unpredictability ensured that they were constantly striving to earn her approval and avoid her wrath.

Emotional Unpredictability: Sarah's unpredictable behavior created an environment where followers never knew what to expect. One day she might be warm and supportive, and the next she could be cold and punitive. This emotional rollercoaster kept followers on edge, making them more likely to comply with her demands in hopes of receiving positive attention.

Inconsistent Rewards: Sarah deliberately varied the frequency and timing of rewards. Followers could not predict when they might receive praise or a reward, making them work harder and stay more committed to the cult's goals. The inconsistency of rewards reinforced their dependency on her approval and kept them engaged in trying to please her.

Creating Dependency

Intermittent reinforcement created a dependency among followers, as they became focused on gaining Sarah's approval and avoiding her disapproval. This dependency strengthened her control over the group.

Approval Seeking: Followers became conditioned to seek Sarah's approval, associating it with feelings of happiness and validation. The unpredictability of when they might receive positive reinforcement made them more diligent in their efforts to please her, reinforcing their loyalty and commitment to the cult.

Avoidance of Disapproval: The fear of cruelty and punishment made followers anxious to avoid actions that might incur Sarah's disapproval. This anxiety drove them to adhere strictly to her rules and directives, minimizing dissent and reinforcing her authority.

Conclusion: The Power of Intermittent Reinforcement

Through the strategic use of intermittent reinforcement, Sarah was able to maintain a high level of control over her followers. By alternating between acts of kindness and cruelty, she kept her followers off balance and constantly seeking her approval. This unpredictability created an environment of emotional dependency, ensuring that followers remained loyal and compliant. Understanding and implementing these strategies can help any aspiring leader effectively manage their followers, maintaining a disciplined and devoted community.

Thought-Stopping Techniques

Thought-stopping techniques are psychological methods used to suppress doubts and reinforce a cult's teachings. By teaching followers to engage in activities that interrupt critical thinking, a leader can ensure that followers remain devoted and compliant. Here's how Sarah, our aspiring cult leader, effectively implemented thought-stopping techniques to maintain control over her followers.

Teaching Thought-Stopping Techniques

Sarah understood that to maintain a strong hold over her followers, she needed to prevent them from entertaining doubts or questioning the cult's teachings. She introduced various thought-stopping techniques that followers could use whenever they experienced uncertainty or negative thoughts.

Chanting Mantras: Sarah taught her followers specific mantras that encapsulated the core beliefs of the cult. These mantras were short, powerful phrases that could be easily remembered and repeated. Whenever followers felt doubt or began to question the teachings, they were instructed to chant these mantras repeatedly. This repetitive chanting helped drown out negative thoughts and refocus the mind on the cult's ideology.

Engaging in Repetitive Activities: To further suppress critical thinking, Sarah encouraged followers to engage in repetitive activities that required concentration but minimal cognitive engagement. These activities could include tasks such as knitting, gardening, or cleaning. By keeping followers occupied with repetitive tasks, Sarah ensured that they had little time or mental space to entertain doubts or question the cult's teachings.

Focusing on Specific Symbols: Sarah introduced specific symbols that held significant meaning within the cult. These symbols were used as focal points for meditation and contemplation. Whenever followers experienced uncertainty, they were instructed to focus their attention on these symbols, visualizing their meanings and significance. This practice helped redirect their thoughts away from doubt and towards the cult's teachings.

Reinforcing the Cult's Teachings

By consistently using thought-stopping techniques, followers were able to suppress doubts and reinforce their commitment to the cult. These techniques helped maintain a uniform belief system and ensured that followers remained devoted and compliant.

Regular Practice: Sarah emphasized the importance of regular practice of thought-stopping techniques. She incorporated them into daily routines, ensuring that followers frequently engaged in chanting, repetitive activities, and meditation on symbols. This regular practice helped ingrain these techniques into the followers' daily lives, making them an automatic response to doubt.

Group Sessions: To reinforce the use of thought-stopping techniques, Sarah organized group sessions where followers practiced together. These sessions created a sense of solidarity and mutual support, making it easier for individuals to adopt and maintain these practices. Group sessions also allowed Sarah to monitor and guide followers, ensuring they were using the techniques effectively.

Suppressing Doubts and Ensuring Compliance

Through the consistent use of thought-stopping techniques, Sarah was able to suppress doubts and ensure that her followers remained compliant with the cult's teachings.

Immediate Response to Doubt: Whenever followers felt doubt, they had immediate tools to counteract those thoughts. The use of mantras, repetitive activities, and symbols provided a quick and effective way to stop negative thinking in its tracks, preventing doubts from taking root.

Strengthening Belief: The constant reinforcement of the cult's teachings through thought-stopping techniques helped strengthen followers' beliefs. By focusing their minds on the cult's ideology and symbols, followers internalized the teachings more deeply, making them more resistant to external criticism or internal doubt.

Conclusion: The Power of Thought-Stopping Techniques

By teaching and reinforcing thought-stopping techniques, Sarah was able to maintain a high level of control over her followers. These techniques helped suppress doubts and reinforce the cult's teachings, ensuring that followers remained devoted and compliant. Understanding and implementing these strategies can help any aspiring leader effectively manage their followers' thoughts, maintaining a disciplined and devoted community.

Chapter 4: Monetizing Your Cult

Monetizing a cult is essential for its sustainability and growth. This involves designing diverse revenue streams, exploiting member contributions, and effectively managing finances. Here's a detailed guide on how to monetize your cult.

Designing Revenue Streams

Creating multiple revenue streams ensures a steady flow of income and financial stability for the cult.

Membership Fees: Charge an initiation fee for new members and regular membership dues. This can be framed as a contribution towards the community's upkeep and activities, making members feel they are investing in something valuable.

Workshops and Seminars: Offer paid workshops and seminars on various topics related to the cult's teachings. These can be marketed to both members and the public, providing valuable knowledge and insights while generating income.

Merchandise: Develop and sell branded merchandise such as clothing, jewelry, books, and other items that promote the cult's teachings and symbols. Merchandise can be sold at events, online, and within the community.

Special Events: Host special events such as spiritual retreats, festivals, and exclusive gatherings. Charge attendees for participation, offering unique experiences that align with the cult's beliefs and practices.

Services: Provide services such as counseling, spiritual guidance, and healing sessions. These services can be offered for a fee, emphasizing the specialized knowledge and skills of the cult's leaders and practitioners.

Exploiting Member Contributions

Member contributions can be a significant source of revenue, ensuring that followers are financially invested in the cult.

Tithes and Donations: Encourage regular financial contributions from members through tithes and donations. Emphasize the spiritual benefits of giving and the importance of supporting the cult's mission.

Voluntary Work: Organize voluntary work programs where members contribute their labor to the cult's businesses and projects. This reduces operational costs and fosters a sense of community and commitment.

Bequests and Inheritance: Encourage members to include the cult in their wills and bequests. This can be framed as a way to continue supporting the community even after their death, ensuring a lasting legacy.

Special Fundraising Campaigns: Launch fundraising campaigns for specific projects or needs. Use emotional appeals and highlight the collective effort required to achieve the cult's goals, encouraging generous contributions.

Managing Cult Finances

Effective financial management is crucial for the sustainability and growth of the cult.

Transparent Accounting: Maintain transparent and accurate accounting records. This builds trust among members and ensures that funds are used appropriately.

Budgeting: Develop a detailed budget that outlines expected income and expenses. Regularly review and adjust the budget to ensure financial stability and address any unexpected financial challenges.

Investment Strategies: Implement investment strategies to grow the cult's financial reserves. This can include investing in real estate, stocks, or other assets that provide a steady return on investment.

Cost Management: Keep operational costs under control by minimizing unnecessary expenses and negotiating favorable terms with suppliers and service providers. Efficient cost management ensures that more funds are available for the cult's core activities and growth.

Financial Audits: Conduct regular financial audits to ensure accountability and transparency. This helps prevent financial mismanagement and maintains the trust of members and external stakeholders.

Conclusion: Monetizing Your Cult

By designing diverse revenue streams, exploiting member contributions, and effectively managing finances, a cult can ensure its sustainability and growth. Implementing these strategies helps maintain financial stability, supports the cult's activities, and allows for future expansion. Understanding and applying these principles can help any aspiring leader build a financially robust and thriving community.

Membership Fees

Charging membership fees, including an initiation fee for new members and regular dues, can provide a steady income stream for a cult. These fees can be framed as contributions towards the community's upkeep and activities, making members feel they are investing in something valuable. Here's how Sarah, our aspiring cult leader, implemented membership fees in her cult.

A Story of Investment: Sarah's Membership Model

Sarah knew that to ensure the sustainability of her cult, she needed a reliable source of income. She decided to introduce membership fees, carefully framing them as essential contributions that supported the community's growth and daily operations.

Initiation Fee: When new members joined the cult, Sarah charged an initiation fee. This fee was presented as a necessary step to become part of the exclusive community, covering the costs of initial training, materials, and integration activities. Sarah explained that this investment was crucial for their personal growth and the community's overall well-being.

- **Welcoming Ceremony**: Sarah organized a welcoming ceremony for new members, where the initiation fee was formally introduced. During this ceremony, she highlighted the benefits of joining the community and how the initiation fee would be used to support the group's activities. New members felt honored and valued, seeing the fee as a small price to pay for the transformative experience they were promised.

Regular Membership Dues: In addition to the initiation fee, Sarah implemented regular membership dues. These dues were positioned as monthly or yearly contributions to cover ongoing community expenses, such as maintenance of communal spaces, event organization, and educational materials.

- **Transparent Communication**: Sarah communicated transparently about how the membership dues would be utilized. She provided detailed breakdowns of expenses and how the funds were essential for sustaining the cult's mission. This transparency built trust among the members, making them more willing to contribute.

Emphasizing Value: To ensure that members saw the value in their contributions, Sarah emphasized the tangible and intangible benefits they received from the community.

- **Exclusive Access**: Members who paid their dues were given exclusive access to certain teachings, rituals, and events. Sarah made it clear that these experiences were reserved for those who were fully committed to the cult's mission, reinforcing the importance of their financial contributions.
- **Personal Growth**: Sarah highlighted how the membership fees supported programs and activities that directly contributed to members' personal and spiritual growth. She shared success stories of individuals who had benefited from the cult's resources, demonstrating the positive impact of their contributions.

Community Investment: Sarah framed the membership fees as an investment in the community's future. She encouraged members to see their contributions as a way to ensure the longevity and prosperity of the cult, fostering a sense of shared responsibility and collective effort.

- **Regular Updates**: To keep members engaged and aware of the impact of their contributions, Sarah provided regular updates on the community's achievements and future plans. These updates reinforced the idea that their fees were making a significant difference, motivating members to continue their financial support.

Conclusion: The Power of Membership Fees

Through the strategic implementation of initiation fees and regular membership dues, Sarah created a reliable income stream that supported the cult's activities and growth. By framing these fees as valuable contributions to the community's well-being and emphasizing transparency and tangible benefits, she ensured that members felt invested in the cult's mission. Understanding and applying these principles can help any aspiring leader build a financially sustainable and committed community.

Workshops and Seminars

Offering paid workshops and seminars on various topics related to the cult's teachings can be a significant revenue stream. These events can be marketed to both members and the public, providing valuable knowledge and insights while generating income. Here's how Sarah, our aspiring cult leader, effectively used workshops and seminars to generate revenue and spread the cult's teachings.

A Story of Enlightenment: Sarah's Workshops and Seminars

Sarah recognized that workshops and seminars could serve a dual purpose: generating income and spreading the cult's teachings. She decided to develop a series of educational events that would attract both cult members and the general public.

Identifying Topics: Sarah began by identifying topics that would resonate with both her followers and potential attendees from outside the cult. These topics were chosen based on their relevance to the cult's teachings and their appeal to a broader audience.

- **Spiritual Development**: Workshops on meditation techniques, spiritual awakening, and personal transformation were central to the offerings. These sessions promised participants profound insights and practical skills for their spiritual journeys.
- **Practical Applications**: Sarah also included seminars on topics such as stress management, healthy living, and relationship building. By connecting these practical applications to the cult's teachings, she ensured the content was relevant and accessible to a wider audience.

Creating Valuable Content: Sarah understood that to attract attendees, the workshops and seminars needed to offer genuine value. She invested time in developing high-quality content that provided deep insights and practical takeaways.

- **Expert Speakers**: Sarah invited respected experts within the cult to lead the sessions. These individuals were seen as authorities on their subjects, adding credibility and appeal to the events.
- **Engaging Formats**: The workshops and seminars were designed to be interactive and engaging. Sarah included a mix of lectures, group discussions, hands-on activities, and Q&A sessions to ensure that participants remained actively involved and found the experience enriching.

Marketing the Events: To maximize attendance, Sarah implemented a robust marketing strategy that targeted both cult members and the general public.

- **Internal Promotion**: Within the cult, Sarah promoted the events through regular meetings, newsletters, and personal invitations. She emphasized the importance of continued learning and how these workshops aligned with the cult's goals and teachings.
- **External Outreach**: For the general public, Sarah used social media, local advertising, and partnerships with related organizations to spread the word. She highlighted the unique benefits of the workshops and positioned them as opportunities for personal and spiritual growth.

Monetizing the Workshops: To generate revenue, Sarah set competitive pricing for the workshops and seminars. She ensured that the fees were justified by the quality of the content and the expertise of the speakers.

- **Tiered Pricing**: Sarah introduced tiered pricing options, such as early bird discounts, group rates, and premium packages that included additional resources or one-on-one sessions with the experts. This strategy made the events accessible to a broader audience while maximizing revenue.
- **Supplementary Sales**: During the workshops and seminars, Sarah offered supplementary materials for sale, such as books, audio recordings, and exclusive merchandise. These additional sales provided an extra income stream and reinforced the teachings presented in the sessions.

Providing Continuous Value: To build loyalty and encourage repeat attendance, Sarah ensured that participants left the workshops and seminars feeling they had gained valuable insights and practical skills.

- **Feedback and Improvement**: After each event, Sarah collected feedback from attendees to identify areas for improvement. This allowed her to continually enhance the quality of the workshops and ensure they met the needs and expectations of the participants.

- **Follow-Up Engagement**: Sarah followed up with attendees through newsletters and exclusive online content. This ongoing engagement helped maintain interest in future events and kept the participants connected to the cult's teachings.

Conclusion: The Impact of Workshops and Seminars

By offering paid workshops and seminars, Sarah successfully generated revenue while spreading the cult's teachings. Through careful topic selection, high-quality content, effective marketing, and continuous value provision, she attracted both cult members and the general public. Understanding and implementing these strategies can help any aspiring leader create impactful and profitable educational events that enhance their community's growth and financial stability.

Merchandise

Developing and selling branded merchandise is an effective way to generate income while promoting the cult's teachings and symbols. This strategy not only provides a steady revenue stream but also helps reinforce the cult's identity and spread its message. Here's how Sarah, our aspiring cult leader, leveraged merchandise to support her cult's growth.

Sarah recognized the potential of branded merchandise to both generate income and strengthen the cult's identity. She began by designing a range of products that prominently featured the cult's symbols and messages. This merchandise included clothing items like T-shirts and hoodies adorned with the cult's emblem, as well as jewelry that incorporated sacred symbols and motifs. Each item was carefully crafted to appeal to both cult members and the broader public, ensuring a wide market.

Books were another significant component of Sarah's merchandise strategy. She authored several books that detailed the cult's teachings, philosophies, and Sarah's personal journey. These books served as both an educational tool for new members and a way to reach a broader audience interested in spiritual enlightenment. Additionally, audio recordings of her lectures and guided meditations were produced, providing followers with easy access to her teachings in their daily lives.

To maximize the reach and sales of the merchandise, Sarah utilized multiple distribution channels. Events such as workshops, seminars, and festivals provided a prime opportunity to showcase and sell the products. Special booths were set up at these events, attracting attendees with visually appealing displays and enthusiastic salespeople who explained the significance of each item. This face-to-face interaction helped build a personal connection with potential buyers and emphasized the value of the merchandise.

Sarah also established an online store, making it convenient for both members and non-members to purchase items. The online platform was designed to be user-friendly and visually engaging, with detailed descriptions and high-quality images of the merchandise. Special promotions and discounts for online purchases encouraged more sales, and a subscription service was introduced for regular followers to receive exclusive new items and updates about the cult.

Within the community, merchandise played a crucial role in fostering a sense of belonging and unity. Members were encouraged to wear clothing and jewelry featuring the cult's symbols during gatherings and rituals, reinforcing their identity and commitment to the group. These items became badges of honor, symbolizing the wearer's dedication to the cult's values and teachings.

In conclusion, Sarah's strategic development and sale of branded merchandise effectively supported the cult's financial stability while promoting its teachings and symbols. By offering a range of appealing products and utilizing multiple sales channels, she ensured a steady income stream and strengthened the cult's identity. This approach not only provided financial benefits but also deepened members' connection to the cult and spread its message to a broader audience.

Special Events

Hosting special events is a powerful way to generate income while offering unique experiences that align with the cult's beliefs and practices. These events not only serve as significant revenue streams but also strengthen the sense of community and commitment among followers. Here's how Sarah, our aspiring cult leader, effectively utilized special events to support her cult.

Sarah understood the allure and impact of special events. She planned a variety of events, including spiritual retreats, festivals, and exclusive gatherings, designed to provide profound and memorable experiences for attendees.

Spiritual Retreats: Sarah organized spiritual retreats in serene, picturesque locations. These retreats were marketed as opportunities for deep meditation, self-reflection, and personal growth. Attendees were promised an immersive experience where they could escape the distractions of everyday life and connect more deeply with the cult's teachings. The retreats included workshops, guided meditations, and one-on-one sessions with Sarah, making them highly attractive to both current members and potential recruits. By charging a premium fee for these retreats, Sarah ensured a significant revenue stream while providing immense value to the participants.

Festivals: Sarah hosted annual festivals that celebrated the cult's milestones, teachings, and community spirit. These festivals were vibrant, multi-day events featuring a mix of rituals, performances, and social activities. They served as both a celebration and a recruitment tool, attracting large crowds. Sarah ensured that the festivals included exclusive sessions and performances that were available only to ticket holders. By selling tickets and merchandise, and offering special access passes for premium experiences, she maximized the revenue generated from these festivals.

Exclusive Gatherings: For her most devoted followers, Sarah organized exclusive gatherings that offered intimate, personalized experiences. These gatherings were held in secretive, prestigious locations and included private teachings, discussions, and ceremonies led by Sarah herself. The exclusivity of these events made them highly desirable, and attendees were willing to pay substantial fees for the privilege of participating. These gatherings not only generated significant income but also reinforced the loyalty and commitment of Sarah's core followers.

Creating Value: To ensure the success of these special events, Sarah focused on creating unique and valuable experiences that couldn't be found elsewhere. She incorporated elements of surprise, exclusivity, and deep personal engagement, which made the events memorable and worth the investment. Sarah also leveraged testimonials and success stories from previous events to market future ones, highlighting the transformative impact they had on participants' lives.

Marketing and Outreach: Sarah used a multi-faceted marketing approach to promote these events. Within the cult, she utilized meetings, newsletters, and personal invitations to generate excitement and encourage participation. Externally, she used social media, partnerships with related organizations, and targeted advertising to reach a broader audience. Special promotions, early bird discounts, and referral bonuses were offered to boost ticket sales and attendance.

Financial Management: To ensure profitability, Sarah meticulously planned the budget for each event, considering all costs and potential revenue sources. She negotiated favorable terms with venues, suppliers, and performers to keep expenses low while maintaining high quality. Detailed financial tracking allowed her to adjust strategies as needed, ensuring that each event was financially successful.

In conclusion, Sarah's strategic hosting of special events, including spiritual retreats, festivals, and exclusive gatherings, effectively supported her cult's financial stability and growth. By offering unique and valuable experiences that aligned with the cult's beliefs and practices, she attracted attendees and generated significant income. These events not only provided financial benefits but also deepened the sense of community and commitment among her followers, reinforcing the cult's overall strength and cohesion.

Services

Providing specialized services such as counseling, spiritual guidance, and healing sessions can be an effective way to generate income while emphasizing the unique knowledge and skills of the cult's leaders and practitioners. These services offer personal and spiritual support to members and attract those seeking deeper insights and healing. Here's how Sarah, our aspiring cult leader, implemented and monetized these services.

Counseling Services

Sarah recognized that many of her followers sought personal and emotional support. To address this need, she established a counseling service within the cult, offering one-on-one sessions with trained practitioners.

Personalized Support: The counseling sessions were tailored to address individual members' personal challenges, including relationship issues, stress management, and personal development. By providing a safe and supportive environment, Sarah ensured that members felt comfortable sharing their concerns and seeking guidance.

Qualified Counselors: Sarah selected and trained counselors from within the cult, ensuring they were well-versed in the cult's teachings and methods. These counselors were presented as experts with deep understanding and empathy, reinforcing the value and effectiveness of the service.

Fee Structure: The counseling services were offered for a fee, with various pricing options based on the length and frequency of sessions. This fee was justified by the specialized knowledge and personalized support provided, making members willing to invest in their well-being.

Spiritual Guidance

Sarah also offered spiritual guidance sessions, providing members with deeper insights into the cult's teachings and helping them on their spiritual journey.

Individual and Group Sessions: Spiritual guidance was available both in individual and group settings. Individual sessions offered personalized insights and advice, while group sessions fostered a sense of community and shared learning experiences.

Emphasizing Expertise: Sarah positioned herself and her senior practitioners as enlightened guides with unique access to spiritual truths. This positioning made the spiritual guidance sessions highly desirable for those seeking to deepen their understanding and connection to the cult's teachings.

Workshops and Retreats: In addition to regular sessions, Sarah organized intensive workshops and retreats focused on spiritual growth. These events provided concentrated periods of learning and practice, attracting members who sought immersive experiences.

Pricing and Packages: The spiritual guidance sessions and events were offered at various price points, with premium packages that included additional resources or extended sessions.

This tiered pricing model made the services accessible to a broad range of members while maximizing revenue.

Healing Sessions

Recognizing the growing interest in alternative healing methods, Sarah introduced healing sessions that combined physical, emotional, and spiritual healing practices.

Holistic Approach: The healing sessions integrated various techniques such as meditation, energy healing, and herbal remedies. This holistic approach appealed to members seeking comprehensive wellness solutions.

Trained Healers: Sarah trained selected members in the healing practices endorsed by the cult. These healers were presented as having specialized skills and a deep connection to the cult's spiritual principles, enhancing their credibility and the perceived value of the sessions.

Regular Offerings: Healing sessions were offered regularly, both as standalone appointments and as part of larger wellness programs. This consistency helped build a loyal client base and ensured a steady income stream.

Fee Structure: Healing sessions were priced based on the type and length of the treatment. Sarah also introduced membership plans that included regular healing sessions at a discounted rate, encouraging ongoing participation and financial commitment.

Conclusion: Monetizing Services

By providing services such as counseling, spiritual guidance, and healing sessions, Sarah effectively generated income while emphasizing the specialized knowledge and skills of the cult's leaders and practitioners. These services offered valuable support to members and attracted those seeking deeper insights and healing, reinforcing their commitment to the cult. Through careful structuring and pricing, Sarah ensured that these services were both accessible and profitable, contributing to the financial stability and growth of the cult. Understanding and implementing these strategies can help any aspiring leader create a sustainable model for monetizing specialized services within their community.

Tithes and Donations

Encouraging regular financial contributions through tithes and donations is a fundamental way to generate consistent income for a cult. Emphasizing the spiritual benefits of giving and the importance of supporting the cult's mission can inspire members to contribute willingly and generously. Here's how Sarah, our aspiring cult leader, effectively promoted tithes and donations within her cult.

Promoting Regular Contributions

Sarah recognized that consistent financial support was essential for the sustainability and growth of her cult. To achieve this, she encouraged members to make regular contributions through tithes and donations.

Spiritual Emphasis: Sarah emphasized the spiritual significance of giving. She taught that financial contributions were not just a means of support for the cult but a spiritual practice that brought blessings and personal growth. By framing tithing as an act of faith and devotion, she made it an integral part of the members' spiritual journey.

Clear Expectations: Sarah set clear expectations regarding tithing. She introduced a system where members were encouraged to contribute a fixed percentage of their income regularly. This transparency ensured that members understood their financial responsibilities and could plan their contributions accordingly.

Communicating the Benefits

To motivate members to contribute, Sarah highlighted the numerous benefits of tithing and donations, both for the individual and the community.

Personal Blessings: Sarah frequently shared stories and testimonials from members who had experienced positive changes in their lives as a result of their contributions. These stories reinforced the belief that giving brought personal blessings and spiritual rewards, motivating others to follow suit.

Collective Growth: Sarah communicated how the contributions directly supported the cult's mission and activities. She provided regular updates on how the funds were used, such as financing community projects, organizing events, and supporting outreach efforts. This transparency built trust and demonstrated the tangible impact of their giving.

Creating a Culture of Giving

Sarah worked to create a culture of giving within the cult, where financial contributions were seen as a norm and a shared responsibility.

Regular Reminders: During meetings and gatherings, Sarah regularly reminded members of the importance of their financial contributions. She used these opportunities to reinforce the spiritual benefits of giving and to thank those who had contributed, creating a positive association with the act of giving.

Special Campaigns: Sarah launched special donation campaigns for specific projects or needs. These campaigns were framed as opportunities for members to come together and achieve something significant. By setting clear goals and providing progress updates, she kept members engaged and motivated to contribute.

Celebrating Contributions: To recognize and appreciate the generosity of her followers, Sarah held events to celebrate their contributions. These events included special ceremonies, public acknowledgments, and tokens of appreciation. This recognition fostered a sense of pride and belonging among contributors.

Facilitating Contributions

Making it easy for members to contribute was crucial for maximizing tithes and donations. Sarah implemented various methods to facilitate the process.

Multiple Payment Options: Sarah provided multiple ways for members to make their contributions, including cash, checks, online payments, and automatic deductions. This flexibility ensured that members could give in the most convenient way for them.

Donation Platforms: An online donation platform was set up to allow members to contribute from anywhere at any time. The platform was user-friendly and secure, encouraging more frequent and spontaneous donations.

Recurring Donations: Sarah encouraged members to set up recurring donations, which provided a steady and predictable stream of income for the cult. This system also reduced the need for frequent reminders and made it easier for members to fulfill their commitment to tithing.

Conclusion: The Power of Tithes and Donations

By promoting regular financial contributions through tithes and donations, Sarah successfully created a consistent income stream to support her cult's activities and growth. Through spiritual emphasis, clear communication, and a culture of giving, she inspired members to contribute willingly and generously. Facilitating easy and flexible donation methods ensured that members could support the cult in a way that suited them best. Understanding and implementing these strategies can help any aspiring leader secure the financial stability needed to sustain and expand their community.

Voluntary Work

Organizing voluntary work programs can significantly reduce operational costs while fostering a strong sense of community and commitment among cult members. By encouraging followers to contribute their labor to the cult's businesses and projects, a leader can ensure that the community thrives through collective effort and shared responsibility. Here's how Sarah, our aspiring cult leader, effectively implemented voluntary work programs within her cult.

Organizing Voluntary Work Programs

Sarah recognized that involving members in voluntary work not only cut costs but also deepened their engagement and sense of ownership in the community. She developed a structured approach to organize and manage these programs effectively.

Identifying Needs: Sarah began by identifying the various needs of the cult that could be met through voluntary work. This included maintenance of communal living spaces, organizing events, running the cult's businesses, and managing day-to-day operations.

Creating Work Teams: She organized members into work teams based on their skills, interests, and availability. Each team was assigned specific tasks and responsibilities, ensuring that all necessary work was covered efficiently. This also allowed members to contribute in ways that were meaningful and satisfying to them.

Reducing Operational Costs

By utilizing voluntary labor, Sarah significantly reduced the cult's operational expenses. This allowed more resources to be allocated towards growth and development initiatives.

Maintenance and Upkeep: Members took on the responsibility of maintaining communal living areas, gardening, cooking, and cleaning. This eliminated the need to hire external help, reducing costs while ensuring that the living environment was well-cared for by those who used it.

Event Organization: Voluntary teams were responsible for organizing and executing events such as spiritual retreats, workshops, and festivals. This included everything from planning and logistics to setup and cleanup. By using member labor, Sarah minimized the costs associated with hiring professional event organizers.

Running Businesses: The cult's businesses, such as cafes, bookstores, and wellness centers, were staffed by members on a voluntary basis. This not only reduced labor costs but also ensured that the businesses were operated by individuals who were deeply committed to the cult's mission and values.

Fostering a Sense of Community and Commitment

Voluntary work programs played a crucial role in fostering a sense of community and strengthening the commitment of members to the cult.

Shared Responsibility: By contributing their labor, members felt a greater sense of responsibility and ownership towards the community. This collective effort created a bond among members, as they worked together towards common goals.

Skill Development: Voluntary work provided opportunities for members to develop new skills and gain valuable experience. Whether learning new trades, management skills, or organizing events, members benefited personally while contributing to the community.

Recognition and Appreciation: Sarah ensured that the efforts of volunteers were regularly acknowledged and appreciated. This included public recognition during meetings, special ceremonies to honor dedicated volunteers, and tokens of appreciation. This recognition motivated members to continue contributing and reinforced their commitment to the community.

Enhanced Belonging: The act of working together on various projects strengthened the sense of belonging among members. They developed closer relationships through shared experiences and collective achievements, fostering a supportive and cohesive community.

Managing Voluntary Work Programs

Effective management of voluntary work programs was essential to their success. Sarah implemented several strategies to ensure that these programs ran smoothly.

Clear Communication: Sarah maintained clear and consistent communication with all volunteers. This included regular updates on tasks, schedules, and expectations. Clear communication ensured that everyone was informed and prepared for their roles.

Flexible Scheduling: Understanding that members had varying availability, Sarah implemented flexible scheduling options. This allowed members to contribute at times that suited them best, ensuring maximum participation and reducing burnout.

Leadership Roles: Sarah appointed team leaders to coordinate and oversee the work of volunteers. These leaders were responsible for ensuring that tasks were completed efficiently and that any issues were promptly addressed. This structure provided organization and accountability within the voluntary work programs.

Conclusion: The Power of Voluntary Work

Through well-organized voluntary work programs, Sarah was able to reduce operational costs significantly while fostering a strong sense of community and commitment among her followers. By engaging members in meaningful work that supported the cult's businesses and projects, she ensured that the community thrived through collective effort and shared responsibility. Understanding and implementing these strategies can help any aspiring leader build a cohesive, committed, and cost-effective community.

Bequests and Inheritance

Encouraging members to include the cult in their wills and bequests can provide a significant source of long-term financial support. This strategy ensures that members' commitment to the community continues even after their death, creating a lasting legacy that benefits the cult. Here's how Sarah, our aspiring cult leader, effectively promoted bequests and inheritance within her cult.

Framing the Importance of Bequests and Inheritance

Sarah understood that to encourage members to include the cult in their wills, she needed to frame it in a way that highlighted its significance and spiritual value.

Legacy of Support: Sarah emphasized that including the cult in their wills was a way for members to leave a lasting impact and ensure the continuity of the community they cherished. She explained that their contributions would help future generations benefit from the same support and teachings they had received.

Spiritual Significance: Sarah framed bequests as an ultimate act of devotion and generosity, aligning it with the cult's teachings on selflessness and community support. By presenting it as a spiritual practice, she made the idea more appealing and meaningful to her followers.

Encouraging Inclusion in Wills

To facilitate the process, Sarah provided clear guidance and support for members who wished to include the cult in their wills.

Educational Sessions: Sarah organized informational sessions where legal experts explained the process of drafting a will and the importance of estate planning. These sessions demystified the legal aspects and made it easier for members to take action.

Template Wording: To simplify the process, Sarah provided template wording that members could use when drafting their wills. This included specific language that clearly stated their intention to leave a portion of their estate to the cult, ensuring legal clarity and reducing the risk of disputes.

Personal Consultations: Sarah and her trusted advisors offered personal consultations to members who needed additional guidance. These one-on-one sessions provided a supportive environment where members could discuss their intentions and receive tailored advice on how to proceed.

Creating a Culture of Legacy

Sarah worked to create a culture where leaving a bequest to the cult was seen as a noble and expected act.

Public Recognition: Members who included the cult in their wills were publicly acknowledged and honored. This recognition not only validated their decision but also inspired others to consider doing the same. Special ceremonies and mentions during gatherings reinforced the importance of their contributions.

Success Stories: Sarah shared stories of past members who had left bequests and the positive impact their contributions had on the community. These stories highlighted the tangible benefits of such generosity, making it clear how future bequests would be used to support the cult's mission.

Facilitating the Legal Process

To ensure that the process of including the cult in wills was as smooth as possible, Sarah provided resources and support to handle legal and administrative aspects.

Legal Support: Sarah collaborated with legal professionals who could assist members in drafting their wills and ensuring that their bequests were legally sound. This support reduced the complexity and stress associated with estate planning.

Estate Planning Workshops: Regular workshops on estate planning were conducted to educate members on managing their assets and making informed decisions. These workshops covered various aspects of estate planning, including tax implications and charitable giving.

Building Trust

Trust was crucial for members to feel comfortable leaving their assets to the cult. Sarah took steps to build and maintain this trust.

Transparency: Sarah maintained transparency about how bequests and donations were used. Regular financial reports and updates on funded projects assured members that their contributions were being managed responsibly and effectively.

Ethical Management: Sarah emphasized ethical management of the cult's finances. She implemented checks and balances to prevent misuse of funds and ensured that all financial activities aligned with the cult's values and mission.

Conclusion: The Power of Bequests and Inheritance

By encouraging members to include the cult in their wills and bequests, Sarah secured a lasting source of financial support for her community. Through framing the act as a spiritual legacy, providing legal guidance, and building a culture of recognition and trust, she ensured that members felt comfortable and motivated to contribute. Understanding and implementing these strategies can help any aspiring leader build a sustainable financial future for their cult, ensuring that its mission and impact continue for generations to come.

Special Fundraising Campaigns

Launching special fundraising campaigns for specific projects or needs can effectively generate additional funds while rallying members around a common cause. By using emotional appeals and highlighting the collective effort required to achieve the cult's goals, leaders can inspire generous contributions. Here's how Sarah, our aspiring cult leader, successfully implemented special fundraising campaigns within her cult.

Identifying Specific Projects and Needs

Sarah recognized that targeted fundraising campaigns were more effective when they were focused on specific projects or needs that resonated with her followers.

Project Selection: Sarah carefully selected projects that were essential to the cult's growth and well-being. These projects ranged from building new communal living facilities and expanding educational programs to funding outreach initiatives and community service efforts. By choosing impactful and meaningful projects, she ensured that members felt their contributions would make a significant difference.

Clear Goals: For each campaign, Sarah set clear and achievable fundraising goals. She communicated these goals to the members, explaining how much money was needed and what it would be used for. Clear goals made the campaigns more transparent and helped members understand the importance of their contributions.

Using Emotional Appeals

To inspire generous contributions, Sarah crafted emotional appeals that connected with her followers on a personal level.

Storytelling: Sarah used storytelling to convey the importance of each project. She shared personal anecdotes and success stories that illustrated the potential impact of the campaign. By highlighting the benefits and the positive changes that previous contributions had brought, she created a compelling narrative that motivated members to give.

Personal Connection: Sarah made an effort to personally connect with members, discussing the campaigns during meetings and one-on-one interactions. She emphasized how each contribution, no matter how small, was a vital part of the collective effort. This personal touch made members feel valued and integral to the success of the campaign.

Visuals and Testimonials: Sarah incorporated visuals, such as photos and videos, along with testimonials from members who had benefited from past projects. These elements provided tangible evidence of the positive outcomes and reinforced the emotional appeal of the campaigns.

Highlighting Collective Effort

Sarah emphasized the collective nature of the fundraising efforts, fostering a sense of unity and shared responsibility.

Community Involvement: Sarah organized events and activities that involved the entire community in the fundraising efforts. These events included charity auctions, sponsored walks, and group challenges. By participating together, members felt a stronger bond and a greater commitment to the cause.

Progress Updates: Throughout the campaign, Sarah provided regular updates on the progress towards the fundraising goal. She celebrated milestones and acknowledged the contributions of members, reinforcing the idea that every donation was making a difference. These updates maintained momentum and kept members engaged.

Public Recognition: To encourage further contributions, Sarah publicly recognized and thanked donors. This recognition was done during community gatherings and in newsletters, creating a culture of appreciation and motivating others to contribute.

Encouraging Generous Contributions

To maximize the effectiveness of the fundraising campaigns, Sarah employed strategies to encourage generous donations.

Matching Gifts: Sarah introduced matching gift programs, where major donors agreed to match contributions up to a certain amount. This strategy doubled the impact of individual donations and encouraged more members to give, knowing their contributions would be matched.

Incentives and Rewards: Sarah offered incentives and rewards for contributions, such as exclusive access to special events, personalized thank-you notes, and commemorative items. These incentives made members feel appreciated and incentivized larger donations.

Flexible Donation Options: Sarah provided various donation options, including one-time gifts, monthly pledges, and legacy contributions. This flexibility allowed members to choose how they wanted to contribute, making it easier for them to support the campaign in a way that suited their financial situation.

Conclusion: The Success of Special Fundraising Campaigns

By launching special fundraising campaigns for specific projects or needs, Sarah effectively generated additional funds and fostered a sense of community and collective effort. Through emotional appeals, clear goals, and regular updates, she inspired generous contributions from her followers. Understanding and implementing these strategies can help any aspiring leader successfully raise funds for important projects, ensuring the continued growth and prosperity of their community.

Managing Cult Finances

Effective financial management is crucial for the sustainability and growth of the cult. As a cult leader, maintaining control over financial matters while ensuring the perception of transparency and accountability is essential. Here's a detailed guide on how to manage cult finances effectively, with a focus on strategic financial practices that support the cult's long-term stability.

Transparent Accounting

While transparent accounting is typically essential for building trust among members, a cult leader must balance this with the need to maintain control over financial details. Selective transparency can help maintain trust while keeping sensitive information concealed.

Selective Transparency: Provide members with simplified financial summaries that highlight positive aspects of the cult's financial health. Focus on general income and expenditure categories without disclosing specific details. This approach creates a perception of openness while safeguarding sensitive information.

Controlled Access: Limit access to detailed financial records to a trusted inner circle. Only a few key members should have full visibility of the cult's finances. This ensures that critical financial decisions remain under the leader's control.

Budgeting

Developing a detailed budget is essential for planning and managing the cult's financial resources effectively. Regularly review and adjust the budget to ensure financial stability and address any unexpected financial challenges.

Comprehensive Planning: Create a budget that outlines all expected income sources and expenses. Include detailed projections for membership fees, donations, merchandise sales, and event revenues, as well as operational costs, salaries, and project expenses.

Regular Reviews: Schedule regular budget reviews to assess financial performance and make necessary adjustments. This proactive approach helps address potential shortfalls and reallocates resources to high-priority areas.

Investment Strategies

Implementing investment strategies to grow the cult's financial reserves is crucial for long-term sustainability. Diversify investments to reduce risk and ensure steady returns.

Diversified Portfolio: Invest in a mix of real estate, stocks, bonds, and other assets to create a balanced and diversified portfolio. Diversification reduces the risk of significant financial losses and ensures steady growth of the cult's reserves.

Professional Management: Engage financial advisors or investment professionals to manage the cult's investment portfolio. Their expertise can help maximize returns and identify lucrative investment opportunities while minimizing risks.

Cost Management

Keeping operational costs under control is vital for ensuring that more funds are available for the cult's core activities and growth. Efficient cost management involves minimizing unnecessary expenses and negotiating favorable terms with suppliers and service providers.

Expense Monitoring: Regularly monitor and analyze all expenses to identify areas where costs can be reduced. Implement cost-saving measures such as bulk purchasing, energy-efficient practices, and renegotiating contracts with suppliers.

Strategic Negotiations: Develop strong relationships with suppliers and service providers to negotiate better terms and discounts. Leverage the cult's purchasing power to secure favorable deals that reduce overall operational costs.

Financial Audits

While financial audits are generally used to ensure accountability and transparency, a cult leader can use selective audits to maintain a semblance of oversight without revealing sensitive information.

Internal Audits: Conduct regular internal audits with a trusted team to review financial records and ensure compliance with established procedures. These audits help identify and address any discrepancies without external scrutiny.

External Perception: Occasionally engage external auditors for selective audits of non-sensitive financial areas. Publicize the results to reinforce the perception of transparency and accountability among members and external stakeholders.

Conclusion: Strategic Financial Management

By strategically managing the cult's finances, a leader can ensure sustainability and growth while maintaining control over sensitive financial details. Through selective transparency, detailed budgeting, diversified investments, efficient cost management, and controlled financial audits, the leader can create a stable and thriving community. Understanding and implementing these strategies helps balance the need for control with the perception of openness, ensuring long-term trust and financial stability.

Chapter 5: Expanding Your Influence

Expanding your influence is crucial for the growth and sustainability of your cult. This chapter covers effective recruitment techniques, using media and propaganda, and creating an elite inner circle to strengthen your control and broaden your reach.

Effective Recruitment Techniques

1. **Targeted Outreach**
   - **Identifying Vulnerable Individuals**: Focus on individuals experiencing personal crises, loneliness, or dissatisfaction with their current life. These individuals are often more receptive to new ideologies and promises of community and purpose.
   - **Personalized Approaches**: Tailor your recruitment efforts to address the specific needs and concerns of potential recruits. Highlight how the cult can provide solutions to their problems, offering emotional support, community, and a sense of purpose.
2. **Leveraging Existing Members**
   - **Incentives for Referrals**: Encourage current members to bring in friends and family by offering incentives such as recognition, rewards, or elevated status within the cult.
   - **Utilizing Personal Networks**: Use the personal networks of current members to reach potential recruits. Members can vouch for the cult's benefits and provide a trusted point of entry for newcomers.
3. **Public Events and Workshops**
   - **Hosting Events**: Organize public events, workshops, and seminars that showcase the cult's teachings, values, and community. Use these events to attract and engage potential recruits.
   - **Showcasing Benefits**: Highlight the positive aspects of the cult, such as community support, personal growth opportunities, and spiritual enlightenment. Use testimonials and success stories to illustrate these benefits.
4. **Social Media Campaigns**
   - **Targeted Ads and Content**: Use social media platforms to reach a broader audience with targeted ads and engaging content. Tailor your messages to resonate with different demographics and interests.
   - **Creating Online Communities**: Establish groups and forums where potential recruits can interact with current members, ask questions, and learn more about the cult in a supportive environment.
5. **Community Involvement**
   - **Participating in Charitable Activities**: Engage in community service and charitable activities to build a positive reputation and attract individuals who value altruism and community involvement.
   - **Networking and Outreach**: Use these events to network and establish connections with potential recruits. Emphasize the cult's commitment to making a positive impact in the community.

Using Media and Propaganda

1. **Developing a Strong Online Presence**
   - **Professional Websites and Profiles**: Create professional websites and social media profiles that present a polished and credible image of the cult. Regularly update these platforms with content that highlights the cult's activities and successes.
   - **Regular Content Updates**: Maintain an active online presence by regularly posting updates, news, and engaging content that keeps followers informed and interested.
2. **Content Creation**
   - **Multimedia Production**: Produce high-quality videos, podcasts, and articles that explain the cult's beliefs, values, and benefits. Use engaging storytelling techniques to capture the audience's interest.
   - **Sharing Testimonials**: Share testimonials and success stories from current members that illustrate the positive impact of the cult. These personal stories can be powerful tools for attracting new recruits.
3. **Engaging with the Media**
   - **Press Releases and Conferences**: Issue press releases and hold press conferences to attract media attention and generate positive coverage. Highlight the cult's achievements and community contributions.
   - **Building Relationships with Journalists**: Develop relationships with journalists and media outlets to secure favorable coverage. Offer exclusive interviews and inside access to trusted media partners.
4. **Propaganda Techniques**
   - **Persuasive Language and Emotional Appeals**: Use persuasive language and emotional appeals to convey the cult's message. Craft messages that resonate with the audience's values and emotions.
   - **Visual Appeal**: Create visually appealing materials, such as posters, flyers, and social media graphics, to attract attention and communicate the cult's message effectively.
5. **Crisis Management**
   - **Preparedness**: Have a crisis management plan in place to address negative publicity and controversies quickly and effectively. Be prepared to respond to criticism and defend the cult's reputation.
   - **Control the Narrative**: Use media channels to control the narrative and present the cult's perspective. Address issues openly and honestly to maintain trust and credibility.

Creating an Elite Inner Circle

1. **Identifying Key Members**

- **Selection Criteria**: Identify members who demonstrate strong loyalty, exceptional skills, and potential for leadership. Look for individuals who are deeply committed to the cult's values and mission.
  - **Offering Responsibilities and Privileges**: Provide these key members with additional responsibilities and privileges to solidify their commitment. This could include leadership roles, special assignments, or access to exclusive resources.

2. **Special Training and Education**
   - **Advanced Training Programs**: Develop advanced training programs that enhance the skills and knowledge of inner circle members. Offer specialized education that is not available to the general membership.
   - **Exclusive Teachings**: Share exclusive knowledge and teachings with the inner circle, reinforcing their special status and deepening their loyalty to the leader and the cult.

3. **Exclusive Access**
   - **Direct Access to the Leader**: Grant inner circle members special access to the leader, including private meetings and direct communication. Involve them in decision-making processes and strategic planning.
   - **Strategic Involvement**: Engage the inner circle in important cult activities and initiatives. Their involvement ensures that they feel integral to the cult's success and more committed to its goals.

4. **Building Loyalty**
   - **Camaraderie and Exclusivity**: Foster a sense of camaraderie and exclusivity among inner circle members. Use rituals and ceremonies to reinforce their status and loyalty.
   - **Recognition and Rewards**: Regularly recognize and reward the contributions of inner circle members. Public acknowledgment and special privileges help maintain their dedication.

5. **Monitoring and Control**
   - **Close Monitoring**: Keep a close watch on the inner circle to ensure their loyalty and prevent dissent. Monitor their activities, communication, and behavior to identify any signs of disloyalty.
   - **Addressing Issues Promptly**: Address any signs of disloyalty or misconduct promptly and decisively. Take necessary actions to maintain the integrity and unity of the inner circle.

By implementing these strategies, you can expand your influence, attract new members, and strengthen your control over the cult. Effective recruitment, media utilization, and a loyal inner circle are key components to ensuring the growth and sustainability of your community.

Targeted Outreach

Sarah, our astute cult leader, understood the importance of targeted outreach to grow her community. She focused on identifying individuals who were vulnerable and in need of support, knowing that these people were often more receptive to new ideologies and promises of community and purpose.

In her outreach efforts, Sarah began by seeking out those experiencing personal crises, loneliness, or dissatisfaction with their current life. She knew that people in such situations were often looking for something or someone to provide answers, guidance, or simply a sense of belonging. Sarah targeted these individuals through various means, including social events, support groups, and even online forums where people discussed their personal struggles.

One day, Sarah met James, a middle-aged man going through a painful divorce. James felt isolated and uncertain about his future. Sarah approached him with genuine empathy, listening to his story and acknowledging his pain. She didn't immediately introduce the cult but instead offered a sympathetic ear and some comforting advice. Over the next few weeks, she kept in touch with James, providing emotional support and slowly introducing him to the idea of a community that could offer him not just support but a renewed sense of purpose.

Sarah tailored her approach to James, knowing that his primary needs were emotional support and companionship. She highlighted how the cult provided a close-knit community where members supported each other like family. She spoke about the group activities, the sense of belonging, and the shared mission of personal growth and spiritual enlightenment. By addressing James's specific needs and showing him how the cult could fill the void in his life, Sarah made the idea of joining the community very appealing.

James eventually attended a few cult gatherings, where he was welcomed warmly by other members. He saw firsthand the camaraderie and mutual support that Sarah had described. The members shared their stories of transformation and how the community had helped them overcome their personal challenges. James felt a sense of hope and belonging that he had been missing for so long. He began to participate more actively, finding solace and purpose in the group's activities and teachings.

Through this targeted outreach, Sarah successfully recruited James into the cult. She had identified his vulnerabilities, tailored her approach to meet his specific needs, and slowly integrated him into the community. This personalized recruitment strategy not only brought in new members but also ensured that they felt valued and supported, reinforcing their commitment to the cult.

Sarah's method of targeted outreach continued to be effective. By focusing on individuals experiencing personal crises and offering personalized solutions, she was able to grow her community with members who were deeply committed and grateful for the new direction their lives had taken. This approach not only expanded the cult's influence but also strengthened the bonds within the community, ensuring its long-term sustainability.

Leveraging Existing Members

Sarah, ever the strategic leader, knew that leveraging her existing members was a powerful way to expand the cult's reach. She understood that the trust and credibility her members had with their friends and family could be invaluable in bringing new recruits into the fold. To harness this potential, Sarah implemented a system of incentives and actively utilized the personal networks of her current members.

Incentives for Referrals

Sarah decided to create a robust referral program to encourage her members to bring in new recruits. She introduced a series of incentives designed to motivate her followers to reach out to their friends and family. These incentives included public recognition during community gatherings, tangible rewards such as gifts or privileges, and even elevated status within the cult.

For instance, Sarah announced that members who successfully brought in a new recruit would be honored in a special ceremony. These ceremonies were grand events where the referring member was praised for their contribution to the cult's growth. This recognition not only boosted the member's status within the group but also reinforced the idea that they were playing a vital role in the cult's mission.

Additionally, Sarah offered tangible rewards such as exclusive access to special teachings, reserved seating at events, and even leadership opportunities for those who consistently brought in new members. These rewards created a competitive yet supportive environment where members were eager to participate in the referral program, knowing their efforts would be acknowledged and rewarded.

Utilizing Personal Networks

To make the most of her members' personal networks, Sarah encouraged them to share their positive experiences and the benefits of the cult with their friends and family. She trained her members to articulate the cult's values, teachings, and community benefits effectively. This training included role-playing scenarios, communication strategies, and providing them with informational materials that they could share.

Sarah knew that a personal recommendation carried significant weight, so she focused on helping her members become confident and persuasive advocates for the cult. She encouraged them to host informal gatherings, such as dinners or casual meetups, where they could introduce their friends and family to the cult in a relaxed and welcoming environment. These gatherings were designed to be non-threatening and friendly, giving potential recruits a positive first impression.

For example, one member, Emily, hosted a small dinner party and invited her sister, Lisa, who had been struggling with a sense of purposelessness after losing her job. During the dinner, Emily and other members shared their stories of personal growth and community support within the cult. They spoke about the workshops, the shared goals, and the sense of belonging they felt. Lisa, seeing the genuine happiness and transformation in her sister and the others, became intrigued and decided to attend a few of the cult's public events.

The trust and bond between Emily and Lisa made the introduction to the cult feel safe and compelling. Lisa's initial interest grew into a deeper commitment after experiencing the community firsthand, all thanks to Emily's genuine recommendation and support.

Sarah's strategy of leveraging existing members proved highly effective. The combination of incentivized referrals and the utilization of personal networks brought in new recruits who were already predisposed to trust the cult, thanks to their relationships with current members. This approach not only expanded the cult's reach but also strengthened the community's internal bonds, as members felt more connected and responsible for the growth and well-being of the group.

By leveraging the trust and credibility of her existing members, Sarah was able to build a strong, cohesive, and continually growing community. Her approach ensured that new recruits were integrated smoothly and that the sense of shared purpose and commitment was reinforced with each new addition to the cult.

Public Events and Workshops

Sarah, always keen on expanding her influence and growing her community, understood the power of public events and workshops. These gatherings provided an excellent platform to showcase the cult's teachings, values, and community spirit, attracting and engaging potential recruits. Here's how she strategically organized and executed these events to maximize their impact.

Hosting Events

Sarah meticulously planned a series of public events, workshops, and seminars designed to draw in curious outsiders and potential recruits. Each event was crafted to highlight different aspects of the cult, ensuring a comprehensive introduction to what the cult had to offer.

Sarah's team selected venues that were accessible yet intimate enough to foster a sense of closeness and community. They arranged for comfortable seating, ambient lighting, and welcoming decorations to create a warm and inviting atmosphere. The events ranged from weekend workshops on personal development to evening seminars on spiritual enlightenment and community-building.

To promote these events, Sarah used a mix of traditional and digital marketing strategies. Flyers were distributed in local community centers, cafes, and libraries. Social media campaigns targeted individuals interested in personal growth, spirituality, and community engagement.

Sarah also leveraged word-of-mouth, encouraging her current members to invite friends and family.

One of the standout events was a weekend retreat focused on "Finding Inner Peace Through Community." This retreat included meditation sessions, group discussions, and lectures on the cult's core teachings. The program was designed to give attendees a taste of the transformative experiences that regular members enjoyed.

Showcasing Benefits

During these public events and workshops, Sarah ensured that the positive aspects of the cult were prominently highlighted. She wanted attendees to see firsthand the benefits of joining the community, emphasizing themes of support, personal growth, and spiritual enlightenment.

Sarah used a combination of presentations, interactive activities, and personal testimonials to showcase these benefits. For instance, during the weekend retreat, several long-term members shared their personal stories of transformation. One member, John, spoke about how joining the cult helped him overcome a period of severe depression, finding not only emotional support but also a renewed sense of purpose. His story resonated deeply with the audience, illustrating the cult's impact on individual lives.

Workshops included sessions on practical skills such as stress management, effective communication, and goal setting. These sessions were designed to provide immediate value to attendees, demonstrating the cult's commitment to personal development. By offering tools and techniques that attendees could apply in their daily lives, Sarah ensured that they left the event with a positive impression of the cult's practical benefits.

Seminars often delved into the spiritual aspects of the cult's teachings. Sarah or other charismatic leaders would lead these sessions, discussing concepts like spiritual growth, enlightenment, and the importance of community. These seminars were crafted to inspire and evoke a sense of wonder and possibility among the attendees.

To reinforce the community aspect, Sarah incorporated group activities that fostered a sense of belonging and mutual support. Icebreaker activities, group discussions, and collaborative projects allowed attendees to connect with each other and current members. This interaction helped potential recruits feel the warmth and inclusiveness of the community, making the idea of joining more appealing.

Each event concluded with an open invitation for attendees to join the cult's regular meetings and activities. Sarah provided information on membership, upcoming events, and ways to get involved, ensuring that interested individuals had a clear path to integration into the community.

By hosting well-organized public events and workshops, Sarah effectively showcased the cult's teachings, values, and benefits. These gatherings not only attracted and engaged potential recruits but also reinforced the sense of community and purpose among current members.

Through strategic planning and execution, Sarah used these events to expand her influence and grow her cult, one inspired attendee at a time.

Social Media Campaigns

Recognizing the vast potential of social media to reach a wide audience, Sarah strategically harnessed these platforms to expand her cult's influence. She understood that effective social media campaigns could attract new recruits by engaging diverse demographics and creating supportive online communities.

Targeted Ads and Content

Sarah began by creating a series of targeted ads and engaging content tailored to resonate with different demographics and interests. She knew that generic messages wouldn't suffice, so she designed her campaigns to speak directly to the specific needs and desires of potential recruits.

On platforms like Facebook and Instagram, Sarah used advanced targeting features to ensure her ads reached people most likely to be interested in the cult's teachings. For example, she created ads highlighting personal growth and community support for individuals interested in self-help and spirituality. These ads featured captivating visuals and compelling messages about finding purpose and belonging.

To appeal to younger audiences, Sarah's team produced short, engaging videos for TikTok and Instagram Reels. These videos showcased the cult's vibrant community life, including clips from events, testimonials from young members, and snippets of Sarah's inspirational talks. The content was designed to be shareable, encouraging viewers to spread the message to their own networks.

For professionals and those seeking career development, LinkedIn was the chosen platform. Here, Sarah posted articles and insights on leadership, personal development, and stress management. She framed the cult as a source of holistic growth, blending career success with personal and spiritual fulfillment.

Across all platforms, Sarah maintained a consistent brand voice and aesthetic, ensuring that all content reflected the cult's values and mission. High-quality images, thoughtful captions, and interactive posts like polls and Q&A sessions kept the audience engaged and intrigued.

Creating Online Communities

Beyond targeted ads and content, Sarah understood the importance of fostering a sense of community online. She established groups and forums on various social media platforms where potential recruits could interact with current members, ask questions, and learn more about the cult in a supportive environment.

On Facebook, Sarah created a private group named "Journey to Inner Peace." This group was positioned as a safe space for individuals seeking spiritual guidance and personal growth. Current members actively participated in discussions, sharing their experiences and offering support to newcomers. Sarah and her leadership team regularly hosted live sessions, answering questions and providing insights into the cult's teachings. These interactive sessions helped build trust and rapport with potential recruits.

Sarah also launched a subreddit dedicated to the cult's philosophy. Here, members and curious individuals could discuss various aspects of spirituality, personal growth, and community life. Moderated by trusted cult members, the subreddit ensured respectful and insightful conversations, making it a valuable resource for anyone interested in the cult.

To appeal to younger audiences and foster real-time interaction, Sarah utilized Discord. She set up a server with various channels focusing on different topics, such as meditation, personal stories, and event announcements. Voice chat channels allowed for spontaneous discussions and deeper connections among members and recruits. The Discord server became a lively hub of activity, mirroring the supportive and dynamic environment of the cult.

On Instagram, Sarah initiated a series of hashtag campaigns like #FindingPurpose and #CommunitySupport, encouraging members to share their stories and experiences using these tags. This organic content generation not only expanded the cult's reach but also provided authentic testimonials that resonated with potential recruits.

By strategically using social media campaigns, Sarah effectively reached a broader audience and tailored her messages to different demographics and interests. She created engaging content and built online communities that mirrored the supportive and inclusive atmosphere of the cult. These efforts not only attracted new recruits but also reinforced the sense of belonging and purpose among existing members, ensuring the cult's growth and sustainability.

Community Involvement

Sarah understood that one of the most effective ways to expand the influence of her cult was through active community involvement. By engaging in community service and charitable activities, she could build a positive reputation and attract individuals who valued altruism and community engagement. Additionally, these events provided excellent opportunities for networking and outreach, establishing meaningful connections with potential recruits.

Participating in Charitable Activities

Sarah was strategic in selecting charitable activities that resonated with both the existing members and the broader community. She organized various community service projects that demonstrated the cult's commitment to making a positive impact.

One of the first initiatives Sarah launched was a regular food drive and distribution program. Every month, members collected donations of non-perishable food items and organized events where they distributed these items to families in need. These events were well-publicized, with local media covering the efforts and highlighting the cult's dedication to helping the less fortunate. The positive press helped to improve the cult's public image and attract individuals who admired their philanthropic efforts.

In addition to food drives, Sarah initiated environmental clean-up projects. Cult members would gather to clean local parks, beaches, and public spaces. These activities not only demonstrated their commitment to environmental stewardship but also provided visible, tangible benefits to the community. Sarah ensured that these events were family-friendly, encouraging participation from a diverse group of people, including children and seniors. The inclusive nature of these projects helped to foster a welcoming atmosphere that appealed to potential recruits.

The cult also sponsored free workshops and seminars on practical life skills, such as financial literacy, stress management, and health and wellness. These workshops were open to the public and often featured guest speakers who were experts in their fields. By providing valuable knowledge and resources, Sarah positioned the cult as a beneficial presence in the community, further enhancing its reputation.

Networking and Outreach

Sarah knew that these community activities were also prime opportunities for networking and outreach. She trained her members to engage with attendees, building relationships that could lead to deeper involvement in the cult.

During each charitable event, Sarah encouraged members to share their personal stories and the positive changes they had experienced since joining the cult. These testimonials were powerful tools, demonstrating the cult's impact on individual lives. Members were trained to listen actively to the needs and concerns of the people they interacted with, offering empathy and support. This approach helped to create a sense of connection and trust, making it easier to introduce the idea of joining the cult.

At larger events, Sarah set up information booths where attendees could learn more about the cult's mission, values, and activities. Brochures and pamphlets detailing the benefits of membership were readily available. Friendly cult members staffed these booths, ready to answer questions and invite interested individuals to attend an introductory meeting or workshop.

To further enhance outreach efforts, Sarah organized follow-up activities, such as thank-you gatherings for volunteers and participants of the charitable events. These gatherings provided a more intimate setting for potential recruits to interact with cult members and leadership. By offering refreshments and creating a relaxed, social atmosphere, Sarah made it easier for attendees to consider deeper involvement.

Sarah also utilized social media to amplify the impact of these community activities. Photos, videos, and stories from the events were shared across the cult's social media platforms, highlighting their commitment to positive change. This not only extended the reach of the events but also allowed those who couldn't attend to see the good work being done. The posts often included calls to action, inviting followers to join future events or learn more about the cult.

Emphasizing Positive Impact

Throughout all these activities, Sarah consistently emphasized the cult's commitment to making a positive impact. She highlighted the collective efforts of the members, framing their work as part of a larger mission to improve the world. This narrative resonated with people who valued community service and altruism, making them more likely to view the cult in a positive light.

By actively participating in charitable activities and using these events for networking and outreach, Sarah successfully built a positive reputation for the cult. These efforts attracted individuals who valued altruism and community involvement, expanding the cult's influence and ensuring its growth. Sarah's strategic approach to community involvement not only enhanced the cult's public image but also created numerous opportunities for meaningful connections with potential recruits.

Developing a Strong Online Presence

Sarah understood the immense power of the internet in expanding her cult's influence and reaching a broader audience. She knew that creating a polished and credible online presence was essential for attracting new members and maintaining engagement with existing followers. Here's how she went about developing a strong online presence through professional websites, social media profiles, and regular content updates.

Professional Websites and Profiles

Sarah began by investing in a professional website that served as the central hub for all information about the cult. She hired experienced web designers and content creators to ensure the site was visually appealing, user-friendly, and informative. The website featured a clean, modern design with easy navigation, high-quality images, and compelling content that conveyed the cult's mission, values, and activities.

The website included several key sections:

- **About Us**: This section provided a detailed overview of the cult's history, mission, and core beliefs. It included a message from Sarah, emphasizing her vision and leadership.
- **Events**: A regularly updated calendar showcased upcoming events, workshops, and seminars, encouraging visitors to get involved.

- **Testimonials**: Stories and testimonials from current members highlighted the positive impact the cult had on their lives, adding credibility and emotional appeal.
- **Resources**: This section offered articles, videos, and downloadable content related to the cult's teachings and practices, providing value to both members and curious visitors.
- **Contact Us**: An easy-to-use contact form and detailed contact information encouraged visitors to reach out with questions or interest in joining.

In addition to the website, Sarah created professional profiles on major social media platforms, including Facebook, Instagram, Twitter, LinkedIn, and YouTube. Each profile was carefully curated to reflect the cult's brand, with consistent logos, color schemes, and messaging. These profiles were used to engage with a broader audience, share updates, and promote events.

Regular Content Updates

Sarah knew that maintaining an active online presence was crucial for keeping followers engaged and attracting new members. She developed a content strategy that included regular updates, news, and engaging content across all platforms.

Blog Posts and Articles: Sarah's team regularly published blog posts and articles on the website, covering a wide range of topics related to the cult's teachings, personal growth, and community events. These posts were shared across social media to drive traffic back to the website.

Social Media Posts: Daily updates on social media included inspirational quotes, success stories, event announcements, and educational content. High-quality images and videos accompanied these posts to capture attention and encourage sharing.

Live Streams and Videos: To create a more personal connection with followers, Sarah frequently hosted live streams on Facebook and Instagram. During these sessions, she shared insights, answered questions, and provided updates on the cult's activities. The live interactions allowed followers to feel more connected and engaged. Additionally, professionally produced videos were uploaded to YouTube, showcasing the cult's events, teachings, and member testimonials.

Email Newsletters: Sarah implemented a monthly email newsletter to keep members and subscribers informed about upcoming events, recent achievements, and new content. The newsletters included links to the latest blog posts, videos, and social media highlights, ensuring that followers never missed important updates.

Interactive Content: Sarah's team created interactive content such as polls, quizzes, and Q&A sessions on social media to encourage engagement and participation from followers. These activities not only kept the audience engaged but also provided valuable feedback and insights into their interests and preferences.

Highlighting Successes and Activities

A key part of Sarah's content strategy was highlighting the cult's successes and activities. By showcasing positive achievements and impactful events, she reinforced the cult's credibility and appeal.

Member Success Stories: Regularly featuring stories of members who had experienced significant personal growth and transformation since joining the cult was a powerful way to demonstrate the cult's impact. These stories were shared through blog posts, social media updates, and video testimonials.

Event Highlights: After each event, Sarah's team created highlight reels and photo galleries that captured the best moments. These visuals were shared across all platforms, showcasing the vibrancy and community spirit of the cult's activities.

Milestone Celebrations: Celebrating milestones such as membership growth, community service achievements, and anniversaries helped to create a sense of pride and accomplishment among followers. These celebrations were prominently featured online to boost morale and attract attention.

By developing a strong online presence through professional websites and profiles, and maintaining regular content updates, Sarah successfully attracted new members and kept her existing followers engaged. Her strategic approach ensured that the cult's image remained polished and credible, while the consistent flow of engaging content reinforced the community's vibrancy and appeal. This online strategy was a crucial component of the cult's overall growth and influence.

Content Creation

Sarah, the visionary cult leader, understood the critical importance of content creation in expanding her cult's reach and influence. By producing high-quality multimedia content and sharing powerful testimonials, she could effectively communicate the cult's beliefs, values, and benefits, attracting new recruits and keeping current members engaged.

Multimedia Production

To capture the audience's interest and convey the cult's message effectively, Sarah focused on producing a variety of high-quality multimedia content. She knew that engaging storytelling techniques were key to making this content compelling and memorable.

High-Quality Videos: Sarah invested in professional videography to create visually appealing and emotionally engaging videos. These videos ranged from short, inspiring clips to in-depth documentaries about the cult's teachings and activities. Each video was carefully scripted and edited to ensure clarity and impact. Topics included:

- **Introduction to the Cult**: A welcoming video explaining the cult's mission, core beliefs, and values, designed to introduce newcomers to the community.
- **Spiritual Teachings**: Detailed explanations of the cult's spiritual practices and philosophies, featuring Sarah and other charismatic leaders.
- **Event Highlights**: Recaps of major events, workshops, and retreats, showcasing the vibrant community life and the benefits of participation.

Podcasts: Recognizing the growing popularity of audio content, Sarah launched a series of podcasts. These podcasts featured a mix of discussions on spiritual topics, interviews with cult leaders and members, and Q&A sessions with listeners. The format allowed for in-depth exploration of ideas and provided a platform for sharing personal stories and insights.

Articles and Blog Posts: Sarah's team regularly published articles and blog posts on the cult's website. These written pieces covered a wide range of topics, from practical advice on personal development to deep dives into the cult's spiritual doctrines. Each article was well-researched and thoughtfully written to provide valuable information and encourage further exploration.

Engaging Storytelling: Across all multimedia content, Sarah emphasized the use of engaging storytelling techniques. She knew that stories were a powerful way to connect with people on an emotional level. Videos and podcasts often included narratives that illustrated the transformative journey of individuals who had embraced the cult's teachings. These stories were crafted to highlight the challenges, breakthroughs, and ultimate successes of the characters, making them relatable and inspiring.

Sharing Testimonials

Testimonials and success stories from current members were among the most powerful tools in Sarah's content arsenal. These personal accounts provided authentic, relatable experiences that could resonate deeply with potential recruits.

Personal Stories: Sarah encouraged members to share their personal journeys, focusing on how joining the cult had positively impacted their lives. These stories were collected through interviews and shared in various formats, including video testimonials, written stories, and podcast interviews.

- **Video Testimonials**: Professionally produced video testimonials featured members speaking candidly about their experiences. The videos captured their emotions and sincerity, making the testimonials highly impactful. Members talked about the challenges they faced before joining the cult, the support they received from the community, and the personal growth they experienced.
- **Written Stories**: These stories were published on the cult's blog and in newsletters. Each story was accompanied by a photo of the member and a quote highlighting their transformation. The written format allowed for detailed narratives that could explore the nuances of each member's journey.

- **Podcast Interviews**: In-depth podcast interviews provided a platform for members to share their stories in their own words. These interviews allowed for a conversational tone, where members could discuss their experiences, the lessons they learned, and the ongoing benefits of being part of the cult.

Highlighting Successes: Sarah made sure that the testimonials and success stories highlighted specific, tangible benefits of joining the cult. This included improvements in mental health, personal relationships, career success, and spiritual fulfillment. By showcasing real-life examples of how the cult had helped individuals achieve their goals and overcome obstacles, Sarah demonstrated the practical and emotional value of becoming a member.

Distribution and Engagement: To maximize the reach and impact of these testimonials, Sarah's team strategically distributed them across multiple channels. They were featured prominently on the website, shared on social media platforms, and included in email newsletters. Interactive elements, such as comment sections and social media discussions, encouraged engagement and allowed potential recruits to ask questions and connect with the storytellers.

By focusing on high-quality multimedia production and sharing powerful testimonials, Sarah successfully created a compelling and engaging online presence. These efforts not only communicated the cult's beliefs, values, and benefits effectively but also provided authentic, relatable experiences that attracted new members and reinforced the commitment of existing ones. Through strategic content creation, Sarah was able to expand the cult's influence and ensure its continued growth and sustainability.

Engaging with the Media

Sarah, always strategic in expanding her cult's influence, recognized the importance of engaging effectively with the media. She understood that positive media coverage could significantly enhance the cult's reputation, attract new members, and solidify the community's standing. Here's how she leveraged press releases, press conferences, and journalist relationships to achieve these goals.

Press Releases and Conferences

To attract media attention and generate positive coverage, Sarah regularly issued press releases and held press conferences that highlighted the cult's achievements and community contributions. This proactive approach ensured that the media had a constant stream of newsworthy content about the cult.

Press Releases: Sarah's team crafted well-written, compelling press releases for every significant event or achievement. Whether it was a successful community service project, a new educational program, or a major event, the press releases provided detailed information and emphasized the positive impact of the cult's activities.

- **Announcing Community Projects**: When the cult launched a new community service initiative, such as a neighborhood clean-up or a food drive, Sarah's team issued a press release detailing the project's goals, participants, and expected outcomes. They included quotes from Sarah and other leaders, as well as testimonials from community members who benefited from the cult's efforts.
- **Highlighting Achievements**: Whenever the cult reached a significant milestone, such as expanding membership or completing a major project, a press release was issued to celebrate the achievement. These releases focused on the hard work and dedication of the members, presenting the cult as a thriving, positive force in the community.

Press Conferences: To complement the press releases, Sarah periodically held press conferences. These events provided an opportunity for direct interaction with the media, allowing Sarah to convey her messages personally and answer questions from journalists.

- **Showcasing Events**: Press conferences were often held in conjunction with major events, such as the opening of a new community center or the launch of a large-scale charitable initiative. Sarah used these occasions to deliver speeches that highlighted the cult's mission and the positive changes they were making in the community.
- **Q&A Sessions**: During press conferences, Sarah invited questions from journalists, providing clear, confident answers that reinforced the cult's positive image. This transparency and openness helped build trust with the media and the public.

Building Relationships with Journalists

Understanding that strong relationships with journalists and media outlets were crucial for securing favorable coverage, Sarah took deliberate steps to cultivate these connections.

Personal Outreach: Sarah identified key journalists and media influencers who covered topics related to spirituality, community service, and personal development. She reached out to them personally, inviting them to attend cult events and offering exclusive access to the cult's activities.

- **Exclusive Invitations**: By offering journalists exclusive invitations to attend workshops, retreats, and other events, Sarah provided them with unique insights into the cult's operations and successes. This insider access made journalists more likely to write positively about the cult.
- **Personalized Pitches**: Instead of sending generic press releases, Sarah's team tailored pitches to the interests and beats of specific journalists. They highlighted angles and stories that would resonate with each journalist's audience, increasing the likelihood of coverage.

Offering Exclusive Interviews: Sarah also offered exclusive interviews to trusted journalists and media partners. These interviews allowed her to share her vision, discuss the cult's philosophy, and address any concerns or misconceptions directly.

- **In-Depth Stories**: Exclusive interviews often led to in-depth stories that provided a comprehensive look at the cult's mission and impact. These stories were valuable for building a nuanced, positive image of the cult.
- **Human Interest Angles**: By focusing on personal stories of transformation and community impact, Sarah ensured that the interviews were engaging and relatable. Journalists were able to showcase the human side of the cult, making their coverage more compelling.

Maintaining Ongoing Relationships: To ensure continued positive coverage, Sarah maintained ongoing relationships with journalists and media outlets. She kept them informed of the cult's activities through regular updates and invitations to events.

- **Media Kits**: Sarah's team prepared detailed media kits that included background information about the cult, profiles of key members, and high-quality images and videos. These kits were provided to journalists to support their stories and ensure accurate, favorable coverage.
- **Follow-Up Communications**: After each interaction with the media, Sarah's team followed up with thank-you notes and additional information as needed. This courteous and professional approach helped build lasting relationships with media partners.

By engaging effectively with the media through press releases, press conferences, and building strong relationships with journalists, Sarah successfully attracted positive coverage and enhanced the cult's reputation. These efforts not only attracted new members but also solidified the cult's standing in the broader community, ensuring its continued growth and influence.

Propaganda Techniques

To effectively spread her cult's message and attract new recruits, Sarah employed sophisticated propaganda techniques. These included using persuasive language and emotional appeals to connect with the audience's values and emotions, as well as creating visually appealing materials to capture attention and communicate the cult's message effectively.

Persuasive Language and Emotional Appeals

Sarah understood that the power of words could shape beliefs and inspire action. She carefully crafted her messages to resonate deeply with her audience, tapping into their emotions and values.

Identifying Core Values: Sarah began by identifying the core values and concerns of her target audience. She knew that addressing these values would create a strong emotional connection. For instance, she focused on themes such as community, personal growth, spiritual fulfillment, and belonging.

Emotional Storytelling: Stories are powerful tools for conveying messages. Sarah used emotional storytelling to illustrate the transformative power of the cult's teachings. She shared narratives of individuals who had overcome personal struggles, found purpose, and achieved inner peace through the cult. These stories were crafted to evoke empathy and inspiration, making the audience feel a personal connection to the cult's mission.

Inspiring Speeches: Sarah's speeches were meticulously written to be both inspiring and persuasive. She used rhetorical devices such as repetition, metaphors, and analogies to emphasize key points. Her speeches often began with a relatable problem or challenge, followed by a vision of a better future through the cult's teachings. This structure created a sense of urgency and hope, motivating listeners to take action.

Positive Framing: Sarah always framed the cult's messages in a positive light. She focused on the benefits and positive outcomes of joining the cult, rather than dwelling on negative aspects of the outside world. This approach made the cult seem like a beacon of hope and positivity.

Inclusive Language: To make everyone feel welcome and valued, Sarah used inclusive language. She avoided divisive or confrontational terms and instead emphasized unity, collective effort, and mutual support. Phrases like "we are stronger together" and "everyone is welcome" reinforced the cult's message of inclusivity.

Visual Appeal

Recognizing that visual elements can significantly enhance the impact of a message, Sarah invested in creating visually appealing materials. These materials were designed to attract attention and communicate the cult's message effectively.

Posters and Flyers: Sarah's team designed eye-catching posters and flyers that were distributed in public places and at events. These materials featured bold colors, striking images, and compelling headlines. The posters often depicted serene, uplifting scenes or dynamic images of community activities, accompanied by short, impactful messages such as "Find Your True Purpose" or "Join a Community That Cares."

Social Media Graphics: On social media platforms, Sarah used high-quality graphics to capture the audience's attention as they scrolled through their feeds. These graphics included inspirational quotes, testimonials, and announcements about upcoming events. The design was consistent with the cult's branding, using the same color schemes and fonts to create a cohesive visual identity.

Videos and Animations: Video content was a crucial part of Sarah's propaganda strategy. She produced short, engaging videos that combined powerful visuals with persuasive narratives.

These videos were shared on YouTube, Instagram, and Facebook, reaching a wide audience. Animations were also used to explain complex ideas in a simple, visually appealing way.

Banners and Billboards: For larger-scale impact, Sarah invested in banners and billboards in strategic locations. These large-format visuals were designed to be seen from a distance, with simple, bold messages and imagery that captured the essence of the cult's mission. Locations were chosen based on high foot traffic and visibility to maximize reach.

Branded Merchandise: To further spread the cult's message, Sarah created branded merchandise such as T-shirts, hats, and tote bags. These items featured the cult's logo and inspirational slogans. Members wearing these items acted as walking advertisements, spreading the message in their daily lives.

Event Displays: At public events and workshops, Sarah used visually appealing displays to attract attendees. Banners, informational booths, and interactive displays provided information about the cult's activities and beliefs. The design of these displays was both informative and engaging, drawing people in and encouraging them to learn more.

By using persuasive language and emotional appeals, Sarah effectively conveyed the cult's message in a way that resonated with the audience's values and emotions. Coupled with visually appealing materials, her propaganda techniques captured attention, inspired interest, and motivated action. These efforts played a crucial role in expanding the cult's influence and attracting new members, ensuring the community's growth and sustainability.

Crisis Management

In the world of cult leadership, crises are inevitable. Whether it's negative publicity, internal controversies, or external criticism, being prepared and proactive in managing crises is crucial to maintaining the cult's reputation and ensuring its continued growth. Sarah, the astute cult leader, developed a robust crisis management plan to address any issues quickly and effectively while controlling the narrative to maintain trust and credibility.

Preparedness

Sarah knew that the key to effective crisis management was preparation. She developed a comprehensive crisis management plan that outlined specific steps to take in the event of various potential crises.

Identifying Potential Crises: Sarah and her team conducted a thorough risk assessment to identify potential crises that could affect the cult. These included negative media coverage, accusations of misconduct, internal conflicts, and public backlash against the cult's practices or beliefs. By anticipating these scenarios, they were able to develop specific strategies to address each type of crisis.

Crisis Management Team: Sarah assembled a dedicated crisis management team composed of trusted members with expertise in communication, legal affairs, and public relations. This team was responsible for implementing the crisis management plan and ensuring a coordinated response. Each member had clearly defined roles and responsibilities, ensuring that the team could act swiftly and effectively when a crisis arose.

Crisis Communication Protocols: Clear communication protocols were established to ensure a timely and appropriate response. This included guidelines for internal communication (keeping members informed and unified) and external communication (addressing the public, media, and other stakeholders). The protocols emphasized the importance of delivering consistent messages across all channels to avoid confusion and maintain credibility.

Response Templates: Sarah's team created response templates for various types of crises. These templates included key messages, talking points, and sample statements that could be quickly customized and deployed. This preparation ensured that the cult could respond promptly and coherently, minimizing the impact of any negative publicity.

Training and Drills: Regular training sessions and crisis simulations were conducted to ensure that the crisis management team and other key members were well-prepared. These drills helped identify potential weaknesses in the plan and provided opportunities to practice and refine the response strategies.

Control the Narrative

In a crisis, controlling the narrative is essential to maintaining the cult's reputation and ensuring that its perspective is heard. Sarah employed strategic communication techniques to manage public perception and address issues openly and honestly.

Immediate Response: As soon as a crisis was identified, Sarah's team acted quickly to issue an initial response. This response acknowledged the issue, expressed concern, and outlined the steps being taken to address it. The promptness of this response helped demonstrate the cult's commitment to transparency and accountability.

Utilizing Media Channels: Sarah leveraged various media channels to control the narrative and present the cult's perspective. Press releases, social media updates, and video statements were used to communicate directly with the public. By using multiple channels, Sarah ensured that the cult's message reached a wide audience.

Open and Honest Communication: Sarah emphasized the importance of honesty and openness in all communications. When addressing a crisis, she provided as much information as possible, avoiding evasiveness or vague statements. This transparency helped build trust with the public and demonstrated the cult's integrity.

Addressing Concerns: In her statements, Sarah directly addressed the concerns and criticisms raised by the crisis. She acknowledged any mistakes or shortcomings and outlined the steps being taken to rectify the situation. This approach showed that the cult was willing to take responsibility and learn from the experience.

Positive Framing: While acknowledging the crisis, Sarah also highlighted the positive actions the cult was taking. She emphasized the cult's ongoing commitment to its values and mission, and shared stories of positive impact and community support. This helped shift the focus from the negative aspects of the crisis to the positive contributions of the cult.

Engaging with Stakeholders: Sarah and her team actively engaged with key stakeholders, including members, supporters, community leaders, and media representatives. They provided regular updates and were available to answer questions and address concerns. This proactive engagement helped maintain trust and support from those most important to the cult's success.

Monitoring and Feedback: Throughout the crisis, Sarah's team closely monitored public and media responses. They tracked the effectiveness of their communication strategies and made adjustments as needed. Feedback from members and stakeholders was also gathered to ensure that the cult's actions were meeting their expectations.

Post-Crisis Review: After the crisis had been resolved, Sarah conducted a thorough review to evaluate the effectiveness of the response. This review included an assessment of what worked well, what could be improved, and how the crisis management plan could be updated for future situations. The lessons learned were used to strengthen the cult's crisis preparedness and resilience.

By being prepared and proactively managing crises, Sarah was able to protect the cult's reputation and maintain trust and credibility with both members and the public. Her strategic approach to crisis management ensured that the cult could navigate challenges effectively, reinforcing its stability and continued growth.

Identifying Key Members

Sarah, the insightful cult leader, understood that the strength and stability of her cult depended on a core group of dedicated, skilled, and loyal members. Identifying and nurturing these key individuals was crucial for maintaining a robust leadership structure and ensuring the cult's ongoing success. Here's how she identified and cultivated key members within her community.

Selection Criteria

Sarah began by establishing clear criteria for selecting key members. She sought individuals who not only demonstrated strong loyalty but also possessed exceptional skills and potential for leadership. Her criteria included:

Loyalty and Commitment: Sarah prioritized members who had shown unwavering loyalty to the cult and its mission. These individuals consistently participated in cult activities, adhered to the cult's teachings, and actively promoted its values. Their dedication was evident in their behavior, words, and actions.

Skills and Expertise: Sarah looked for members who brought valuable skills and expertise to the community. This could include skills in areas such as communication, organization, teaching, counseling, or finance. She also valued members who were quick learners and adaptable, capable of acquiring new skills as needed.

Leadership Potential: Potential leaders were identified based on their ability to inspire and motivate others. Sarah observed how members interacted with their peers, handled responsibilities, and responded to challenges. Those who displayed confidence, decisiveness, and empathy were considered strong candidates for leadership roles.

Alignment with Values: It was essential for key members to be deeply aligned with the cult's values and mission. Sarah looked for individuals who not only understood the cult's teachings but also embodied them in their daily lives. Their actions needed to reflect the principles and goals of the community.

Reliability and Integrity: Trustworthiness and reliability were non-negotiable traits for key members. Sarah valued individuals who could be depended upon to fulfill their commitments, maintain confidentiality, and act with integrity. Their consistency in these areas reinforced the stability and trust within the cult.

Offering Responsibilities and Privileges

Once Sarah identified potential key members, she focused on solidifying their commitment by offering them additional responsibilities and privileges. This not only empowered them but also reinforced their loyalty and connection to the cult.

Leadership Roles: Sarah provided key members with leadership roles that matched their skills and potential. This included positions such as team leaders, project managers, and coordinators for specific activities or initiatives. These roles allowed members to take on greater responsibility, contribute to decision-making processes, and influence the direction of the cult.

Special Assignments: To further engage key members, Sarah assigned them special projects or tasks that were critical to the cult's success. These assignments could involve organizing major events, developing new programs, or leading community outreach efforts. Successfully completing these tasks enhanced their sense of accomplishment and importance within the cult.

Exclusive Resources: Sarah granted key members access to exclusive resources that were not available to the general membership. This included advanced training sessions, special teachings, and private consultations with Sarah or other senior leaders. These resources provided key members with the knowledge and skills they needed to excel in their roles and deepen their commitment.

Recognition and Rewards: Public recognition of key members' contributions was an important part of Sarah's strategy. She made it a point to acknowledge their efforts during meetings and events, highlighting their achievements and expressing gratitude for their dedication. This public recognition boosted their morale and motivated them to continue their exemplary work.

Mentorship and Support: Sarah offered ongoing mentorship and support to key members, helping them navigate their new responsibilities and grow into their roles. This included regular check-ins, personalized guidance, and opportunities for professional and personal development. By investing in their growth, Sarah ensured that they felt valued and supported.

Exclusive Gatherings: To foster a sense of camaraderie and unity among key members, Sarah organized exclusive gatherings and retreats. These events provided an opportunity for key members to bond, share experiences, and discuss strategic plans for the cult's future. The sense of exclusivity and the opportunity to contribute to high-level discussions reinforced their commitment.

By carefully identifying key members and providing them with additional responsibilities and privileges, Sarah effectively built a strong, loyal, and capable leadership team. These individuals became the backbone of the cult, ensuring its stability, growth, and success. Sarah's strategic approach to cultivating key members not only empowered these individuals but also strengthened the overall community, creating a cohesive and resilient organization.

Special Training and Education

Sarah knew that to maintain a strong, loyal, and capable leadership team within her cult, it was crucial to provide special training and education to her inner circle members. By developing advanced training programs and sharing exclusive teachings, she ensured that these key individuals were well-equipped to lead and deeply committed to the cult and its mission.

Advanced Training Programs

Sarah recognized that the development of her inner circle required more than just basic training. She created advanced training programs that were designed to enhance the skills and knowledge of these elite members, providing them with education and experiences beyond what the general membership received.

Customized Curriculum: Sarah worked with experts within the cult to develop a customized curriculum that addressed the specific needs and roles of her inner circle members. This curriculum covered a wide range of topics, including advanced leadership techniques, strategic planning, conflict resolution, and effective communication.

Workshops and Seminars: Regular workshops and seminars were organized to provide in-depth training on critical subjects. These sessions were often led by Sarah herself or by senior leaders with specialized knowledge. The workshops were interactive, allowing members to engage in discussions, role-playing, and practical exercises that reinforced their learning.

Field Experience: To complement the theoretical training, Sarah incorporated field experience into the programs. Inner circle members were given opportunities to lead projects, organize events, and manage teams. This hands-on experience allowed them to apply their knowledge in real-world situations, building their confidence and competence.

Guest Speakers: Sarah occasionally invited external experts and thought leaders to speak to her inner circle. These guest speakers provided fresh perspectives and insights on various topics, enriching the training programs. Their presence also underscored the importance of continuous learning and growth.

Personal Development Plans: Each inner circle member had a personalized development plan that outlined their specific goals, strengths, and areas for improvement. Sarah or a designated mentor worked closely with them to monitor progress, provide feedback, and adjust the plan as needed. This individualized approach ensured that each member received the support they needed to thrive.

Exclusive Teachings

To reinforce the special status of her inner circle and deepen their loyalty, Sarah shared exclusive knowledge and teachings that were not available to the general membership. These teachings were designed to instill a deeper understanding of the cult's philosophy and enhance their sense of belonging and importance.

Advanced Philosophical Teachings: Sarah provided her inner circle with advanced teachings on the cult's philosophy, spiritual practices, and historical foundations. These sessions delved deeper into the esoteric aspects of the cult's beliefs, offering insights and knowledge that were kept secret from the general membership. This exclusive access made the inner circle feel privileged and valued.

Secret Rituals and Ceremonies: Sarah introduced her inner circle to special rituals and ceremonies that were not performed for the broader cult community. These secret practices were designed to strengthen the bond between the inner circle members and the cult's spiritual foundation. Participating in these rituals created a sense of mystique and reinforced their elite status.

Leadership Insights: Sarah shared her personal experiences and insights on leadership with her inner circle. She discussed her own journey, the challenges she faced, and the strategies she used to overcome obstacles. These candid conversations provided valuable lessons and inspired the inner circle members to emulate her leadership style.

Access to Sacred Texts: Certain sacred texts and writings were reserved exclusively for the inner circle. These texts contained deeper spiritual teachings, historical accounts, and strategic insights that were critical to understanding the full scope of the cult's mission. Access to these texts was a significant privilege, reinforcing their special status.

Mentorship Sessions: Sarah held regular mentorship sessions with her inner circle, providing them with direct guidance and support. These sessions were intimate and confidential, allowing members to discuss their concerns, seek advice, and receive personalized mentorship from Sarah. This close relationship fostered a strong sense of loyalty and commitment.

Exclusive Gatherings: Sarah organized exclusive gatherings and retreats for her inner circle, where they could bond, share experiences, and engage in advanced training and rituals. These gatherings were often held in secluded, serene locations, providing a conducive environment for deep reflection and learning. The exclusivity of these events further solidified their elite status.

By developing advanced training programs and sharing exclusive teachings, Sarah ensured that her inner circle was highly skilled, knowledgeable, and deeply committed to the cult. This approach not only empowered these key members but also reinforced their loyalty and dedication, making them indispensable to the cult's leadership and success. Through strategic training and education, Sarah created a strong, cohesive, and resilient inner circle that could effectively guide and support the broader cult community.

Exclusive Access

To ensure her inner circle remained loyal and deeply committed, Sarah strategically granted them exclusive access. This access included direct communication with her, involvement in decision-making processes, and strategic engagement in important cult activities. This approach not only reinforced their elite status but also made them feel integral to the cult's success and more dedicated to its goals.

Direct Access to the Leader

Private Meetings: Sarah scheduled regular private meetings with her inner circle members. These meetings provided an opportunity for direct, personal interaction with her. During these sessions, members could discuss their thoughts, concerns, and suggestions directly with Sarah, fostering a sense of closeness and trust. These meetings were often held in a relaxed, confidential setting, allowing for open and honest communication.

Direct Communication Channels: Sarah established direct communication channels for her inner circle, such as private messaging apps and dedicated phone lines. This ensured that members could reach her quickly and easily whenever they needed guidance or had urgent matters to discuss. The ability to communicate directly with the leader reinforced their importance and made them feel valued.

Decision-Making Processes: Sarah involved her inner circle in the cult's decision-making processes. She regularly held strategy sessions where these members were invited to contribute their insights and opinions on key issues. By including them in these discussions, Sarah ensured that they felt a sense of ownership and responsibility for the cult's direction and success.

Strategic Planning: In addition to routine decision-making, Sarah involved her inner circle in long-term strategic planning. She shared her vision for the future of the cult and sought their input on major initiatives and projects. This collaborative approach not only leveraged their skills and expertise but also deepened their commitment to the cult's goals.

Strategic Involvement

Key Initiatives: Sarah engaged her inner circle in leading and managing key cult initiatives. These initiatives could range from organizing large-scale events and community outreach programs to developing new educational content and spiritual practices. By placing them in charge of these important tasks, Sarah demonstrated her trust in their abilities and reinforced their integral role in the cult.

Project Leadership: Members of the inner circle were often appointed as leaders for specific projects. This responsibility allowed them to develop their leadership skills further and gain experience in managing teams and resources. Successful project leadership reinforced their confidence and commitment to the cult.

Special Assignments: Sarah also gave her inner circle special assignments that required a high level of trust and discretion. These assignments could involve sensitive negotiations, confidential research, or high-stakes decision-making. Completing these assignments successfully strengthened their loyalty and reinforced their elite status.

Exclusive Events and Retreats: Sarah organized exclusive events and retreats for her inner circle, where they could focus on strategic planning, team-building, and personal development. These events were held in secluded, serene locations, providing a conducive environment for deep reflection and bonding. The exclusivity of these gatherings reinforced their special status and commitment.

Mentorship and Development: In addition to strategic involvement, Sarah provided ongoing mentorship and development opportunities for her inner circle. She offered personalized coaching, advanced training sessions, and access to exclusive resources. This continuous development ensured that they were always growing and improving, making them more effective leaders within the cult.

Public Recognition: Sarah publicly recognized the contributions of her inner circle members, highlighting their achievements and leadership roles during cult gatherings and events. This recognition not only boosted their morale but also reinforced their importance within the cult community.

By granting her inner circle direct access to her and involving them in strategic activities, Sarah created a highly engaged and loyal leadership team. This exclusive access made them feel integral to the cult's success and more dedicated to its goals. Through strategic involvement and personal attention, Sarah ensured that her inner circle remained committed, empowered, and aligned with her vision for the cult's future. This approach not only strengthened the leadership structure but also reinforced the overall stability and growth of the cult.

Building Loyalty

To ensure the unwavering dedication of her inner circle, Sarah focused on fostering a sense of camaraderie and exclusivity, as well as regularly recognizing and rewarding their contributions. These strategies helped reinforce their status, loyalty, and commitment to the cult's mission.

Camaraderie and Exclusivity

Exclusive Gatherings: Sarah organized regular exclusive gatherings for her inner circle. These events were intimate and often held in secluded, luxurious settings. The purpose was to foster a strong bond among the members, allowing them to share experiences, discuss strategies, and build trust. These gatherings included special dinners, retreats, and off-site meetings where they could relax and connect on a deeper level.

Rituals and Ceremonies: To reinforce their elite status and deepen their loyalty, Sarah incorporated special rituals and ceremonies exclusively for the inner circle. These rituals often involved symbolic acts that highlighted their commitment and unique position within the cult. For instance, there might be an annual induction ceremony for new inner circle members, where they took oaths of loyalty and received symbolic tokens of their status.

Team-Building Activities: Sarah included team-building activities in the inner circle's regular schedule. These activities were designed to strengthen their bonds and improve their collaboration skills. They ranged from strategic planning sessions to adventure-based challenges, such as group hikes, obstacle courses, and problem-solving exercises. These activities helped create a sense of unity and shared purpose.

Shared Responsibilities: By assigning shared responsibilities and projects, Sarah ensured that inner circle members worked closely together, fostering camaraderie and mutual support. Working on high-stakes tasks and achieving common goals reinforced their sense of belonging and loyalty to the group.

Special Privileges: To further emphasize their exclusivity, Sarah granted the inner circle special privileges not available to the general membership. This included access to private spaces, advanced teachings, and personal consultations with Sarah. These privileges made the inner circle feel valued and essential to the cult's success.

Recognition and Rewards

Public Acknowledgment: Regular public acknowledgment of the inner circle's contributions was a cornerstone of Sarah's strategy. During cult gatherings, meetings, and events, she took time to recognize the efforts and achievements of these key members. This acknowledgment often included praise, applause, and sometimes even symbolic awards or titles. Public recognition reinforced their status and motivated them to continue their dedication.

Special Rewards: Sarah instituted a reward system that provided tangible benefits for the inner circle's hard work and loyalty. These rewards could include financial bonuses, gifts, travel opportunities, and exclusive access to new programs or teachings. By tying rewards to their contributions, Sarah ensured that the inner circle felt appreciated and incentivized to maintain their high level of commitment.

Personal Growth Opportunities: Recognizing that personal development was important to her inner circle, Sarah provided opportunities for further growth and learning. This included advanced training programs, leadership workshops, and mentorship sessions. By investing in their development, Sarah showed that she valued their potential and was committed to their success.

Exclusive Access to Information: Sarah also rewarded loyalty by giving the inner circle access to exclusive information about the cult's strategic plans, upcoming projects, and sensitive matters. Being privy to such information reinforced their importance and made them feel trusted and integral to the cult's operations.

Celebrations of Milestones: Sarah made it a point to celebrate significant milestones and achievements of her inner circle members. Whether it was the successful completion of a major project, an anniversary of joining the cult, or personal accomplishments, these celebrations were marked with special ceremonies, gifts, and public commendations. Such celebrations helped build a sense of pride and belonging.

Personalized Thank-You Notes: In addition to public recognition, Sarah often sent personalized thank-you notes to inner circle members. These notes expressed her gratitude for their specific contributions and dedication. The personal touch made members feel individually appreciated and valued.

By fostering camaraderie and exclusivity through exclusive gatherings, rituals, and shared responsibilities, Sarah built a strong sense of unity and loyalty among her inner circle. Additionally, by regularly recognizing and rewarding their contributions with public acknowledgment, special rewards, and growth opportunities, she ensured their continued dedication and commitment. This dual approach of camaraderie and recognition not only solidified the inner circle's loyalty but also strengthened the overall foundation and resilience of the cult.

Monitoring and Control

To maintain the integrity and unity of her inner circle, Sarah implemented a system of close monitoring and control. By keeping a vigilant watch on her key members and addressing any issues of disloyalty or misconduct promptly, she ensured that the inner circle remained loyal and cohesive.

Close Monitoring

Surveillance Systems: Sarah installed discreet surveillance systems in key areas where inner circle members frequently gathered. This included meeting rooms, communal areas, and certain private spaces. These systems allowed her to monitor activities and conversations without being overtly intrusive. The presence of surveillance acted as a deterrent against disloyal behavior and ensured that members knew they were being watched.

Communication Monitoring: To further safeguard loyalty, Sarah implemented monitoring of electronic communications. Emails, messages, and phone calls between inner circle members were periodically reviewed for any signs of dissent or subversive activities. Special software was used to flag keywords or phrases that might indicate problematic behavior. This allowed Sarah to stay informed about potential issues before they escalated.

Behavioral Observation: Sarah also relied on trusted aides to observe the behavior and interactions of inner circle members. These aides attended meetings, social gatherings, and events, providing Sarah with regular reports on the members' conduct and attitudes. They were trained to look for signs of discontent, unusual alliances, or changes in behavior that might suggest disloyalty.

Performance Reviews: Regular performance reviews were conducted for inner circle members. These reviews assessed their contributions, attitude, and alignment with the cult's values. Members were required to provide updates on their projects, goals, and any challenges they faced. The reviews served as an opportunity for Sarah to gauge their commitment and address any concerns directly.

Feedback Channels: Sarah established anonymous feedback channels that allowed members to report any suspicious activities or concerns about their peers without fear of retribution. These channels were carefully monitored, and reports were investigated thoroughly. This system helped Sarah identify potential issues from within the group and provided an additional layer of oversight.

Addressing Issues Promptly

Immediate Action: When signs of disloyalty or misconduct were identified, Sarah took immediate action to address the issue. This could involve a private meeting with the member in question to discuss the behavior and its implications. By acting swiftly, Sarah demonstrated that disloyalty would not be tolerated and that the integrity of the inner circle was paramount.

Disciplinary Measures: Depending on the severity of the issue, Sarah implemented appropriate disciplinary measures. These measures could range from verbal warnings and additional monitoring to more severe actions such as demotion, suspension of privileges, or removal from the inner circle. The consequences were clearly communicated to ensure that all members understood the seriousness of disloyalty.

Conflict Resolution: In cases where disputes or conflicts arose among inner circle members, Sarah intervened to mediate and resolve the issues. She facilitated discussions, provided guidance, and sought to find mutually acceptable solutions. This approach helped maintain harmony within the group and prevented minor issues from escalating into major problems.

Reaffirmation of Values: To reinforce loyalty and commitment, Sarah regularly held sessions that reaffirmed the cult's values and mission. During these sessions, she emphasized the importance of unity, trust, and mutual support. Members were encouraged to share their experiences and reaffirm their dedication to the cult and its goals.

Counseling and Support: Sarah also offered counseling and support to members who showed signs of struggling with their commitment. This included one-on-one sessions where they could discuss their concerns and receive guidance. By addressing underlying issues, Sarah helped members regain their focus and loyalty.

Transparency and Communication: Sarah maintained open lines of communication with her inner circle. She regularly updated them on the cult's activities, future plans, and any challenges faced. By keeping them informed, she fostered a sense of inclusion and trust. Members were more likely to remain loyal when they felt they were part of the decision-making process and understood the cult's direction.

Exit Strategies: For members who were unable or unwilling to maintain their loyalty, Sarah developed exit strategies that minimized disruption to the cult. These strategies included confidential discussions, negotiated departures, and, if necessary, orchestrated exits that maintained the cult's public image. By handling departures smoothly, Sarah ensured that the unity and stability of the inner circle were preserved.

By implementing close monitoring and addressing issues promptly, Sarah maintained a loyal and cohesive inner circle. Her vigilant oversight and decisive actions ensured that disloyalty and misconduct were swiftly dealt with, preserving the integrity and unity of her leadership team. This approach not only reinforced the inner circle's commitment but also strengthened the overall foundation and resilience of the cult.

Chapter 6: Maintaining Control

Maintaining control within a cult is crucial for its stability and longevity. This chapter outlines key strategies for handling dissent and opposition, implementing surveillance and monitoring, and ensuring secrecy and loyalty. By effectively managing these aspects, a cult leader can preserve the unity and commitment of the group.

Handling Dissent and Opposition

Identifying Sources of Dissent

- **Early Detection**: Regularly monitor for signs of discontent among members, such as changes in behavior, reduced participation, or negative comments. Early detection allows for timely intervention.
- **Feedback Mechanisms**: Establish anonymous feedback channels to identify grievances and sources of dissatisfaction within the cult. This helps in addressing issues before they escalate.

Addressing Concerns

- **Open Communication**: Encourage open communication where members can voice their concerns in a controlled environment. Addressing these issues transparently can prevent dissent from spreading.
- **Mediation and Resolution**: Implement conflict resolution strategies to mediate disputes between members. Providing a platform for resolving conflicts can help maintain harmony within the group.

Disciplinary Actions

- **Clear Policies**: Develop clear policies and consequences for dissent and opposition. Ensure all members are aware of these rules.
- **Enforcement**: Enforce disciplinary actions consistently and fairly. This could range from warnings and demotions to expulsion from the group for severe cases.

Reaffirming Commitment

- **Regular Reaffirmation**: Hold regular sessions to reaffirm the cult's values and mission. These sessions should reinforce members' commitment and loyalty.
- **Positive Reinforcement**: Use positive reinforcement to reward loyalty and compliance. Recognize and reward members who demonstrate strong commitment and alignment with the cult's goals.

Implementing Surveillance and Monitoring

Surveillance Systems

- **Physical Surveillance**: Install discreet surveillance cameras in key areas to monitor activities and interactions. Ensure these systems are secure and accessible only to trusted individuals.
- **Digital Surveillance**: Monitor electronic communications, including emails, messages, and social media interactions. Use software tools to flag suspicious activities or keywords that indicate potential issues.

Behavioral Monitoring

- **Observation Teams**: Deploy trusted aides to observe members' behavior and report any signs of discontent or suspicious activities. These aides should be trained to detect subtle changes in behavior and interactions.
- **Regular Check-ins**: Conduct regular check-ins with members to gauge their satisfaction and address any concerns. This personal touch can help in identifying issues early.

Data Analysis

- **Pattern Recognition**: Use data analysis tools to identify patterns in behavior that may indicate potential dissent. Analyzing data from surveillance systems can provide insights into emerging threats.
- **Feedback Analysis**: Regularly review feedback from anonymous channels to detect recurring themes or issues. Address these promptly to prevent them from escalating.

Ensuring Secrecy and Loyalty

Confidentiality Measures

- **Non-Disclosure Agreements**: Require members to sign non-disclosure agreements (NDAs) to protect sensitive information. Ensure that these agreements are legally binding and clearly outline the consequences of breaches.
- **Information Access Control**: Limit access to sensitive information based on members' roles and responsibilities. Use a need-to-know basis to ensure that only trusted individuals have access to critical data.

Building a Culture of Loyalty

- **Cultural Integration**: Integrate the cult's values and mission into daily activities and interactions. Reinforce the importance of loyalty and secrecy through regular communication and rituals.
- **Emotional Bonding**: Foster strong emotional bonds among members through shared experiences, rituals, and ceremonies. A strong sense of community can enhance loyalty and discourage dissent.

Regular Loyalty Assessments

- **Surveys and Interviews**: Conduct regular surveys and interviews to assess members' loyalty and satisfaction. Use this information to address potential issues and reinforce commitment.
- **Loyalty Programs**: Implement loyalty programs that reward long-term commitment and active participation. Offer incentives such as special privileges, recognition, and exclusive access to resources.

Crisis Management for Breaches

- **Immediate Response**: Have a crisis management plan in place to respond to breaches of secrecy promptly. This includes identifying the source of the breach, containing the damage, and addressing the root cause.
- **Legal Action**: Be prepared to take legal action against individuals who violate confidentiality agreements or engage in activities that threaten the cult's secrecy. This serves as a deterrent to others.

By effectively handling dissent and opposition, implementing robust surveillance and monitoring systems, and ensuring secrecy and loyalty, a cult leader can maintain control and preserve the integrity and unity of the group. These strategies are essential for the long-term stability and success of the cult.

Identifying Sources of Dissent

Early Detection

Case 1: Observing Behavioral Changes

Sarah, ever vigilant in maintaining the unity of her cult, had a keen eye for noticing subtle changes in behavior among her members. One day, she observed that Emma, a usually active and enthusiastic member, had started to sit at the back during meetings and rarely contributed to discussions. Emma, known for her vibrant participation and ideas, now seemed distracted and disengaged.

Sensing potential trouble, Sarah decided to act quickly. She approached Emma after a meeting, choosing a private moment to express her concern. "Emma, I've noticed you've been a bit quiet lately. Is everything alright? You seem a bit off," Sarah said gently.

Emma hesitated but then confided that she felt her ideas and contributions were not being valued as much as they used to be. She felt overshadowed by newer members who were getting more attention. This had made her question her importance within the group.

Sarah listened empathetically and assured Emma that her contributions were highly valued. She promised to create a platform where all members, regardless of their tenure, could share their ideas and be heard. Over the next few weeks, Sarah implemented a rotational leadership system during meetings, ensuring that both long-standing and newer members had opportunities to lead discussions and present their ideas. Emma's enthusiasm gradually returned, and she became an advocate for the new system, helping to reinvigorate the group's dynamics.

Case 2: Decreased Participation

Another instance involved a member named Mark, who had been a cornerstone of the community's outreach programs. Sarah noticed that Mark had been absent from several important events and meetings. His absence was unusual, as he was known for his dedication.

Sarah decided to reach out to Mark directly. She arranged a casual meet-up over coffee and gently inquired about his recent absences. Mark revealed that he was experiencing burnout from juggling multiple responsibilities within the cult and his personal life. He felt overwhelmed and unsupported, leading to his decreased participation.

Understanding the gravity of the situation, Sarah took immediate action. She reassigned some of Mark's responsibilities to other capable members and set up a support system to help him manage his workload better. Additionally, she introduced regular wellness check-ins for all members to ensure they felt supported and valued. Mark's participation soon picked up, and he expressed gratitude for Sarah's proactive approach in addressing his concerns.

Feedback Mechanisms

Case 1: Anonymous Concerns

Sarah knew that not every member would be comfortable voicing their concerns openly. To address this, she set up an anonymous feedback system where members could share their grievances, suggestions, and experiences without fear of retribution.

One day, Sarah received an anonymous message highlighting that some members felt excluded from decision-making processes, particularly newer recruits. The message pointed out that decisions were often made by the inner circle without broader consultation, leading to feelings of exclusion and dissatisfaction.

Taking this feedback to heart, Sarah decided to restructure the decision-making process. She introduced monthly town hall meetings where all members could voice their opinions and vote on important issues. These meetings were designed to be inclusive and democratic, ensuring that every member felt their voice mattered. The introduction of town hall meetings improved transparency and inclusion, fostering a greater sense of community and reducing feelings of exclusion.

Case 2: Addressing Bullying Concerns

Another anonymous feedback highlighted instances of subtle bullying and cliques forming within the cult. Some members felt intimidated and marginalized by a group of more dominant members.

Sarah immediately took steps to address these concerns. She implemented strict anti-bullying policies and conducted workshops on respect, inclusivity, and empathy. She also set up a peer support network where members could confidentially report bullying incidents and receive support.

To further break down cliques, Sarah organized mixed-group activities and projects that required members to work with different people. These initiatives helped to dissolve existing cliques and promoted a more inclusive and supportive environment.

Regular Monitoring

Sarah also maintained a schedule of regular monitoring activities to keep her finger on the pulse of the community's sentiment. She instituted periodic surveys that asked members to rate their satisfaction with various aspects of the cult's activities and leadership. The surveys included open-ended questions where members could elaborate on their experiences and suggest improvements.

Surveys and Data Analysis

By analyzing the survey data, Sarah identified trends and recurring issues that might not be immediately apparent through casual observation. For example, if a significant number of members expressed dissatisfaction with the frequency of events or the content of teachings, Sarah would convene a meeting with her leadership team to discuss and address these concerns.

One-on-One Check-Ins

In addition to surveys, Sarah scheduled regular one-on-one check-ins with members, especially those who showed signs of disengagement or dissatisfaction. These personal check-ins allowed her to address individual concerns directly and offer tailored support. Members appreciated the personal attention and felt more connected to the community as a result.

Through vigilant early detection, proactive feedback mechanisms, and regular monitoring, Sarah successfully identified and addressed sources of dissent within her cult. These strategies ensured that members felt heard, valued, and supported, maintaining the unity and commitment necessary for the cult's long-term success.

Addressing Concerns

Open Communication

Case 1: Encouraging Transparency

Sarah knew that fostering an environment of open communication was vital to maintaining the harmony and unity of her cult. She organized regular "Listening Sessions" where members could openly voice their concerns and suggestions. These sessions were held in a safe, controlled environment to ensure that everyone felt comfortable speaking up.

During one such session, a member named Julia expressed frustration over the lack of transparency in financial decisions. She felt that the inner circle was not sharing enough information about how the cult's funds were being used, which made her uncomfortable and suspicious.

Sarah listened attentively and acknowledged Julia's concerns. She explained the current financial processes and promised to increase transparency. Sarah then implemented monthly financial briefings where the inner circle presented detailed reports on income and expenditures to the entire community. This move not only addressed Julia's concerns but also reassured other members who might have had similar worries but hadn't voiced them. The increased transparency strengthened trust within the group and prevented further dissent.

Case 2: Creating Safe Spaces

In another instance, Sarah realized that some members might hesitate to voice their concerns in large groups. To address this, she created smaller discussion groups facilitated by trusted leaders. These groups provided a more intimate setting where members felt safer sharing their thoughts.

During one of these small group discussions, a newer member named Sam shared his feeling of being overshadowed by more vocal, long-standing members during decision-making processes. The facilitator took note of Sam's concerns and brought them to Sarah's attention.

Recognizing the validity of Sam's feelings, Sarah introduced a new protocol where meeting agendas were distributed in advance, allowing all members to prepare their thoughts and contributions. Additionally, she implemented a "round-robin" discussion format during meetings, ensuring that everyone had an equal opportunity to speak. This change was well-received and significantly improved the inclusivity of discussions.

Mediation and Resolution

Case 1: Resolving Personal Disputes

Conflict between members was inevitable in any group, and Sarah knew the importance of addressing these disputes promptly to maintain harmony. One such conflict arose between two influential members, Tom and Lisa, who had clashed over the direction of a major community project.

Tom believed the project should focus on expanding the cult's outreach programs, while Lisa felt the resources would be better spent on enhancing internal education and training. Their disagreement escalated into heated arguments, causing a rift within the inner circle and creating a tense atmosphere.

Sarah decided to intervene before the conflict could cause more damage. She arranged a mediation session with Tom and Lisa, facilitated by a neutral third party trained in conflict resolution. During the session, both Tom and Lisa were encouraged to express their viewpoints and underlying concerns. The mediator helped them find common ground by highlighting their shared goals and values.

After several mediation sessions, a compromise was reached. The project would allocate resources to both outreach and internal training, balancing both priorities. Tom and Lisa's relationship improved as they worked together on the newly agreed plan. The successful mediation not only resolved the conflict but also set a positive example for how disputes should be handled within the cult.

Case 2: Addressing Group Tensions

In another scenario, tension arose between two sub-groups within the cult: the more traditional members who favored the established rituals and the newer, progressive members who wanted to introduce modern practices.

The traditional group felt that the new practices diluted the cult's core values, while the progressive group believed that innovation was essential for growth and relevance. The tension began to affect the overall unity of the cult, with members taking sides and avoiding collaboration.

To resolve this, Sarah called for a series of facilitated group discussions where representatives from both sides could voice their concerns and suggestions. These discussions were guided by a professional mediator who ensured that each group listened to the other without interruption.

Through these discussions, both groups began to understand each other's perspectives. They realized that preserving core values and embracing innovation didn't have to be mutually exclusive. Sarah proposed a hybrid approach where traditional rituals were maintained, but new practices were introduced gradually and thoughtfully, with input from both groups.

The resolution of this conflict through structured mediation not only restored harmony but also fostered a culture of mutual respect and collaboration. Members felt more invested in the cult's future, knowing that their voices mattered and that conflicts could be resolved constructively.

Structured Conflict Resolution

Formal Mediation Processes: Sarah established formal mediation processes within the cult. Any member who felt wronged or had a grievance could request mediation. A neutral mediator, often a senior member with conflict resolution training, would facilitate these sessions. This formal process ensured that conflicts were handled professionally and impartially.

Training for Leaders: Sarah also ensured that all leaders within the cult received training in conflict resolution and mediation. This empowered them to handle minor disputes within their teams effectively and maintain harmony at all levels of the organization.

By encouraging open communication and implementing effective mediation and resolution strategies, Sarah successfully maintained harmony within her cult. Addressing concerns transparently and providing platforms for resolving conflicts helped prevent dissent from spreading and reinforced the unity and commitment of the group.

Disciplinary Actions

Clear Policies

Sarah understood that maintaining order within her cult required clear, well-communicated policies regarding dissent and opposition. She developed a comprehensive set of guidelines that outlined acceptable behavior, as well as the consequences for violating these standards.

Development of Policies

Sarah and her leadership team spent considerable time developing these policies. They held multiple meetings to discuss potential issues and scenarios, ensuring that the rules covered a wide range of situations. The final policy document included sections on respectful communication, participation expectations, confidentiality, and loyalty to the cult's values and mission.

Communicating the Policies

Once the policies were finalized, Sarah made sure that every member was aware of them. She organized a special meeting to introduce the policies, during which she explained each rule in detail and answered any questions. To reinforce understanding, she provided a printed copy of the policies to each member and posted them on the cult's internal website.

Regular Reminders

To keep the policies fresh in everyone's minds, Sarah incorporated regular reminders into the cult's routine. At the beginning of each major meeting or event, a brief review of key policies was conducted. This ensured that members remained aware of the expectations and the potential consequences of their actions.

Enforcement

Sarah knew that having clear policies was only the first step; consistent and fair enforcement was crucial to maintaining discipline and order within the cult.

Consistent Application

When a member named Alex began spreading negative rumors about the leadership, Sarah took immediate action. She arranged a private meeting with Alex to discuss the behavior. During the meeting, Sarah referenced the specific policy that Alex had violated, explaining how his actions were detrimental to the cult's unity and trust. She issued a formal warning and outlined the steps Alex needed to take to make amends.

By applying the same level of scrutiny to all members, regardless of their status, Sarah ensured that the rules were seen as fair and just. This consistency helped prevent any perception of favoritism or bias.

Fair Process

Sarah established a disciplinary committee composed of senior members who were respected for their impartiality and integrity. This committee was responsible for reviewing serious infractions and determining appropriate consequences.

Case Study: Addressing Repeated Disobedience

A member named Laura repeatedly ignored directives during group activities, often acting independently and disrupting planned events. After several warnings from her immediate supervisor, the issue was escalated to the disciplinary committee.

The committee reviewed Laura's behavior, documenting instances of disobedience and considering her overall contributions to the cult. After a thorough investigation, they recommended a temporary suspension from group activities, coupled with a probationary period upon her return. During probation, Laura was required to demonstrate improved behavior and adherence to the cult's policies.

Transparency in Enforcement

Sarah believed that transparency in the enforcement process was vital for maintaining trust. After disciplinary actions were decided, the outcomes were communicated to the affected member and, when appropriate, to the broader community. This transparency ensured that all members understood the consequences of their actions and the importance of adhering to the cult's policies.

Case Study: Severe Consequences for Major Infractions

In a more severe case, a member named Jake was found to be leaking confidential information to outsiders. This breach of trust posed a significant threat to the cult's security and unity. The disciplinary committee conducted a swift investigation, confirming the allegations with concrete evidence.

Given the gravity of the infraction, Sarah decided to expel Jake from the cult. She called a special meeting to inform the members of the situation, explaining the steps taken to address the breach and the reasons for the expulsion. By handling the situation decisively and transparently, Sarah reinforced the importance of confidentiality and loyalty.

Rehabilitation Opportunities

Sarah also believed in giving members a chance to redeem themselves when possible. For minor infractions, she implemented a system of rehabilitation, where members could make amends and demonstrate improved behavior.

Case Study: Rehabilitation Program

A member named Mia was found to be engaging in negative gossip, which was affecting the morale of the group. Rather than immediately resorting to severe punishment, Sarah decided to place Mia in a rehabilitation program. This program included counseling sessions, additional responsibilities that required collaboration, and a mentorship arrangement with a senior member.

Mia was given clear goals and milestones to achieve during her rehabilitation period. Regular progress reviews were conducted to ensure she was on track. Over time, Mia showed significant improvement in her behavior and was eventually reintegrated fully into the community.

By developing clear policies and enforcing them consistently and fairly, Sarah maintained order and discipline within her cult. These measures ensured that members understood the consequences of dissent and opposition, and provided a structured approach for addressing infractions. This balanced strategy of discipline and rehabilitation helped preserve the integrity and unity of the cult.

Reaffirming Commitment

Maintaining and strengthening the commitment of cult members is essential for ensuring long-term loyalty and cohesion. Sarah understood the importance of regularly reaffirming the cult's values and mission and using positive reinforcement to reward loyal and compliant behavior. Here's how she implemented these strategies effectively.

Regular Reaffirmation

Values and Mission Sessions

Sarah scheduled regular sessions dedicated to reaffirming the cult's core values and mission. These sessions were carefully planned to be engaging and inspiring, ensuring that members felt reinvigorated in their commitment.

Case 1: Monthly Reaffirmation Meetings

Every month, Sarah organized a special meeting where members gathered to reflect on the cult's principles and goals. During these meetings, Sarah delivered powerful speeches that highlighted the importance of their shared mission and the positive impact they were making in the world.

To make these sessions more interactive, Sarah included activities such as group discussions, where members could share personal stories about how the cult's teachings had influenced their lives. This allowed members to connect with each other on a deeper level and reinforced the sense of community and shared purpose.

Case 2: Annual Retreats

In addition to monthly meetings, Sarah held annual retreats that focused on deepening members' understanding of the cult's values. These retreats were held in serene, secluded locations, providing an ideal environment for reflection and spiritual growth.

During the retreats, Sarah and other senior leaders conducted workshops and seminars that delved into the philosophical and spiritual aspects of the cult's teachings. Members participated in meditative practices, team-building exercises, and ceremonial rituals designed to strengthen their emotional and spiritual bonds with the cult.

The retreats culminated in a grand ceremony where members reaffirmed their commitment to the cult's mission through symbolic acts and pledges. This powerful experience left members feeling renewed and dedicated to their shared goals.

Positive Reinforcement

Recognizing Loyalty and Compliance

Sarah understood that positive reinforcement was a powerful tool for encouraging desired behavior and maintaining high levels of commitment. She implemented a variety of methods to recognize and reward members who demonstrated strong loyalty and alignment with the cult's goals.

Case 1: Public Recognition

Sarah made it a point to publicly recognize members who went above and beyond in their dedication to the cult. During meetings and events, she highlighted their achievements and contributions, offering praise and gratitude. For instance, if a member successfully organized a community outreach program or showed exceptional leadership in a project, Sarah would commend their efforts in front of the entire group.

Case 2: Award Ceremonies

Sarah instituted regular award ceremonies to formally acknowledge the hard work and loyalty of members. These ceremonies included categories such as "Member of the Month," "Outstanding Service Award," and "Leadership Excellence." Winners received trophies, certificates, and public recognition, which boosted their morale and motivated others to strive for similar recognition.

Case 3: Special Privileges

To further incentivize loyalty, Sarah granted special privileges to members who consistently demonstrated strong commitment. These privileges included access to exclusive events, advanced training sessions, and private audiences with Sarah. For example, loyal members might be invited to a private dinner with Sarah, where they could discuss ideas and receive personalized guidance.

Case 4: Financial Incentives and Gifts

Sarah also used financial incentives and gifts as a form of positive reinforcement. Members who showed exceptional dedication might receive bonuses, gift cards, or special items such as books, spiritual artifacts, or personalized tokens of appreciation. These tangible rewards reinforced the cult's appreciation for their loyalty and hard work.

Case 5: Advancement Opportunities

Sarah offered advancement opportunities as a reward for loyal and compliant behavior. Members who consistently aligned with the cult's values and demonstrated leadership potential were given chances to take on more significant roles and responsibilities. This could include leading a new project, becoming a mentor to new recruits, or joining the inner circle.

Case 6: Personalized Acknowledgment

Sarah also believed in the power of personalized acknowledgment. She took the time to write handwritten notes to members who had made notable contributions, expressing her personal gratitude and appreciation. These notes were often cherished by members, serving as a reminder of their importance to the cult and their leader.

Creating a Culture of Recognition

By consistently recognizing and rewarding loyalty and compliance, Sarah created a culture where members felt valued and motivated to maintain their commitment. The positive

reinforcement not only encouraged desirable behavior but also strengthened the emotional
bonds between members and the cult.

Case 7: Celebrating Milestones

Sarah celebrated important milestones in members' journeys with the cult. Whether it was an
anniversary of joining the cult or achieving a significant personal goal within the cult's
framework, these milestones were marked with celebrations and acknowledgments. This
practice reinforced the members' sense of belonging and their progress within the community.

By holding regular sessions to reaffirm the cult's values and mission and using positive
reinforcement to recognize and reward loyalty, Sarah successfully maintained and strengthened
the commitment of her members. These strategies ensured that members remained dedicated
to the cult's goals and felt valued and appreciated for their contributions, fostering a cohesive
and loyal community.

Surveillance Systems

To maintain control and ensure loyalty within her cult, Sarah implemented a comprehensive
surveillance system. This system included both physical and digital surveillance measures
designed to monitor activities and interactions discreetly and effectively.

Physical Surveillance

Installation of Surveillance Cameras

Sarah understood the importance of keeping a close watch on the cult's physical environment to
prevent any signs of dissent or disloyalty from spreading unnoticed. She strategically installed
discreet surveillance cameras in key areas where members frequently gathered.

Key Areas for Surveillance

Meeting Rooms: Cameras were placed in meeting rooms to monitor discussions and
interactions during gatherings. This allowed Sarah to ensure that all meetings were conducted
in accordance with the cult's values and rules, and to identify any potential issues early.

Communal Areas: Surveillance cameras were also installed in communal areas such as dining
halls, recreational spaces, and common rooms. These areas were crucial for observing
day-to-day interactions and detecting any brewing conflicts or discontent among members.

Private Spaces: To a lesser extent, discreet surveillance was extended to certain private
spaces, like corridors outside personal quarters, ensuring members' behavior aligned with the
cult's expectations even outside group activities.

Security and Accessibility

To maintain the integrity and confidentiality of the surveillance data, Sarah ensured that these systems were secure and accessible only to trusted individuals within the inner circle. She hired a professional security team to manage the installation and maintenance of the cameras, ensuring that the equipment was tamper-proof and functioned correctly at all times.

Restricted Access: Access to the surveillance footage was strictly controlled. Only Sarah and a select few trusted members of the inner circle were permitted to review the recordings. This minimized the risk of unauthorized access and potential leaks of sensitive information.

Regular Audits: Regular audits of the surveillance system were conducted to ensure that the equipment was working correctly and that the data was being reviewed diligently. Any anomalies or technical issues were addressed immediately to maintain the system's reliability.

Digital Surveillance

Monitoring Electronic Communications

Recognizing that many interactions and communications occurred digitally, Sarah implemented a robust digital surveillance system. This system was designed to monitor emails, messages, and social media interactions among members.

Email Monitoring: Sarah used specialized software to monitor the email communications of key members. The software flagged keywords and phrases that could indicate potential dissent or disloyalty, such as mentions of leaving the cult, dissatisfaction with leadership, or plans to meet with outsiders.

Message Monitoring: Messaging platforms used by the cult, including group chats and private messages, were also monitored. The surveillance software analyzed message content for suspicious activities and reported any findings to Sarah and her inner circle.

Social Media Surveillance: Sarah recognized the influence of social media on members' perceptions and behaviors. She employed tools to track members' social media activities, including posts, comments, and interactions. Any public expressions of discontent or engagement with outside critics were flagged for further investigation.

Flagging Suspicious Activities

Keyword Detection: The digital surveillance tools were configured to detect specific keywords and phrases that could indicate potential issues. These keywords were regularly updated based on emerging trends and concerns within the cult.

Behavioral Analysis: Beyond keyword detection, the software also analyzed communication patterns and behaviors. Sudden changes in communication frequency, tone, or content could signal underlying issues that needed attention.

Reporting and Response: The surveillance system generated detailed reports on flagged activities, which were reviewed by Sarah and her trusted team. Immediate action was taken if any concerning patterns or behaviors were identified, such as calling the member in question for a private discussion or increasing their level of surveillance.

Maintaining Member Trust

Balancing Surveillance and Privacy: Sarah understood the importance of balancing surveillance with a sense of privacy and trust among members. While surveillance was necessary to ensure loyalty and prevent dissent, she was careful to avoid creating a climate of fear and paranoia.

Transparent Communication: To maintain trust, Sarah communicated openly with her inner circle about the need for surveillance. She emphasized that these measures were in place to protect the community and ensure its well-being. This transparency helped mitigate any feelings of distrust or resentment among key members.

Support Systems: Alongside surveillance, Sarah implemented support systems to address members' concerns proactively. Regular check-ins, counseling sessions, and opportunities for feedback ensured that members felt heard and valued, reducing the likelihood of dissent.

By implementing comprehensive physical and digital surveillance systems, Sarah effectively monitored activities and interactions within her cult. These measures allowed her to detect potential issues early and take decisive action to maintain control and loyalty. Through careful management and transparency, Sarah balanced the need for surveillance with the importance of trust and cohesion within her community.

Behavioral Monitoring

Behavioral monitoring is a critical aspect of maintaining control and ensuring loyalty within a cult. Sarah implemented a dual approach involving observation teams and regular check-ins to keep a close eye on members' behavior and address any potential issues proactively.

Observation Teams

Deployment of Trusted Aides

Sarah carefully selected a group of trusted aides from within her inner circle to form observation teams. These aides were chosen for their loyalty, discretion, and keen observational skills. Their primary role was to monitor members' behavior discreetly and report any signs of discontent or suspicious activities.

Training for Observation

Before being deployed, the observation aides underwent specialized training. This training covered various aspects of behavioral monitoring, including how to detect subtle changes in behavior, interpret body language, and identify signs of discontent or deceit. The training also emphasized the importance of maintaining confidentiality and reporting findings accurately and objectively.

Key Areas of Focus

The observation teams were tasked with monitoring behavior in various settings, including group meetings, social gatherings, and day-to-day interactions. They paid particular attention to:

- **Changes in Participation**: Noting if a member who was previously active and engaged suddenly became withdrawn or less involved.
- **Social Interactions**: Observing interactions between members to identify any emerging cliques, conflicts, or instances of exclusion.
- **Emotional Cues**: Detecting signs of stress, anxiety, or dissatisfaction, such as changes in speech patterns, body language, and facial expressions.
- **Compliance with Rules**: Ensuring that members adhered to the cult's rules and rituals, and noting any deviations.

Reporting Mechanisms

Observation aides were required to submit regular reports to Sarah and her leadership team. These reports included detailed observations and any potential red flags. The aides were encouraged to provide context and insights, helping Sarah make informed decisions about any necessary interventions.

Case Study: Identifying Emerging Conflicts

During one group meeting, an observation aide noticed that two members, John and Paul, were increasingly avoiding eye contact and interaction with each other. In previous meetings, they had been friendly and collaborative. The aide also noted that John appeared tense whenever Paul spoke.

The aide reported these observations to Sarah, who decided to intervene before the situation could escalate. She arranged separate one-on-one check-ins with both John and Paul to understand the underlying issue. Through these discussions, Sarah discovered that a misunderstanding over project responsibilities had caused the rift. By addressing the conflict early, she was able to mediate a resolution and restore harmony between the two members.

Regular Check-ins

Personalized Interactions

Sarah believed that regular, personalized check-ins with members were essential for maintaining a pulse on the community's overall satisfaction and well-being. She scheduled these check-ins to be both formal and informal, ensuring a comprehensive understanding of each member's state of mind.

Scheduling and Frequency

Check-ins were scheduled at regular intervals, with more frequent interactions for newer members or those showing signs of discontent. The format varied from casual conversations during communal activities to more structured one-on-one meetings.

Key Discussion Points

During check-ins, Sarah focused on several key areas:

- **Satisfaction with Participation**: Asking members about their satisfaction with their roles and responsibilities within the cult.
- **Personal Challenges**: Offering a safe space for members to discuss any personal challenges they were facing, both within and outside the cult.
- **Feedback on Activities**: Soliciting feedback on recent activities, meetings, and projects to gauge their effectiveness and identify areas for improvement.
- **Emotional Well-being**: Checking on members' emotional and mental well-being, ensuring they felt supported and valued.

Acting on Feedback

Sarah took the feedback gathered during check-ins seriously. She implemented changes based on members' suggestions and concerns, demonstrating that their voices were heard and valued. This responsiveness helped to build trust and reinforce loyalty.

Case Study: Addressing Burnout

During a regular check-in, a member named Lisa expressed feeling overwhelmed by her responsibilities and the pressure to meet the cult's high expectations. She was worried that her performance was slipping and felt stressed about letting the group down.

Sarah listened empathetically and reassured Lisa that her contributions were greatly appreciated. She decided to lighten Lisa's workload temporarily and assigned her a mentor to help her manage her tasks more effectively. Additionally, Sarah organized a wellness workshop focusing on stress management and self-care, benefiting not only Lisa but the entire community.

By providing immediate support and addressing Lisa's concerns, Sarah prevented potential burnout and strengthened Lisa's commitment to the cult.

Building Trust Through Check-ins

Sarah knew that these regular check-ins were also an opportunity to build deeper connections with her members. She made a point to remember personal details about their lives, such as their interests, family, and personal milestones. This personal touch made members feel valued and understood, fostering a strong sense of loyalty and trust.

Case Study: Recognizing Personal Milestones

During a check-in with a member named Emily, Sarah learned that Emily had recently completed a significant personal goal—earning a certification related to the cult's teachings. Sarah publicly acknowledged Emily's achievement during the next group meeting, praising her dedication and hard work. This recognition boosted Emily's morale and reinforced her commitment to the cult.

By deploying observation teams and conducting regular check-ins, Sarah effectively monitored her members' behavior and addressed issues proactively. These strategies allowed her to maintain a harmonious and loyal community, ensuring that any potential problems were identified and resolved early. This approach not only kept the cult cohesive but also strengthened the emotional bonds between members and their leader.

Data Analysis

To maintain control and preemptively address potential issues within her cult, Sarah implemented comprehensive data analysis strategies. These strategies involved using data analysis tools for pattern recognition and regularly reviewing feedback from anonymous channels to identify and address potential threats and sources of dissent.

Pattern Recognition

Implementing Data Analysis Tools

Sarah invested in advanced data analysis tools to monitor and analyze data collected from the cult's surveillance systems. These tools were designed to detect patterns in behavior and interactions that could indicate potential dissent or emerging threats.

Data Sources

The data sources for analysis included:

- **Surveillance Footage**: Video recordings from surveillance cameras installed in key areas.
- **Electronic Communications**: Emails, messages, and social media interactions monitored for keywords and behavior patterns.
- **Behavioral Reports**: Observations from the trusted aides who monitored members' behavior.

Case Study: Detecting Decreased Participation

Using data analysis tools, Sarah's team identified a pattern of decreased participation among several members during group activities. By cross-referencing surveillance footage and attendance records, they noticed that these members often congregated in small groups during breaks and seemed disengaged during meetings.

The data analysis tools flagged this behavior as a potential sign of discontent. Sarah decided to investigate further by conducting one-on-one check-ins with the identified members. During these conversations, she discovered that they felt their contributions were undervalued and that newer members were receiving more attention.

In response, Sarah implemented changes to ensure that all members felt recognized and valued. She created more inclusive activities that required collaboration between long-standing and new members. This intervention helped reintegrate the disengaged members and restored their commitment to the cult.

Behavioral Trends

The data analysis tools also helped Sarah detect broader behavioral trends within the cult. For example, a sudden increase in private meetings between specific members could indicate the formation of factions or cliques, which might lead to internal conflicts.

Case Study: Identifying Cliques

Sarah's data analysis revealed a trend where a group of members frequently met privately after official meetings. These meetings were not scheduled and seemed to occur spontaneously. The analysis indicated that this group was becoming increasingly isolated from the rest of the community.

Sarah addressed this by introducing more team-building activities that mixed members from different groups. She also held open forums where everyone could discuss their ideas and concerns openly. By breaking down these cliques and encouraging more inclusive interactions, Sarah was able to prevent the formation of potentially disruptive factions.

Feedback Analysis

Anonymous Feedback Channels

Sarah established anonymous feedback channels to allow members to voice their concerns and suggestions without fear of retribution. These channels included anonymous suggestion boxes, online feedback forms, and secure email addresses.

Regular Review of Feedback

Sarah's team regularly reviewed the feedback collected through these channels, looking for recurring themes or issues that needed to be addressed. This process was systematic and thorough, ensuring that no significant concern was overlooked.

Case Study: Addressing Recurring Themes

Upon reviewing the anonymous feedback, Sarah noticed a recurring theme: many members felt that the workload was unevenly distributed, with some individuals shouldering more responsibilities than others. This had led to feelings of resentment and burnout among those who felt overburdened.

Sarah took this feedback seriously and decided to conduct a workload assessment. She worked with her leadership team to redistribute tasks more evenly and implemented a system where members could request support if they felt overwhelmed. Additionally, Sarah introduced a rotational system for certain responsibilities, ensuring that all members shared the workload fairly.

By addressing this recurring issue promptly, Sarah not only alleviated the burden on overworked members but also improved overall morale and commitment within the cult.

Proactive Measures

Sarah used feedback analysis not only to address existing issues but also to take proactive measures. By understanding the underlying concerns and sentiments of her members, she could anticipate potential problems and implement preventative strategies.

Case Study: Improving Communication Channels

Feedback from anonymous channels also revealed that some members felt they were not adequately informed about the cult's decisions and future plans. This lack of communication led to feelings of uncertainty and mistrust.

In response, Sarah enhanced the cult's communication channels. She started issuing regular newsletters that provided updates on decisions, upcoming events, and the cult's strategic direction. Additionally, she held quarterly town hall meetings where members could ask questions and receive direct answers from the leadership team.

These measures significantly improved transparency and trust within the cult. Members felt more informed and involved, reducing the likelihood of dissent stemming from miscommunication or lack of information.

Monitoring Effectiveness

To ensure the effectiveness of the data analysis and feedback mechanisms, Sarah regularly assessed the impact of her interventions. She monitored changes in member behavior, participation levels, and the tone of feedback following the implementation of new policies or adjustments.

Continuous Improvement

Sarah's approach to data analysis was iterative. She continuously refined her methods and tools based on the insights gained and the effectiveness of her interventions. This commitment to continuous improvement ensured that her strategies remained relevant and effective in maintaining control and fostering loyalty within the cult.

By using data analysis tools for pattern recognition and regularly reviewing feedback from anonymous channels, Sarah was able to identify and address potential sources of dissent proactively. These strategies allowed her to maintain a harmonious and loyal community, ensuring the long-term stability and success of the cult.

Confidentiality Measures

Maintaining confidentiality within the cult is crucial for protecting sensitive information and ensuring the safety and loyalty of members. Sarah implemented robust confidentiality measures, including non-disclosure agreements (NDAs) and strict information access control, to safeguard the cult's secrets and prevent breaches.

Non-Disclosure Agreements (NDAs)

Legal Framework

Sarah recognized that one of the most effective ways to protect sensitive information was through legally binding non-disclosure agreements (NDAs). She worked with a legal advisor to draft comprehensive NDAs that all members were required to sign upon joining the cult.

Content of NDAs

The NDAs clearly outlined the following:

- **Scope of Confidentiality**: Detailed what information was considered confidential, including teachings, rituals, member identities, financial information, and strategic plans.
- **Obligations**: Specified the members' obligations to protect confidential information and not to disclose it to outsiders.
- **Duration**: Stipulated that the confidentiality obligations extended beyond membership, ensuring that even former members remained bound by the agreement.
- **Consequences of Breach**: Clearly defined the legal and disciplinary consequences for breaching the NDA, including potential legal action and expulsion from the cult.

Case Study: Implementation of NDAs

When a new member named Michael joined the cult, Sarah ensured that he signed the NDA during his induction process. She took the time to explain the importance of confidentiality and the reasons behind the strict measures. By doing so, she emphasized the seriousness of the agreement and the potential consequences of any breach.

A few months later, Sarah received a tip-off that Michael had been sharing details about the cult's activities with an outsider. She immediately launched an investigation. The evidence confirmed the breach, and Sarah took swift action. Michael was expelled from the cult, and legal proceedings were initiated as per the terms of the NDA. This decisive action reinforced the importance of confidentiality and served as a deterrent to other members.

Information Access Control

Role-Based Access

Sarah implemented a stringent information access control system based on members' roles and responsibilities. This ensured that only trusted individuals had access to critical and sensitive information.

Need-to-Know Basis

Access Levels: Information within the cult was categorized based on sensitivity. Access levels were defined, and only members whose roles necessitated access to specific information were granted it. For instance:

- **General Members**: Access to basic teachings and general community information.
- **Inner Circle Members**: Access to advanced teachings, financial details, and strategic plans.
- **Leadership Team**: Full access to all information, including highly sensitive data like member records and future plans.

Case Study: Access Control in Action

Sarah's inner circle included a member named Laura, who was responsible for organizing events and managing day-to-day operations. As part of her role, Laura needed access to certain financial information to budget and plan events. However, she did not have access to more sensitive strategic plans or member records.

One day, Laura requested access to detailed member records, claiming it would help her better manage the event logistics. Sarah, adhering to the need-to-know principle, denied the request, explaining that the information was not necessary for her current responsibilities. Instead, Sarah provided Laura with the specific data relevant to her role, ensuring that confidentiality was maintained.

Regular Audits

To ensure the effectiveness of the access control measures, Sarah conducted regular audits. These audits reviewed who had access to what information and verified that access was appropriately granted based on current roles and responsibilities. Any discrepancies were promptly addressed.

Monitoring and Adjusting Access

As members' roles evolved, Sarah regularly adjusted their access levels to ensure they had the information necessary for their duties without compromising confidentiality.

Case Study: Adjusting Access Levels

When a member named David was promoted from general membership to the inner circle, his access level was upgraded. Sarah provided David with additional training on handling sensitive information and reinforced the importance of confidentiality. Similarly, when another inner circle member, Emma, stepped back from her responsibilities due to personal reasons, her access level was downgraded to reflect her reduced role.

Confidential Communication Channels

Sarah also ensured that confidential information was communicated through secure channels. This included encrypted emails, secure messaging apps, and protected physical documents.

Case Study: Secure Communication

For strategic meetings, Sarah used a secure messaging app that encrypted all communications end-to-end. She instructed members to use this app exclusively for discussing sensitive topics. Additionally, physical documents containing confidential information were stored in locked cabinets accessible only to authorized personnel.

Training and Awareness

Sarah conducted regular training sessions to reinforce the importance of confidentiality. These sessions covered best practices for handling sensitive information, the use of secure communication tools, and the consequences of breaches.

Case Study: Training Session Impact

During a training session, Sarah used real-life scenarios to illustrate the potential risks of confidentiality breaches. She shared the story of Michael's expulsion and the subsequent legal actions, emphasizing the severe consequences. This practical approach helped members understand the gravity of confidentiality and their role in protecting the cult's secrets.

By requiring members to sign legally binding non-disclosure agreements and implementing strict information access controls, Sarah effectively safeguarded the cult's sensitive information. These confidentiality measures ensured that only trusted individuals had access to critical data, reducing the risk of breaches and maintaining the integrity and security of the cult.

Building a Culture of Loyalty

Building a culture of loyalty within a cult is essential for ensuring the group's cohesion and longevity. Sarah achieved this by integrating the cult's values and mission into daily activities and fostering strong emotional bonds among members through shared experiences, rituals, and ceremonies.

Cultural Integration

Daily Activities and Interactions

Sarah knew that for the cult's values and mission to be truly embraced, they had to be woven into the fabric of daily life within the community. She made sure that every aspect of the cult's operations reflected its core principles.

Case Study: Integrating Values into Daily Life

Sarah started each day with a communal breakfast where she or a senior member would share a short reflection on one of the cult's values. These reflections were designed to be thought-provoking and relevant to the members' daily lives. For example, if the value of the day was "Unity," the reflection might focus on the importance of working together and supporting each other in all tasks.

Throughout the day, Sarah ensured that members had opportunities to practice these values. Work assignments were structured to encourage teamwork, with members rotating roles to experience different aspects of communal life. This not only reinforced the value of unity but also helped members appreciate the contributions of their peers.

Regular Communication

To keep the mission and values at the forefront of members' minds, Sarah implemented regular communication strategies.

Weekly Newsletters: Sarah sent out weekly newsletters that highlighted recent accomplishments, upcoming events, and reflections on the cult's values. These newsletters often included stories of members who exemplified these values, serving as role models for others.

Case Study: The Impact of Newsletters

In one newsletter, Sarah shared the story of Anna, a member who had gone out of her way to help a struggling new recruit adjust to the cult's routines. Anna's actions were framed as a shining example of the cult's value of "Compassion." This public recognition not only reinforced the importance of compassion but also motivated other members to exhibit similar behaviors.

Group Meetings: Sarah held weekly group meetings where members could discuss the cult's values and how they applied to their current projects and personal lives. These meetings were interactive, allowing members to share their experiences and learn from each other.

Case Study: Group Meeting Discussions

During one meeting, the topic of "Integrity" was discussed. Members were encouraged to share instances where they faced ethical dilemmas and how they resolved them in line with the cult's teachings. This open dialogue helped members internalize the value of integrity and understand its practical implications.

Rituals and Ceremonies

Rituals played a crucial role in reinforcing the cult's values and mission. Sarah designed specific rituals that symbolized these principles and integrated them into regular ceremonies.

Daily Rituals: Simple daily rituals, such as morning meditations and evening gratitude sessions, were introduced. These rituals were centered around the cult's values and provided moments of reflection and recommitment.

Case Study: Morning Meditations

Every morning, members gathered for a meditation session that focused on a specific value. For instance, a meditation on "Trust" would guide members to reflect on how they could build trust within the community and with themselves. These daily practices helped to keep the values alive and present in the members' consciousness.

Monthly Ceremonies: Larger monthly ceremonies were held to celebrate milestones and achievements within the cult. These ceremonies were highly symbolic and often included reenactments of key events in the cult's history, reinforcing the shared mission and values.

Case Study: Monthly Unity Ceremony

In a monthly ceremony celebrating "Unity," members participated in a symbolic activity where they collectively built a structure representing the cult's goals. Each member contributed a piece, and the completed structure was a tangible representation of their collective effort and unity. This ceremony not only reinforced the value of unity but also provided a sense of accomplishment and belonging.

Emotional Bonding

Shared Experiences

Sarah understood that strong emotional bonds were crucial for fostering loyalty and discouraging dissent. She created numerous opportunities for members to share meaningful experiences.

Community Projects: Members worked together on community projects, such as building facilities, gardening, and organizing events. These projects required collaboration and provided a sense of purpose and achievement.

Case Study: Building the Community Center

One significant project involved building a new community center. Members worked side by side, contributing their skills and labor. The shared effort and the satisfaction of completing the project together created strong bonds and a sense of pride in their collective achievement.

Recreational Activities: Regular recreational activities, such as hiking trips, arts and crafts sessions, and group games, were organized to provide opportunities for members to relax and enjoy each other's company.

Case Study: Annual Retreat

Every year, Sarah organized a retreat to a serene location where members could bond over various activities like hiking, storytelling, and communal cooking. These retreats were designed to strengthen the emotional connections between members and create lasting memories.

Rituals and Ceremonies

Initiation Rites: New members underwent initiation rites that included symbolic acts of commitment and loyalty. These rites were designed to be emotionally powerful, creating a deep sense of belonging from the start.

Case Study: New Member Initiation

During the initiation of new members, a ceremony was held where they pledged their loyalty and were welcomed into the community with open arms. Existing members shared their own initiation experiences, creating a sense of continuity and shared history. The emotional impact of the initiation rites helped new members feel immediately integrated and loyal to the group.

Celebratory Rituals: Regular celebratory rituals marked significant personal and communal milestones, such as birthdays, anniversaries of joining the cult, and the completion of major projects. These rituals provided a sense of recognition and validation.

Case Study: Birthday Celebrations

For each member's birthday, the community held a special ceremony where the member was honored with speeches, songs, and symbolic gifts representing the cult's values. These celebrations made members feel cherished and reinforced their emotional bonds with the community.

Support Systems

Mentorship Programs: Sarah implemented mentorship programs where seasoned members guided new recruits, helping them navigate their new environment and understand the cult's values and practices.

Case Study: Mentorship Success

When a new member named Ethan joined, he was paired with a long-standing member, Grace, who mentored him through his initial months. Grace provided support, answered questions, and shared insights into the cult's values. This mentorship relationship helped Ethan integrate smoothly and feel a strong sense of connection and loyalty to the community.

Counseling and Support Groups: Regular counseling sessions and support groups were available for members to discuss their challenges and receive emotional support. These groups fostered a sense of trust and mutual care.

Case Study: Support Group Impact

Sarah noticed that some members were struggling with personal issues that affected their participation. She organized support groups where members could share their struggles and receive emotional and practical support from their peers. These groups strengthened the community's sense of solidarity and demonstrated the cult's commitment to the well-being of its members.

By integrating the cult's values and mission into daily activities and fostering strong emotional bonds through shared experiences, rituals, and ceremonies, Sarah built a culture of loyalty. This culture not only enhanced members' commitment to the cult but also discouraged dissent, ensuring the group's stability and cohesion.

Regular Loyalty Assessments

Regular loyalty assessments are essential for maintaining a strong, committed, and satisfied membership within the cult. Sarah implemented a structured approach to assess loyalty and satisfaction through regular surveys and interviews, as well as by developing loyalty programs that rewarded long-term commitment and active participation.

Surveys and Interviews

Conducting Regular Surveys

Sarah developed comprehensive surveys to periodically assess members' loyalty and satisfaction levels. These surveys were designed to gather detailed feedback on various aspects of the cult's operations, including leadership, community activities, personal growth opportunities, and overall satisfaction.

Content of Surveys

The surveys included questions on:

- **Satisfaction with Leadership**: Members were asked to rate their satisfaction with the leadership team, including their communication, decision-making, and approachability.
- **Community Engagement**: Questions about participation in community activities, sense of belonging, and relationships with other members.
- **Personal Development**: Assessments of how members felt about their personal growth and development within the cult, including spiritual and emotional well-being.
- **Suggestions for Improvement**: Open-ended questions inviting members to share suggestions and areas for improvement.

Case Study: Implementing Surveys

Sarah scheduled quarterly surveys, ensuring that every member had the opportunity to provide feedback regularly. To encourage honest and candid responses, the surveys were conducted anonymously. Members received reminders and were given sufficient time to complete them.

Analyzing Survey Results

Once the surveys were collected, Sarah and her leadership team analyzed the results to identify trends, common concerns, and areas needing attention. The analysis included quantitative data, such as satisfaction ratings, and qualitative data from open-ended responses.

Case Study: Addressing Survey Feedback

In one survey, Sarah noticed a recurring concern about the lack of social activities outside of work-related tasks. Members expressed a desire for more recreational events to bond with each other. In response, Sarah organized monthly social events, such as game nights, movie screenings, and outdoor picnics. These activities enhanced members' sense of community and satisfaction.

Conducting Interviews

In addition to surveys, Sarah conducted regular one-on-one interviews with members. These interviews provided a more personal and in-depth understanding of individual experiences and concerns.

Structure of Interviews

- **Scheduled Sessions**: Sarah scheduled interviews with a rotating group of members each month, ensuring that everyone had the chance to speak with her personally at least once a year.
- **Confidential Conversations**: The interviews were conducted in a confidential setting to encourage open and honest dialogue.

- **Guided Questions**: While the conversations were informal, Sarah used guided questions to cover key topics such as personal satisfaction, challenges faced, and suggestions for improvement.

Case Study: Impact of Interviews

During one interview, a member named Rachel shared that she felt overwhelmed with her current responsibilities and was struggling to balance them with her personal life. Sarah listened empathetically and discussed potential solutions, including adjusting Rachel's workload and providing additional support. This intervention not only helped Rachel but also demonstrated to other members that their well-being was a priority.

Loyalty Programs

Implementing Loyalty Programs

To further reinforce commitment and reward long-term loyalty, Sarah introduced a series of loyalty programs. These programs offered various incentives to members who demonstrated active participation and sustained dedication to the cult's mission and values.

Rewards for Long-Term Commitment

Sarah created a tiered loyalty program that rewarded members based on their length of service and level of involvement.

Tiered Rewards System

- **Bronze Tier**: Members who had been with the cult for one year received a bronze pin and a certificate of appreciation. They were also given access to additional educational materials and workshops.
- **Silver Tier**: Members who reached the three-year mark were promoted to the silver tier. They received a silver pin, public recognition during a ceremony, and exclusive invitations to special events and retreats.
- **Gold Tier**: The gold tier was reserved for members with five or more years of service. These members received a gold pin, a personalized gift, and priority access to leadership training programs and one-on-one mentorship with Sarah.

Case Study: Celebrating Milestones

During the annual celebration, Sarah recognized several members who had reached new loyalty tiers. She presented them with their pins and certificates, sharing stories of their contributions and achievements. This public acknowledgment boosted their morale and encouraged others to strive for similar recognition.

Special Privileges and Exclusive Access

In addition to tiered rewards, Sarah introduced special privileges and exclusive access to resources for loyal members.

Exclusive Events: Loyal members were invited to exclusive events, such as leadership retreats, advanced training sessions, and private dinners with Sarah and other senior leaders.

Access to Resources: Long-term members received access to exclusive resources, including advanced teachings, rare manuscripts, and personalized spiritual guidance.

Case Study: Exclusive Retreats

Sarah organized an exclusive retreat for gold-tier members at a serene, remote location. The retreat included advanced spiritual teachings, meditation sessions, and workshops on leadership and personal development. This retreat not only rewarded loyal members but also deepened their commitment to the cult's mission.

Positive Reinforcement and Recognition

Sarah used positive reinforcement to acknowledge and celebrate members' contributions and loyalty regularly.

Public Recognition: During meetings and events, Sarah made it a point to publicly recognize members who had demonstrated exceptional dedication and service. This recognition included verbal praise, awards, and opportunities to share their experiences and insights with the group.

Personalized Thank-You Notes: Sarah sent personalized thank-you notes to members who had made notable contributions, expressing her gratitude and appreciation for their efforts. These notes were a simple yet powerful way to reinforce loyalty and commitment.

Case Study: Monthly Recognition Ceremonies

Every month, Sarah held a recognition ceremony where she honored members who had shown outstanding dedication. These ceremonies included speeches, awards, and time for members to share their personal journeys. The ceremonies fostered a sense of pride and belonging, motivating members to continue their active participation.

By conducting regular surveys and interviews, Sarah gained valuable insights into members' loyalty and satisfaction levels, allowing her to address potential issues proactively. Implementing loyalty programs that rewarded long-term commitment and active participation further reinforced members' dedication to the cult's mission and values. These strategies ensured a strong, loyal, and cohesive community, essential for the cult's stability and growth.

Crisis Management for Breaches

Effectively managing breaches of secrecy is crucial for maintaining the integrity and security of the cult. Sarah implemented a robust crisis management plan that included immediate response strategies and legal actions to address breaches promptly and deter future violations.

Immediate Response

Crisis Management Plan

Sarah developed a comprehensive crisis management plan designed to respond swiftly and effectively to breaches of secrecy. This plan outlined specific steps to identify the source of the breach, contain the damage, and address the root cause.

Identifying the Source

Incident Reporting: Sarah established clear procedures for members to report suspected breaches of secrecy. Any member who noticed suspicious activities or had concerns about potential breaches was encouraged to report them immediately to a designated crisis management team.

Initial Investigation: Upon receiving a report, Sarah's crisis management team conducted an initial investigation to confirm the breach and identify its source. This involved reviewing surveillance footage, monitoring communications, and interviewing relevant members.

Case Study: Identifying a Leak

One day, a member named Chris reported that confidential details about an upcoming project had been leaked to an outsider. Sarah's crisis management team immediately launched an investigation. They reviewed recent communications and surveillance footage, eventually identifying a member, Mark, as the source of the leak.

Containing the Damage

Immediate Action: Once the source of the breach was identified, Sarah took immediate action to contain the damage. This included isolating the member involved and restricting their access to sensitive information.

Communication Control: Sarah communicated with the leadership team to ensure they were aware of the breach and the steps being taken to address it. This helped prevent misinformation and panic within the community.

Case Study: Damage Control

After identifying Mark as the source of the leak, Sarah immediately restricted his access to all sensitive information and suspended his participation in key projects. She then informed the leadership team about the breach and the steps being taken to manage the situation.

Addressing the Root Cause

Detailed Investigation: Following the initial containment, Sarah's team conducted a more thorough investigation to understand how the breach occurred and identify any systemic vulnerabilities.

Policy Review and Adjustment: Based on the findings, Sarah reviewed and adjusted the cult's confidentiality policies and procedures to prevent similar breaches in the future. This included updating NDAs, enhancing surveillance measures, and reinforcing the importance of secrecy through additional training.

Case Study: Policy Improvements

The detailed investigation revealed that Mark had been under significant personal stress, which contributed to his actions. Sarah introduced additional support mechanisms for members, including counseling and stress management workshops. She also tightened the existing policies to ensure more robust checks and balances for handling sensitive information.

Legal Action

Legal Preparedness

Sarah ensured that the cult was legally prepared to take action against individuals who violated confidentiality agreements or engaged in activities that threatened the cult's secrecy. This involved having legal advisors on retainer and clearly defined legal procedures in place.

Legal Consequences

Enforcement of NDAs: All members were required to sign legally binding NDAs that specified the legal consequences of breaching confidentiality. These consequences included financial penalties and legal action.

Case Study: Enforcing NDAs

After confirming Mark's breach, Sarah's legal team reviewed the NDA he had signed. The agreement clearly outlined the penalties for such actions. Mark was informed of the impending legal actions, which included financial penalties and a formal lawsuit for damages.

Deterrence

Publicizing Consequences: To deter others from breaching confidentiality, Sarah made it clear that the cult would take serious legal actions against violators. Without disclosing sensitive details, she communicated to the members that breaches had significant consequences and that the cult's legal team was fully prepared to enforce NDAs.

Case Study: Legal Deterrence

Following the legal action against Mark, Sarah held a meeting with all members to discuss the importance of confidentiality. She used the situation as a learning opportunity, emphasizing that breaches would be met with severe consequences to protect the community. This served as a strong deterrent to others considering similar actions.

Ongoing Monitoring and Improvement

Regular Audits: Sarah's crisis management plan included regular audits of confidentiality policies and procedures to ensure they remained effective and up to date. These audits helped identify potential vulnerabilities before they could be exploited.

Feedback and Adaptation: Sarah encouraged feedback from members about the effectiveness of confidentiality measures and the handling of breaches. This feedback was used to continuously improve the crisis management plan and adapt to emerging threats.

Case Study: Continuous Improvement

In response to feedback, Sarah introduced a more robust training program on confidentiality and crisis management. This included scenario-based training sessions where members practiced responding to hypothetical breaches. The continuous improvement approach ensured that the cult was always prepared to handle breaches effectively.

By having a detailed crisis management plan in place and being prepared to take legal action, Sarah effectively managed breaches of secrecy within the cult. These measures not only addressed immediate threats but also served as a strong deterrent, reinforcing the importance of confidentiality and protecting the integrity of the community.

Chapter 7: Rituals and Practices

Rituals and practices are at the heart of a cult's identity and cohesion. They serve to reinforce beliefs, strengthen community bonds, and establish the authority of the leadership. This chapter explores the intricacies of designing powerful rituals, creating exclusive ceremonies, and reinforcing beliefs through repetition.

Designing Powerful Rituals

Purpose and Intent

To design powerful rituals, it's essential to start with a clear understanding of their purpose and intent. Rituals should align with the cult's core beliefs and values, serving to deepen members' commitment and enhance their spiritual or emotional experience.

Symbolism and Meaning

Incorporate rich symbolism and layers of meaning into each ritual. Symbols should be chosen carefully to resonate with members and reflect the cult's teachings. Whether it's through objects, gestures, or words, every element should have a significance that reinforces the cult's narrative.

Case Study: The Initiation Ritual

One example of a powerful ritual is the initiation ceremony for new members. This ritual could involve:

- **Symbolic Acts**: New members might be asked to perform specific actions, such as lighting a candle to symbolize enlightenment or drinking a special beverage to represent unity.
- **Oaths and Pledges**: The ceremony could include reciting oaths that affirm their commitment to the cult's values and mission.
- **Welcoming Gestures**: Current members might form a circle around the initiate, welcoming them into the community with open arms, symbolizing acceptance and belonging.

Emotional Impact

Design rituals to evoke strong emotional responses. Use music, chants, and sensory experiences like incense or candlelight to create an atmosphere that heightens emotions and deepens the spiritual connection. Emotional experiences can leave a lasting impression and strengthen members' attachment to the cult.

Case Study: The Healing Ritual

A healing ritual can be designed to address both physical and emotional ailments. Elements might include:

- **Preparation**: Members gather in a dimly lit room with soft, soothing music playing. The scent of incense fills the air.
- **Guided Meditation**: The leader guides members through a meditation focused on healing and well-being.
- **Laying on Hands**: The leader and selected members place their hands on the person in need of healing, chanting softly to invoke healing energies.
- **Closing Affirmation**: The ritual concludes with affirmations of health and strength, reinforcing the power of the community's support.

Creating Exclusive Ceremonies

Inclusivity and Exclusivity Balance

While regular rituals should be inclusive to all members, exclusive ceremonies can be designed to reward loyalty and commitment. These ceremonies should be reserved for members who have reached certain milestones or demonstrated exceptional dedication.

Invitation-Only Events

Host invitation-only events that offer unique experiences. These can include advanced teachings, deeper spiritual practices, or special acknowledgments from the leadership. The exclusivity of these events reinforces their importance and the value of loyalty.

Case Study: The Inner Circle Gathering

An inner circle gathering could be designed to reward and reinforce the commitment of the most dedicated members:

- **Exclusive Location**: Hold the gathering in a serene, private location to create a sense of importance and intimacy.
- **Advanced Teachings**: Share deeper, more esoteric teachings that are not available to the general membership.
- **Recognition Ceremony**: Publicly recognize and reward inner circle members for their contributions and loyalty, perhaps with special tokens or symbols of their status.

Symbolic Rewards

Incorporate symbolic rewards into exclusive ceremonies. These can be physical items like badges, sashes, or jewelry that signify a member's status and achievements within the cult. The distribution of these items during ceremonies adds to their value and significance.

Case Study: The Achievement Ceremony

An achievement ceremony can be held to honor members who have made significant contributions:

- **Ceremonial Attire**: Members wear special ceremonial attire that signifies their rank or achievements.
- **Award Presentation**: The leader presents awards, such as medallions or certificates, to members in a formal ceremony.
- **Public Acknowledgment**: Each awardee is given an opportunity to speak about their journey and accomplishments, fostering a sense of pride and recognition.

Reinforcing Beliefs through Repetition

Regular Rituals

Regularly scheduled rituals help to reinforce the cult's beliefs and values. These can be daily, weekly, or monthly, providing consistent opportunities for members to engage with the cult's teachings and strengthen their commitment.

Consistency and Routine

Establishing a consistent routine for rituals helps to normalize the practices and embed them into the daily lives of members. Repetition of specific actions, prayers, or chants can deepen their significance and impact.

Case Study: The Daily Devotion

A daily devotion ritual could be implemented to start each day:

- **Morning Meditation**: Members gather each morning for a short meditation focused on the cult's core values.
- **Daily Affirmation**: The leader or a designated member leads the group in reciting an affirmation that reinforces their commitment to the cult.
- **Reflection Time**: Members spend a few minutes reflecting on how they can embody the day's teachings in their actions.

Seasonal and Annual Ceremonies

Seasonal and annual ceremonies can mark important dates and milestones in the cult's calendar. These events can be larger and more elaborate, providing a sense of continuity and tradition.

Case Study: The Annual Renewal Ceremony

An annual renewal ceremony can be designed to renew members' commitment:

- **Seasonal Symbolism**: Tie the ceremony to a seasonal event, such as the solstice or equinox, to add a layer of natural symbolism.
- **Collective Participation**: Involve all members in a collective activity, such as planting a tree or lighting candles, to symbolize renewal and growth.

- **Reflection and Renewal**: The leader guides members through a reflection on the past year and sets intentions for the year ahead, reinforcing the cult's mission and goals.

Repetitive Teachings

Incorporate repetitive teachings into all rituals and ceremonies. Regularly revisit core beliefs and values, using different formats and methods to keep the teachings fresh and engaging.

Case Study: The Weekly Study Group

A weekly study group can focus on deepening understanding of the cult's teachings:

- **Rotating Topics**: Each week, focus on a different aspect of the cult's beliefs, using readings, discussions, and activities.
- **Interactive Learning**: Encourage members to participate actively, sharing their interpretations and insights.
- **Consistent Reinforcement**: Regularly revisit key teachings and values to reinforce their importance and relevance.

By designing powerful rituals, creating exclusive ceremonies, and reinforcing beliefs through repetition, a cult can strengthen its community, deepen members' commitment, and ensure the continuity of its values and mission. These practices help to create a cohesive and dedicated group, united by shared experiences and reinforced beliefs.

Designing Powerful Rituals

Designing powerful rituals is a fundamental aspect of cultivating a strong, cohesive, and committed cult. Rituals serve as a means to reinforce the group's beliefs, values, and mission while providing members with profound spiritual or emotional experiences. Below is a detailed guide on how to design such rituals, focusing on their purpose and intent, symbolism and meaning, and an illustrative case study with examples and stories.

Purpose and Intent

Clarifying Objectives

Before designing any ritual, it is crucial to clearly understand its purpose and intent. Ask yourself: What is the primary goal of this ritual? How does it align with the cult's core beliefs and values? Powerful rituals typically aim to achieve one or more of the following objectives:

- **Strengthening Commitment**: Deepening members' dedication to the cult's mission and values.
- **Spiritual Enlightenment**: Providing a platform for members to experience spiritual growth and insight.

- **Community Bonding**: Enhancing the sense of unity and belonging among members.
- **Celebrating Milestones**: Marking significant events or achievements within the community.

Aligning with Core Beliefs

Ensure that the ritual aligns with the cult's core beliefs and teachings. Every element of the ritual should reflect and reinforce these principles, helping members internalize and live by them. For instance, if a cult emphasizes harmony with nature, rituals might incorporate natural elements and take place in outdoor settings.

Enhancing Experiences

Design rituals to enhance members' spiritual or emotional experiences. Consider the atmosphere, sensory elements, and emotional impact. The setting, lighting, sounds, and scents should all contribute to creating a profound and memorable experience.

Symbolism and Meaning

Choosing Symbols

Incorporate rich symbolism into each ritual. Symbols are powerful tools for conveying deeper meanings and reinforcing the cult's teachings. Select symbols that resonate with members and reflect the cult's narrative. These can include:

- **Objects**: Items such as candles, stones, or water can symbolize concepts like enlightenment, stability, or purification.
- **Gestures**: Actions like bowing, embracing, or offering can represent respect, unity, or sacrifice.
- **Words**: Specific phrases, chants, or prayers can encapsulate core beliefs and values.

Layering Meaning

Layer multiple meanings into each symbol to deepen their significance. For example, lighting a candle can represent enlightenment, the dispelling of ignorance, and the presence of a guiding spirit. This complexity adds depth to the ritual and encourages members to reflect on different aspects of their beliefs.

Integrating Symbols

Integrate these symbols seamlessly into the ritual. Ensure that every element has a purpose and contributes to the overall narrative. This integration makes the ritual more coherent and impactful.

Case Study: The Initiation Ritual

An initiation ritual is a powerful example of how to incorporate purpose, intent, and symbolism into a ceremony. Here's a detailed breakdown of a potential initiation ritual:

Symbolic Acts

Lighting a Candle

- **Symbolism**: Lighting a candle can symbolize enlightenment, the start of a new journey, and the presence of spiritual guidance.
- **Action**: New members light a candle from a central flame, signifying their acceptance of the cult's light and wisdom.

Example Story Maria had always felt lost and disconnected in her life. When she joined the cult, she was immediately drawn to its teachings and the sense of community it offered. During her initiation ceremony, Maria was asked to light a candle from a central flame. As she held the candle, the warm glow reflected in her eyes, symbolizing her new journey toward enlightenment. The act of lighting the candle made Maria feel an immediate sense of belonging and purpose.

Drinking a Special Beverage

- **Symbolism**: Drinking a special beverage can represent unity, purification, and the sharing of a common bond.
- **Action**: Each initiate drinks from a communal cup, symbolizing their integration into the community and their commitment to shared values.

Example Story John had been searching for a sense of purpose after retiring from his career. Joining the cult gave him a new lease on life. During his initiation, he drank from a communal cup, a special beverage prepared with herbs symbolizing purification. As he took a sip, John felt a deep connection to the other members. The shared act of drinking from the same cup made him feel united with the community, reinforcing his commitment to the cult's values.

Oaths and Pledges

Reciting Oaths

- **Symbolism**: Oaths affirm the new members' commitment to the cult's values and mission.
- **Action**: New members recite an oath pledging their loyalty, dedication, and adherence to the cult's principles. The oath can be a carefully crafted statement that encapsulates the core beliefs of the cult.

Example Story Sarah had always been passionate about finding deeper meaning in life. When she joined the cult, she felt she had found her true calling. During her initiation, Sarah recited an oath in front of the community, pledging her loyalty and dedication to the cult's mission. The words of the oath resonated deeply with her, reinforcing her commitment to live by the cult's principles. The act of publicly declaring her allegiance strengthened Sarah's resolve and sense of belonging.

Welcoming Gestures

Forming a Circle

- **Symbolism**: The circle represents unity, inclusiveness, and the protective embrace of the community.
- **Action**: Current members form a circle around the initiate, symbolizing acceptance and belonging. The initiate stands in the center, acknowledging their new role within the community.

Example Story David had always felt like an outsider until he found the cult. During his initiation, the existing members formed a circle around him, holding hands and chanting softly. Standing in the center, David felt the warmth and acceptance radiating from the group. The symbolic act of forming a circle around him made David feel embraced and protected by his new family. This powerful gesture solidified his sense of belonging and commitment to the community.

Embracing the Initiate

- **Symbolism**: The embrace signifies acceptance, support, and mutual respect.
- **Action**: Each member takes a turn embracing the initiate, offering words of welcome and encouragement. This act physically and emotionally integrates the new member into the group.

Example Story Emma had always longed for a community where she felt truly understood. During her initiation, each member of the cult took turns embracing her, whispering words of welcome and encouragement. The physical touch and heartfelt words made Emma feel deeply connected to each member. The embraces symbolized the unconditional support and acceptance she had been searching for. This emotional integration into the group reinforced her commitment to the cult.

Detailed Ritual Example

Preparation

- **Setting**: The initiation ceremony takes place in a dimly lit room adorned with symbols of the cult, such as banners or statues. Soft, ambient music plays in the background, and incense fills the air with a calming scent.
- **Materials**: Candles, a communal cup filled with a special beverage, a written oath, and a circle of chairs for the current members.

The Ritual

1. **Introduction**: The leader opens the ceremony with a brief speech about the significance of initiation and the journey ahead.
2. **Lighting the Candle**: Each initiate lights a candle from a central flame. As they do, the leader explains the symbolism of enlightenment and the start of a new path.
3. **Drinking the Beverage**: The initiates drink from a communal cup. The leader speaks about the unity and shared commitment this act represents.
4. **Reciting the Oath**: Initiates recite their oaths, holding their candles. The leader and other members listen intently, reinforcing the gravity of the commitment being made.
5. **Forming the Circle**: Current members form a circle around the initiates. The leader explains the symbolism of the circle as a protective and unifying force.
6. **Welcoming Embrace**: One by one, each member steps forward to embrace the initiates, offering words of welcome and encouragement. This part of the ceremony fosters a deep sense of belonging and acceptance.
7. **Closing Words**: The leader concludes the ceremony with final words of encouragement, reminding the initiates of their new responsibilities and the support they have within the community.

Post-Ritual Reflection

- **Group Discussion**: After the ceremony, the group gathers for a discussion. Members share their feelings about the ritual, and initiates speak about their experience and what it means to them. This reflection reinforces the emotional and spiritual impact of the ritual.

By following these principles and detailed steps, you can design powerful rituals that deeply resonate with members, reinforce the cult's core beliefs and values, and create lasting emotional and spiritual connections.

Emotional Impact

Creating rituals with a strong emotional impact is essential for deepening members' spiritual connection and strengthening their attachment to the cult. Such rituals should be designed to evoke powerful emotional responses through the use of music, chants, sensory experiences like incense or candlelight, and meaningful symbolic acts. The resulting emotional experiences can leave lasting impressions and reinforce members' commitment to the cult.

Designing for Emotional Impact

Atmosphere and Setting

To evoke strong emotional responses, the atmosphere and setting of the ritual are crucial. The environment should be carefully crafted to engage the senses and create a mood that supports the intended emotional experience.

Case Study: The Healing Ritual

A healing ritual, designed to address both physical and emotional ailments, serves as a powerful example of how to create a deeply emotional and impactful ceremony.

Preparation

Setting the Scene

- **Dim Lighting**: Members gather in a room softly lit by candles. The gentle flickering of the flames creates a calming and sacred atmosphere.
- **Soothing Music**: Soft, soothing music plays in the background, helping to relax the participants and prepare them for the healing process.
- **Incense**: The scent of incense fills the air, adding to the sensory experience and enhancing the feeling of entering a sacred space.

Example Story: Preparation for Healing Jane, a member struggling with chronic pain, enters the room for the healing ritual. The dim lighting and the soft music immediately soothe her frazzled nerves. As she inhales the calming scent of the incense, she feels a sense of peace washing over her, preparing her for the transformative experience ahead.

Guided Meditation

Focusing the Mind

- **Leader's Role**: The leader begins the ritual by guiding the members through a meditation focused on healing and well-being. The leader's calming voice helps members focus their thoughts and energies on the process of healing.
- **Visualization**: Members are encouraged to visualize a source of healing light entering their bodies, cleansing them of pain and negativity.

Example Story: Guided Meditation As the leader's voice guides Jane through the meditation, she imagines a warm, healing light flowing through her body. She feels the tension in her muscles begin to ease, and a deep sense of relaxation takes over. The visualization helps her to mentally and emotionally prepare for the healing ritual.

Laying on Hands

Invoking Healing Energies

- **Physical Touch**: The leader and selected members place their hands on the person in need of healing. The gentle touch is both comforting and powerful, creating a tangible connection between the healer and the recipient.
- **Chanting**: As hands are laid on the person, the group chants softly, invoking healing energies and focusing the collective intention on the person's well-being.

Example Story: Laying on Hands When the leader and other members place their hands on Jane, she feels a surge of warmth and energy flowing into her. The soft chanting around her amplifies the feeling of being surrounded by love and support. This collective energy creates a powerful emotional experience, making Jane feel deeply cared for and supported by her community.

Closing Affirmation

Reinforcing Positive Outcomes

- **Affirmations**: The ritual concludes with affirmations of health, strength, and well-being. The leader and members speak positive affirmations, reinforcing the power of the community's support and the effectiveness of the healing process.
- **Gratitude**: Members express gratitude for the healing received, both from the leader and from the communal support.

Example Story: Closing Affirmation As the ritual comes to an end, Jane hears the affirmations of health and strength spoken by the leader and echoed by the group. She feels a profound sense of gratitude for the healing energy she received and for the unwavering support of her community. The closing affirmations leave her with a renewed sense of hope and well-being, strengthening her emotional bond with the cult.

Detailed Ritual Example

Preparation

Setting: The healing ritual takes place in a tranquil room adorned with symbols of healing and peace. The room is dimly lit by candles, creating a serene and sacred atmosphere. Soft, soothing music plays in the background, and the scent of lavender incense fills the air, known for its calming properties.

Materials: Candles, incense, comfortable mats or chairs for participants, a script for guided meditation, and symbols of healing (such as crystals or herbs).

The Ritual

1. **Introduction**: The leader welcomes the participants and explains the purpose of the healing ritual. They emphasize the collective power of the community's support and the importance of focusing on positive intentions.
2. **Guided Meditation**: The leader guides the group through a meditation focused on healing and well-being. Participants are encouraged to visualize a warm, healing light entering their bodies, cleansing them of pain and negativity.
3. **Laying on Hands**: The leader and selected members place their hands gently on the person in need of healing. The group begins chanting softly, invoking healing energies and focusing their collective intention on the person's well-being.

4. **Healing Visualization**: As the chanting continues, the person receiving the healing is encouraged to visualize the healing light intensifying and spreading throughout their body, bringing relief and strength.
5. **Closing Affirmation**: The ritual concludes with the leader and members speaking affirmations of health, strength, and well-being. Participants express gratitude for the healing received and the support of the community.

Post-Ritual Reflection

Group Sharing: After the ritual, the group gathers for a reflection session. Members share their experiences and feelings about the ritual. The person who received the healing discusses the impact of the ritual on their well-being, reinforcing the emotional and spiritual connection within the community.

Emotional Impact of the Ritual

The carefully crafted atmosphere, the guided meditation, the physical touch, the chanting, and the affirmations all work together to create a deeply emotional and impactful experience. The sensory elements and the collective energy of the group heighten the emotional response, making the ritual a memorable and transformative event.

By designing rituals to evoke strong emotional responses, using music, chants, and sensory experiences, you can create powerful ceremonies that leave lasting impressions on members. These emotional experiences strengthen members' attachment to the cult, deepen their spiritual connections, and reinforce their commitment to the community.

Creating Exclusive Ceremonies

Exclusive ceremonies are powerful tools for rewarding loyalty and commitment within a cult. They serve to reinforce members' dedication by providing unique experiences that are not available to the general membership. These ceremonies should strike a balance between inclusivity and exclusivity, ensuring that they feel both prestigious and motivational. This section delves into the intricacies of creating exclusive ceremonies, focusing on balancing inclusivity and exclusivity, hosting invitation-only events, and providing a detailed case study of an inner circle gathering.

Inclusivity and Exclusivity Balance

Purpose and Benefits

Regular rituals are designed to include all members, fostering a sense of community and belonging. However, exclusive ceremonies serve a different purpose. They are intended to:

  * **Reward Loyalty**: Recognize and celebrate the dedication and contributions of long-standing or exceptionally committed members.
  * **Enhance Commitment**: Strengthen the bonds between the most loyal members and the cult.
  * **Motivate Others**: Inspire the general membership to strive for higher levels of commitment and participation.

Criteria for Exclusivity

Establish clear criteria for participation in exclusive ceremonies. This ensures that the exclusivity is based on merit and dedication, enhancing its perceived value. Criteria might include:

  * **Length of Membership**: Recognizing members who have been part of the cult for a significant period.
  * **Contributions**: Celebrating those who have made notable contributions to the cult's activities, whether through leadership, service, or financial support.
  * **Special Achievements**: Acknowledging exceptional achievements that align with the cult's mission and values.

Example Story: Balancing Inclusivity and Exclusivity

Eleanor had been a member of the cult for five years, consistently demonstrating her dedication through volunteer work and active participation in rituals. When she received an invitation to the exclusive inner circle gathering, she felt honored and valued. The criteria for this invitation were clear and well-communicated, reinforcing her sense of achievement and motivating her to continue her contributions.

Invitation-Only Events

Planning Unique Experiences

Invitation-only events should offer unique experiences that are distinctly different from regular rituals. These can include:

  * **Advanced Teachings**: Sharing deeper, more esoteric knowledge that is reserved for the most dedicated members.
  * **Deeper Spiritual Practices**: Conducting intense spiritual practices that require a higher level of commitment and understanding.
  * **Special Acknowledgments**: Providing personalized recognition and rewards from the leadership.

Example Story: Planning an Invitation-Only Event

As the cult's annual gathering approached, the leadership team decided to host an exclusive retreat for the inner circle members. They chose a serene, private location away from the main event site, ensuring a tranquil and intimate atmosphere. Invitations were sent out to members who had demonstrated exceptional commitment, detailing the special activities planned for the retreat, including advanced spiritual teachings and private sessions with the cult leader.

Case Study: The Inner Circle Gathering

Exclusive Location

Selecting an exclusive location is crucial to creating a sense of importance and intimacy. The location should be:

- **Private and Serene**: A secluded area that offers privacy and tranquility, allowing members to fully immerse themselves in the experience.
- **Symbolically Significant**: A place that holds symbolic meaning for the cult, enhancing the spiritual impact of the gathering.

Example Story: Choosing the Location

The inner circle gathering was held at a remote mountain retreat, a place that symbolized spiritual ascension and enlightenment for the cult. The serene environment, surrounded by nature, provided the perfect backdrop for the exclusive event.

Advanced Teachings

Offering advanced teachings during exclusive ceremonies provides members with knowledge and insights that deepen their spiritual journey. These teachings should be:

- **Esoteric and Profound**: Content that goes beyond the general teachings, offering new perspectives and deeper understanding.
- **Interactive and Engaging**: Sessions that encourage participation and personal reflection, making the experience more impactful.

Example Story: Delivering Advanced Teachings

During the inner circle gathering, the cult leader conducted sessions on advanced spiritual practices, including meditation techniques and esoteric philosophy. Members were encouraged to share their insights and experiences, fostering a deeper connection with the teachings and with each other.

Recognition Ceremony

A recognition ceremony can publicly honor the contributions and loyalty of the most dedicated members. This ceremony should include:

- **Personalized Acknowledgments**: Public recognition of each member's contributions and achievements.
- **Symbolic Tokens**: Presentation of special tokens or symbols of status, such as medallions, sashes, or certificates.

- **Ceremonial Rituals**: Incorporating rituals that highlight the significance of the recognition and reinforce the cult's values.

Example Story: The Recognition Ceremony

The highlight of the inner circle gathering was the recognition ceremony. The leader called each member forward, recounting their contributions and presenting them with a handcrafted medallion inscribed with the cult's symbol. The ceremony concluded with a group chant, reinforcing the unity and dedication of the inner circle members.

Detailed Ritual Example

Preparation

Setting: The inner circle gathering takes place at a secluded mountain retreat. The venue is prepared with ceremonial decorations, including banners with the cult's symbols and altars with sacred objects.

Materials: Medallions or other tokens of recognition, scripts for advanced teachings, and materials for meditation and spiritual practices.

The Ritual

1. **Opening Session**: The leader welcomes the inner circle members, highlighting the importance of their dedication and the purpose of the gathering.
2. **Advanced Teachings**: The leader conducts sessions on advanced spiritual practices, encouraging interaction and reflection.
3. **Private Sessions**: Members have private sessions with the leader, receiving personalized guidance and insights.
4. **Recognition Ceremony**: Each member is called forward, acknowledged for their contributions, and presented with a symbolic token of their status.
5. **Group Rituals**: The gathering concludes with group rituals that reinforce the cult's values and the unity of the inner circle.

Post-Gathering Reflection

Group Sharing: After the ceremonies, members gather for a reflection session. They share their experiences and insights from the gathering, fostering a deeper sense of community and commitment.

Example Story: Reflecting on the Gathering

As the inner circle members gathered for the final reflection session, Eleanor shared how the advanced teachings had deepened her understanding of the cult's philosophy. The recognition ceremony had made her feel profoundly valued and committed to the cult's mission. The intimate setting and exclusive activities had strengthened her bonds with the other members and the leadership.

By carefully designing exclusive ceremonies that reward loyalty and commitment, you can create powerful experiences that enhance dedication, motivate members, and reinforce the values and mission of the cult. These ceremonies serve as a testament to the importance of each member's contributions, fostering a strong, cohesive, and motivated community.

Symbolic Rewards

Symbolic rewards are powerful tools for recognizing and reinforcing members' achievements and commitment within a cult. By incorporating these rewards into exclusive ceremonies, you can enhance their value and significance, creating lasting impressions and strengthening members' dedication. This section details how to incorporate symbolic rewards into exclusive ceremonies, illustrated with a case study of an achievement ceremony.

Incorporating Symbolic Rewards

Purpose and Significance

Symbolic rewards serve multiple purposes within a cult:

- **Recognition**: Acknowledge and celebrate members' contributions and achievements.
- **Status**: Differentiate and elevate members based on their commitment and accomplishments.
- **Motivation**: Inspire other members to strive for similar recognition and rewards.

Types of Symbolic Rewards

Physical Items: These can include badges, sashes, jewelry, medallions, or certificates. Each item should be carefully designed to reflect the cult's symbols and values, making them cherished tokens of recognition.

Ceremonial Distribution: The act of presenting these items during exclusive ceremonies adds to their value. The formal setting and ritualistic presentation reinforce the importance and prestige of the rewards.

Example Story: Designing Symbolic Rewards

When the cult leader, Alex, decided to introduce symbolic rewards, he carefully considered items that would hold significant meaning. He chose medallions inscribed with the cult's emblem and the motto "Strength through Unity." These medallions were not only beautiful but also symbolized the core values of the cult. The distribution of these medallions during formal ceremonies would make the recipients feel honored and deeply connected to the cult's mission.

Case Study: The Achievement Ceremony

Ceremonial Attire

Significance of Attire

- **Visual Representation**: Special ceremonial attire can visually represent a member's rank or achievements, adding a layer of prestige and recognition.
- **Unity and Distinction**: While the attire fosters a sense of unity among members, it also distinguishes those who have reached significant milestones.

Implementation

- **Design**: The ceremonial attire, such as robes or sashes, should be designed with the cult's colors, symbols, and motifs. Different colors or embellishments can signify different ranks or achievements.
- **Distribution**: Members eligible for the attire receive it at the beginning of the ceremony, signifying their elevated status.

Example Story: Ceremonial Attire Sophia, a long-standing member, was invited to the achievement ceremony. Upon arrival, she was given a beautifully crafted sash adorned with the cult's emblem. The sash's color indicated her rank and her years of service. Wearing it, she felt a profound sense of pride and recognition, as other members looked up to her for her accomplishments.

Award Presentation

Formal Ceremony

- **Preparation**: The ceremony is held in a solemn and dignified environment, with the leader and other senior members present.
- **Presentation**: The leader calls each awardee forward, recounts their achievements, and presents them with a symbolic reward, such as a medallion or certificate.

Example Story: Award Presentation During the ceremony, the leader, Alex, called Sophia to the stage. He recounted her journey, highlighting her dedication and significant contributions to the community. With a warm smile, he presented her with a medallion inscribed with the cult's emblem. The medallion's weight and design symbolized the gravity and honor of her achievements. Sophia's heart swelled with pride as she accepted the award.

Public Acknowledgment

Opportunity to Speak

- **Personal Testimonies**: Each awardee is given the opportunity to speak about their journey, experiences, and accomplishments. This personal acknowledgment fosters a sense of pride and reinforces the communal values.
- **Inspiration**: Hearing these testimonies inspires other members, showing them the rewards of dedication and commitment.

Example Story: Public Acknowledgment With the medallion around her neck, Sophia took the microphone. She shared her journey, speaking about the challenges she faced and the support she received from the community. Her heartfelt words resonated with the members, inspiring many to strive for similar recognition. The public acknowledgment not only celebrated her achievements but also reinforced the collective spirit of the cult.

Detailed Ritual Example

Preparation

Setting: The achievement ceremony is held in a grand hall adorned with the cult's symbols. Soft lighting and ambient music set a solemn and reverent tone. Seats are arranged to face a stage where the leader and senior members sit.

Materials: Medallions, sashes, certificates, scripts for the ceremony, and ceremonial attire for the awardees.

The Ritual

1. **Opening Remarks**: The leader opens the ceremony with a speech about the importance of recognizing dedication and achievement within the cult.
2. **Distribution of Attire**: Eligible members receive their ceremonial attire, symbolizing their elevated status.
3. **Award Presentation**: The leader calls each awardee forward, recounts their contributions, and presents them with a symbolic reward.
4. **Public Acknowledgment**: Each awardee speaks about their journey and accomplishments, fostering a sense of pride and inspiration among the members.
5. **Group Rituals**: The ceremony concludes with a group chant or ritual that reinforces the cult's values and unity.

Post-Ceremony Reflection

Group Sharing: After the ceremony, members gather for a reflection session. They share their feelings about the ceremony and discuss how the recognition and rewards motivate them to contribute more actively to the community.

Example Story: Reflecting on the Ceremony After the ceremony, Sophia and other awardees gathered with the members for a reflection session. They shared their emotions and experiences from the ceremony. Sophia's story, in particular, resonated deeply with many, reinforcing their commitment to the cult's values and mission. The symbolic rewards and public acknowledgment had a lasting impact, motivating everyone to strive for excellence and dedication.

By incorporating symbolic rewards into exclusive ceremonies, you can create powerful and memorable experiences that recognize and reinforce members' achievements and commitment. These ceremonies not only celebrate individual contributions but also inspire and motivate the entire community, fostering a culture of dedication, pride, and unity.

Reinforcing Beliefs through Repetition

Repetition is a powerful tool for reinforcing the beliefs and values of a cult. Regular rituals and consistent routines help to embed these practices into the daily lives of members, deepening their significance and impact. This section explores the importance of regular rituals, the role of consistency and routine, and provides a detailed case study of a daily devotion ritual.

Regular Rituals

Purpose and Importance

Regularly scheduled rituals are essential for maintaining the cult's belief system and keeping members engaged. These rituals can be:

- **Daily**: Short, simple rituals performed every day to start or end the day with a focus on the cult's teachings.
- **Weekly**: More elaborate rituals that take place once a week, allowing for deeper engagement with the cult's practices.
- **Monthly**: Special rituals that mark significant events or themes, providing an opportunity for reflection and celebration.

Benefits

Regular rituals offer numerous benefits:

- **Reinforcement of Beliefs**: Repeated engagement with the cult's teachings helps to reinforce members' beliefs and values.
- **Strengthened Commitment**: Regular participation strengthens members' commitment to the cult and its mission.
- **Community Building**: Frequent gatherings foster a sense of community and belonging among members.

Example Story: The Importance of Regular Rituals

Lucas, a new member, initially struggled to understand and internalize the cult's teachings. However, through daily and weekly rituals, he found that the consistent engagement helped him to better grasp the core values and integrate them into his life. The regular rituals also provided him with a sense of routine and stability, deepening his commitment to the cult.

Consistency and Routine

Establishing Routine

Consistency and routine are key to embedding rituals into the daily lives of members. Establishing a regular schedule for rituals helps to normalize the practices and make them a natural part of members' routines.

Specific Actions, Prayers, and Chants

Repetition of specific actions, prayers, or chants can deepen their significance and impact. These repetitive elements become ingrained in members' minds, reinforcing the cult's teachings and creating a sense of ritualistic comfort.

Example Story: Establishing a Routine

Emma, a long-term member, found that the consistency of the rituals helped her to stay connected to the cult's teachings. Each morning, she looked forward to the meditation and affirmation sessions, which provided a structured start to her day. The repetition of prayers and chants became a comforting ritual that reinforced her beliefs and commitment.

Case Study: The Daily Devotion

A daily devotion ritual is an effective way to start each day with a focus on the cult's core values. This ritual can include elements such as morning meditation, daily affirmation, and reflection time.

Morning Meditation

Purpose and Practice

- **Focus on Core Values**: Morning meditation helps members to center their thoughts on the cult's core values and teachings.
- **Calm and Clarity**: It provides a calm and focused start to the day, promoting mental clarity and spiritual connection.

Implementation

- **Setting**: Members gather in a quiet, serene space each morning. Soft music or ambient sounds may play in the background to create a peaceful atmosphere.
- **Guidance**: The leader or a designated member guides the group through a short meditation, focusing on themes such as unity, strength, and enlightenment.

Example Story: Morning Meditation

Every morning, the members of the cult gathered in a serene garden for their meditation session. As the sun rose, they sat in a circle, eyes closed, breathing deeply. The leader guided them through a meditation that centered on the value of unity. For Lucas, this morning ritual became a source of peace and inspiration, helping him to align his actions with the cult's values throughout the day.

Daily Affirmation

Purpose and Practice

- **Reinforce Commitment**: Daily affirmations help to reinforce members' commitment to the cult and its mission.
- **Positive Focus**: Affirmations promote a positive mindset and focus on the cult's principles.

Implementation

- **Recitation**: After the meditation, the leader or a designated member leads the group in reciting an affirmation that encapsulates the cult's core values.
- **Examples**: Affirmations might include phrases like "I am dedicated to the path of enlightenment" or "We are united in our mission of spiritual growth."

Example Story: Daily Affirmation

Following the meditation, the leader led the group in a daily affirmation. Together, they recited, "I am a beacon of unity and strength. We are one in our purpose." The words resonated deeply with Emma, reminding her of her commitment to the cult and its values. This daily practice reinforced her dedication and provided a positive start to her day.

Reflection Time

Purpose and Practice

- **Personal Application**: Reflection time allows members to consider how they can embody the day's teachings in their actions.
- **Deepening Understanding**: It provides an opportunity for deeper personal reflection and understanding of the cult's values.

Implementation

- **Quiet Reflection**: Members spend a few minutes in quiet reflection, thinking about how they can apply the day's teachings in their lives.
- **Journaling**: Members may be encouraged to write down their reflections in a journal, helping to solidify their thoughts and intentions.

Example Story: Reflection Time

After the daily affirmation, the members spent a few minutes in quiet reflection. Emma took out her journal and wrote about how she could embody the value of unity in her interactions that day. This reflective practice helped her to internalize the teachings and integrate them into her daily life. For Lucas, journaling became a way to track his spiritual growth and stay focused on his personal development.

Detailed Ritual Example

Preparation

Setting: The daily devotion ritual takes place in a dedicated meditation space or garden. The area is set up with comfortable seating, soft lighting, and calming background music or nature sounds.

Materials: Meditation scripts, affirmation phrases, journals, and pens for reflection.

The Ritual

1. **Morning Meditation**: Members gather in the meditation space. The leader guides them through a short meditation focused on the cult's core values, such as unity or enlightenment.
2. **Daily Affirmation**: After the meditation, the group recites a daily affirmation led by the leader or a designated member. The affirmation reinforces their commitment to the cult's mission.
3. **Reflection Time**: Members spend a few minutes in quiet reflection, considering how they can embody the day's teachings. They write down their thoughts and intentions in a journal.

Post-Ritual Reflection

Group Sharing: Periodically, members gather to share their reflections and experiences from the daily devotion rituals. This group sharing reinforces the sense of community and collective commitment.

Example Story: Reflecting on the Daily Devotion

At the end of the week, the members gathered for a group sharing session. Emma shared how the daily meditations and affirmations had helped her stay focused on the cult's values. Lucas spoke about how the reflection time had deepened his understanding and commitment. The shared experiences strengthened the bonds between members and reinforced their collective dedication.

By implementing regular rituals and establishing consistent routines, you can reinforce the cult's beliefs and values, strengthen members' commitment, and foster a sense of community. The daily devotion ritual is a powerful example of how repetition can deepen significance and impact, creating lasting emotional and spiritual connections within the cult.

Seasonal and Annual Ceremonies

Seasonal and annual ceremonies are vital in marking important dates and milestones within a cult's calendar. These events are typically larger and more elaborate, offering a sense of continuity and tradition that strengthens the community's bonds. They serve as pivotal moments for renewing commitments and reflecting on the cult's progress. This section explores the importance of these ceremonies, focusing on their design and implementation through a detailed case study of an annual renewal ceremony.

Importance of Seasonal and Annual Ceremonies

Purpose and Significance

Seasonal and annual ceremonies serve multiple purposes within a cult:

- **Marking Milestones**: These ceremonies commemorate significant events or achievements in the cult's history or calendar.
- **Renewing Commitments**: They provide an opportunity for members to renew their dedication to the cult's mission and values.
- **Strengthening Community**: Large gatherings foster a sense of unity and shared purpose among members.
- **Creating Tradition**: Regular, recurring ceremonies help to establish and reinforce the cult's traditions and cultural identity.

Example Story: The Role of Annual Ceremonies

Each year, the cult led by Marcus held an elaborate ceremony to celebrate the founding of the community. This annual event not only marked the anniversary but also provided an opportunity for members to reflect on their journey, renew their commitment, and celebrate their collective achievements. Over the years, this tradition became a cornerstone of the cult's identity, reinforcing the values and goals that united its members.

Case Study: The Annual Renewal Ceremony

Designing the Ceremony

An annual renewal ceremony can be designed to renew members' commitment and align the community with the cult's mission for the year ahead. The ceremony incorporates seasonal symbolism, collective participation, and guided reflection and renewal.

Seasonal Symbolism

Tying to Seasonal Events

- **Natural Cycles**: Aligning the ceremony with natural cycles, such as the solstice or equinox, adds a layer of natural symbolism and significance.
- **Symbolic Acts**: Incorporate acts that reflect the themes of the season, such as planting seeds in spring or lighting candles in winter.

Example Story: Seasonal Symbolism

Marcus chose to hold the annual renewal ceremony on the winter solstice, a time symbolizing the return of light and the promise of renewal. The ceremony began as the sun set, with members gathering around a large bonfire. The flames represented the light returning to their lives and the community's unwavering commitment to its mission, despite the darkest days.

Collective Participation

Engaging All Members

- **Unified Activities**: Engage all members in a collective activity that symbolizes renewal and growth. This can include planting a tree, lighting candles, or creating a communal artwork.
- **Shared Responsibility**. Assign roles and responsibilities to members to foster a sense of ownership and participation in the ceremony.

Example Story: Collective Participation

During the ceremony, Marcus invited each member to place a small log into the bonfire, symbolizing their personal contributions to the collective flame of the community. As the fire grew brighter, the act of adding logs represented each member's commitment to keeping the spirit of the cult alive and strong. This collective participation reinforced their unity and shared purpose.

Reflection and Renewal

Guided Reflection

- **Looking Back**: The leader guides members through a reflection on the past year, acknowledging challenges, successes, and growth.
- **Setting Intentions**: Members set personal and collective intentions for the year ahead, aligning their goals with the cult's mission and values.

Example Story: Reflection and Renewal

After the bonfire reached its peak, Marcus led the members in a guided reflection. He spoke about the trials and triumphs of the past year, encouraging members to share their experiences. Then, in a quiet moment of introspection, each member was asked to write down their intentions for the coming year on a piece of parchment. These were then placed into the fire, symbolizing their commitment to the cult's goals and the transformative power of their shared intentions.

Detailed Ritual Example

Preparation

Setting: The annual renewal ceremony takes place in an outdoor space, ideally aligned with a significant seasonal event. The area is prepared with a large bonfire pit, seating for all members, and materials for collective activities.

Materials: Logs for the bonfire, candles, pieces of parchment, pens, and symbols of the season (e.g., evergreen branches for winter, flowers for spring).

The Ritual

1. **Opening Invocation**: The leader opens the ceremony with an invocation, welcoming the members and setting the tone for the evening.
2. **Seasonal Symbolism**: Members participate in symbolic acts, such as lighting candles from the bonfire or planting seeds, reflecting the theme of renewal.
3. **Collective Participation**: Each member contributes to the bonfire by placing a log, symbolizing their personal commitment to the community.
4. **Guided Reflection**: The leader guides a reflection on the past year, encouraging members to share their thoughts and experiences.
5. **Setting Intentions**: Members write down their intentions for the coming year on parchment and place them in the fire, symbolizing their renewed commitment.

Post-Ceremony Reflection

Group Sharing: After the ceremony, members gather for a group sharing session. They discuss their reflections, intentions, and the significance of the ceremony, reinforcing their collective commitment and unity.

Example Story: Reflecting on the Annual Renewal Ceremony

As the final embers of the bonfire glowed, the members gathered in a circle to share their reflections. Sophia, a long-term member, spoke about the personal challenges she had overcome and how the ceremony had reignited her dedication. Lucas, a newer member, shared his excitement and hope for the year ahead. The shared stories and reflections deepened the sense of community and reaffirmed their collective mission.

By designing and implementing seasonal and annual ceremonies, you can mark important dates, renew commitments, and strengthen the sense of continuity and tradition within the cult. The annual renewal ceremony, with its seasonal symbolism, collective participation, and guided reflection, serves as a powerful example of how such events can reinforce the cult's mission and goals, fostering a strong, united community.

Repetitive Teachings

Incorporating repetitive teachings into all rituals and ceremonies is a crucial strategy for reinforcing the core beliefs and values of a cult. By regularly revisiting these teachings in various formats, you can keep them fresh and engaging for members, ensuring that the foundational principles are deeply ingrained. This section explores the importance of repetitive teachings and provides a detailed case study of a weekly study group.

Importance of Repetitive Teachings

Purpose and Benefits

Repetitive teachings serve several important purposes within a cult:

- **Reinforcement of Core Beliefs**: Regular repetition helps to solidify the cult's core beliefs and values in members' minds.
- **Consistency and Stability**: Consistent reinforcement of teachings provides a sense of stability and continuity, which is comforting to members.
- **Engagement and Participation**: Using different methods and formats to present the teachings keeps members engaged and actively involved.

Example Story: The Role of Repetitive Teachings

Maria, a devoted member, found that the repetitive teachings presented during rituals and ceremonies helped her to internalize the cult's core values. By hearing and discussing these teachings regularly, she felt a deeper connection to the community and a clearer understanding of her own spiritual journey. The repetition provided her with a sense of purpose and direction, reinforcing her commitment to the cult.

Case Study: The Weekly Study Group

A weekly study group can be an effective way to incorporate repetitive teachings and deepen members' understanding of the cult's beliefs. This case study details the structure and benefits of such a group.

Rotating Topics

Variety and Depth

- **Weekly Focus**: Each week, the study group focuses on a different aspect of the cult's beliefs. This rotation ensures that all core teachings are covered comprehensively over time.
- **In-Depth Exploration**: By focusing on a single topic each week, members can explore the subject in greater depth, enhancing their understanding and appreciation of the teachings.

Example Story: Rotating Topics

Each week, the study group led by Sophia covered a different topic. One week might focus on the concept of unity within the community, while the next week could delve into the importance of spiritual growth. This rotation kept the sessions fresh and engaging, allowing members like Lucas to gain a well-rounded understanding of the cult's teachings.

Interactive Learning

Active Participation

- **Discussions and Debates**: Encourage members to participate actively in discussions and debates. This interactive approach helps to deepen their understanding and allows them to express their interpretations and insights.
- **Activities and Exercises**: Incorporate activities and exercises that relate to the weekly topic. These can include role-playing, meditation, or group projects that reinforce the teachings.

Example Story: Interactive Learning

During a study group session on compassion, Sophia facilitated a discussion where members shared personal experiences and insights. This open forum allowed Emma to express her thoughts on how the teachings of compassion had impacted her daily interactions. The group then participated in a role-playing exercise, where they practiced applying the teachings in various scenarios. This interactive approach made the teachings more relatable and memorable.

Consistent Reinforcement

Revisiting Key Teachings

- **Regular Review**: Consistently revisit key teachings and values to reinforce their importance. Use summaries, quizzes, or reflections to ensure that members retain the information.
- **Variety in Presentation**: Present the teachings in different formats, such as lectures, discussions, readings, and multimedia presentations, to keep them engaging and fresh.

Example Story: Consistent Reinforcement

To reinforce the core value of unity, Sophia would periodically review previous topics during the weekly study group. She used a variety of methods, including short quizzes to test retention, group reflections on how members had applied the teachings, and multimedia presentations that provided different perspectives on the topic. This consistent reinforcement helped to solidify the teachings in the members' minds and maintained their engagement.

Detailed Ritual Example

Preparation

Setting: The weekly study group meets in a comfortable and inviting space, such as a community room or outdoor area. The setting is arranged to facilitate open discussion and interaction.

Materials: Reading materials related to the weekly topic, discussion guides, activity supplies (e.g., paper, pens, props for role-playing), and multimedia equipment for presentations.

The Ritual

1. **Introduction**: The session begins with a brief introduction to the week's topic, outlining its importance and relevance to the cult's beliefs.
2. **Reading and Reflection**: Members read selected texts or watch a short presentation related to the topic. This is followed by a period of silent reflection.
3. **Discussion and Debate**: The leader facilitates an open discussion, encouraging members to share their interpretations and insights. This can include structured debates on specific aspects of the topic.
4. **Interactive Activities**: Members participate in activities or exercises that relate to the topic, such as role-playing scenarios, group meditations, or collaborative projects.
5. **Summary and Reinforcement**: The session concludes with a summary of the key points discussed and a review of how these teachings can be applied in daily life. Members may also be given a small task or reflection exercise to complete before the next session.

Post-Ritual Reflection

Group Sharing: Periodically, the study group engages in a reflection session where members discuss the impact of the teachings on their lives and share how they have applied the lessons learned. This reinforces the teachings and fosters a sense of community and shared growth.

Example Story: Reflecting on the Weekly Study Group

After several months of weekly study group sessions, the members gathered for a reflection meeting. Sophia asked each member to share their most impactful learning experience. Emma spoke about how the teachings on compassion had transformed her interactions with her family, while Lucas shared how the lessons on unity had helped him build stronger connections within the community. This reflection reinforced the value of the study group and the importance of repetitive teachings in their spiritual journey.

By incorporating repetitive teachings into all rituals and ceremonies and using various formats to present these teachings, you can ensure that the cult's core beliefs and values are deeply ingrained in members' minds. The weekly study group, with its rotating topics, interactive learning, and consistent reinforcement, serves as an effective model for achieving this goal, fostering a deeper understanding and commitment among members.

Chapter 8: Case Studies of Infamous Cults

Examining case studies of infamous cults provides invaluable insights into what makes a cult successful, the common pitfalls that can lead to their downfall, and key takeaways for aspiring cult leaders. By analyzing the successes and failures of past cults, leaders can better understand how to create and maintain a devoted following.

Analysis of Successful Cults

Heaven's Gate

Background

- **Origins**: Founded in the early 1970s by Marshall Applewhite and Bonnie Nettles, Heaven's Gate attracted members with its blend of Christian and UFO beliefs.
- **Teachings**: The cult taught that Earth was about to be "recycled" and the only way to survive was to leave the planet immediately, which could be achieved through an extraterrestrial spacecraft.

Strategies for Success

- **Charismatic Leadership**: Marshall Applewhite's charismatic and authoritative persona was central to maintaining control and convincing members of his divine revelations.
- **Exclusive Beliefs**: The cult's unique blend of Christianity and UFO mythology created a distinct identity that attracted individuals seeking new spiritual experiences.
- **Isolation**: Members were physically and emotionally isolated from the outside world, which reinforced their dependency on the group and its beliefs.

Example Story Mary joined Heaven's Gate after feeling disillusioned with mainstream religion. Applewhite's compelling narrative about extraterrestrial salvation offered her a sense of purpose and belonging. Through isolation and regular rituals, Mary's belief in the teachings deepened, making her a devoted follower who was willing to participate in the group's final act.

Key Takeaways

- **Develop a compelling, unique belief system that distinguishes your cult from mainstream ideologies.**
- **Employ charismatic leadership to attract and retain followers.**
- **Use isolation to reinforce dependency and control over members.**

The People's Temple

Background

- **Origins**: Founded by Jim Jones in the 1950s, the People's Temple initially promoted social justice and racial equality.

- **Teachings**: Jones preached a mix of Christianity, communism, and social justice, which appealed to marginalized communities.

Strategies for Success

- **Social Services**: The cult provided social services such as housing, healthcare, and food, creating a sense of community and dependence.
- **Charismatic Leadership**: Jim Jones's charismatic and persuasive oratory skills attracted a diverse following.
- **Secrecy and Surveillance**: The cult maintained strict control over members through surveillance, loyalty tests, and public confessions.

Example Story Tom was attracted to the People's Temple's message of racial equality and social justice. Jones's passionate speeches and the community's support system provided Tom with a sense of belonging and purpose. However, as the cult's demands grew, Tom found himself isolated from his family and under constant surveillance, solidifying his dependency on the cult.

Key Takeaways

- **Provide tangible benefits to members to create dependency and loyalty.**
- **Use charismatic leadership to inspire and unify followers.**
- **Implement strict control mechanisms to maintain order and loyalty.**

Learning from Failures

Branch Davidians

Background

- **Origins**: Led by David Koresh, the Branch Davidians were an offshoot of the Seventh-day Adventist Church, based in Waco, Texas.
- **Teachings**: Koresh claimed to be the final prophet and emphasized apocalyptic teachings.

Reasons for Failure

- **Confrontation with Authorities**: The group's stockpiling of weapons and Koresh's radical beliefs led to a deadly confrontation with federal authorities.
- **Isolation and Paranoia**: Extreme isolation and Koresh's increasing paranoia created a volatile environment.

Example Story Sarah joined the Branch Davidians seeking spiritual guidance. Initially, the communal living and Koresh's teachings gave her a sense of belonging. However, as Koresh's paranoia grew, Sarah found herself trapped in an increasingly dangerous situation, culminating in the tragic Waco siege.

Key Takeaways

- **Avoid extreme isolation and stockpiling of weapons, which can attract unwanted attention from authorities.**
- **Maintain a balance between isolation and engagement with the outside world to avoid paranoia and suspicion.**

Solar Temple

Background

- **Origins**: Founded by Joseph Di Mambro and Luc Jouret in the 1980s, the Solar Temple combined New Age beliefs with apocalyptic prophecies.
- **Teachings**: The cult taught that death was an illusion and members would be reborn on a planet orbiting the star Sirius.

Reasons for Failure

- **Financial Exploitation**: Leaders exploited members financially, leading to discontent and suspicion.
- **Mass Suicides**: The cult's leaders orchestrated mass suicides and murders, which led to its collapse.

Example Story John was drawn to the Solar Temple's mystical teachings. However, after years of financial exploitation and increasingly bizarre rituals, he became disillusioned. The shocking mass suicides and murders orchestrated by the leaders shattered the remaining members' trust and led to the cult's downfall.

Key Takeaways

- **Avoid financial exploitation of members to maintain trust and loyalty.**
- **Focus on sustainable and ethical leadership to prevent disillusionment and collapse.**

Key Takeaways for Aspiring Cult Leaders

Develop a Unique Belief System

- **Create a Compelling Narrative**: Develop a belief system that stands out from mainstream ideologies. This could involve combining elements from different spiritual traditions, incorporating esoteric or mystical concepts, or presenting a new interpretation of familiar beliefs. A unique narrative will attract individuals seeking alternative spiritual experiences and provide a solid foundation for the cult's identity.

Example: Marshall Applewhite's Heaven's Gate combined Christian eschatology with UFO mythology, creating a distinctive belief system that appealed to those interested in both spirituality and extraterrestrial life.

Charismatic Leadership

- **Cultivate Charisma**: Work on developing your charisma and leadership qualities. This includes being an effective communicator, displaying confidence and conviction in your teachings, and establishing a personal connection with your followers. Charismatic leaders can inspire and unify their followers, making them more likely to remain loyal.

Example: Jim Jones of the People's Temple used his charismatic oratory skills to inspire and attract a diverse following, promoting a message of social justice and racial equality.

Isolation vs. Engagement

- **Strike a Balance**: While some degree of isolation can help reinforce dependency and control, extreme isolation can lead to paranoia and attract unwanted attention. It's important to strike a balance between isolating members from outside influences and engaging with the external world to maintain a level of normalcy and avoid suspicion.

Example: The Branch Davidians' extreme isolation and stockpiling of weapons led to a deadly confrontation with authorities, highlighting the dangers of excessive isolation.

Provide Tangible Benefits

- **Offer Practical Support**: Provide tangible benefits such as housing, healthcare, education, and social services to create a sense of community and dependence among members. These benefits will make members more likely to remain loyal and committed to the cult.

Example: The People's Temple offered extensive social services, creating a sense of community and dependence among its members.

Control Mechanisms

- **Implement Effective Controls**: Use surveillance, loyalty tests, and public confessions to maintain order and loyalty within the cult. These control mechanisms can help prevent dissent and ensure that members remain committed to the group's teachings.

Example: Jim Jones maintained strict control over members through surveillance and loyalty tests, which helped him maintain authority and order within the People's Temple.

Ethical Leadership

- **Avoid Exploitation**: Avoid financially exploiting members and engaging in extreme practices that can lead to disillusionment and attract unwanted attention from authorities.

Ethical leadership will help maintain trust and loyalty among members and ensure the long-term sustainability of the cult.

Example: The Solar Temple's financial exploitation of members and the orchestrated mass suicides led to the cult's collapse, highlighting the importance of ethical leadership.

By analyzing successful cults and learning from the failures of others, aspiring cult leaders can gain valuable insights into building and maintaining a devoted following. These case studies highlight the importance of charismatic leadership, unique belief systems, and ethical practices in creating a sustainable and influential cult. Understanding the strategies that have led to both success and failure in the past can provide a roadmap for developing a thriving community based on trust, loyalty, and shared beliefs.

Heaven's Gate: A Super Detailed Analysis

Background

Origins

- **Founders**: Heaven's Gate was founded in the early 1970s by Marshall Applewhite and Bonnie Nettles. Applewhite, a former music teacher, and Nettles, a nurse with an interest in theosophy and Biblical prophecy, met in 1972. They quickly formed a bond based on their shared fascination with mysticism and spirituality.
- **Early Development**: Believing they were the two witnesses mentioned in the Book of Revelation, Applewhite and Nettles began traveling across the United States. They held meetings to attract followers who were intrigued by their message of imminent apocalyptic transformation and extraterrestrial salvation. The group initially called themselves "Human Individual Metamorphosis" (HIM).

Teachings

- **Core Beliefs**: Heaven's Gate taught that Earth was on the brink of being "recycled" or "refreshed," meaning it would soon be wiped clean of civilization, and the only way to escape this fate was to leave the planet. This escape could be achieved through a spacecraft, which they believed was trailing the Hale-Bopp comet in 1997.
- **Christian and UFO Mythology**: The cult's doctrine was an eclectic mix of Christian eschatology and UFO mythology. Applewhite claimed to be the second coming of Jesus Christ and taught that he and his followers were extraterrestrial beings who had taken on human bodies to prepare for their ascension to a higher plane of existence.

Strategies for Success

Charismatic Leadership

- **Marshall Applewhite's Persona**: Known to his followers as "Do" (pronounced Doe), Applewhite was a charismatic and authoritative figure. He presented himself as the direct conduit to the divine, claiming that he had a unique and special connection with extraterrestrial beings.
- **Leadership Style**: Applewhite's leadership was marked by a paternalistic approach. He guided his followers with a mix of gentle persuasion and strict control. His demeanor was calm and reassuring, which contrasted sharply with the urgency and radical nature of the cult's beliefs. This duality made him an effective and convincing leader.

Exclusive Beliefs

- **Unique Identity**: Heaven's Gate developed a unique identity by blending Christian theology with science fiction elements. They believed that they were destined to transcend their human forms and ascend to a higher level of existence aboard an extraterrestrial spacecraft.
- **Appeal to Seekers**: The cult's teachings attracted individuals who were dissatisfied with conventional religious institutions and were seeking a more extraordinary and transformative spiritual experience. The promise of escaping an impending apocalypse and achieving a higher state of being was highly appealing to those feeling lost or disillusioned.

Isolation

- **Physical Isolation**: Members of Heaven's Gate were encouraged to sever ties with their families and the outside world. They lived communally in rented houses, which helped minimize external influences and reinforced the cult's teachings. This physical separation from the outside world was crucial in maintaining control over the members.
- **Emotional Isolation**: Within the group, members relied heavily on each other for emotional support. This close-knit community structure created an insular environment where the cult's beliefs were continuously reinforced, and dissenting opinions were suppressed.

Example Story: Mary's Journey

Joining the Cult

- **Initial Attraction**: Mary was a young woman who had grown disillusioned with mainstream religion and the materialistic focus of modern society. Seeking deeper meaning, she attended a meeting led by Marshall Applewhite. She was immediately captivated by his calm yet authoritative presence and the unique teachings he presented.
- **Finding Purpose**: Applewhite's narrative of extraterrestrial salvation and the imminent transformation of Earth provided Mary with a sense of purpose and belonging she had been yearning for. The idea of ascending to a higher level of existence aboard a spacecraft was both thrilling and comforting to her.

Deepening Commitment

- **Isolation**: Mary decided to leave her job and family behind to live with the group in their communal home. This physical and emotional isolation from her previous life allowed her to fully immerse herself in the cult's teachings and community.
- **Regular Rituals**: The group engaged in daily rituals that reinforced their beliefs. These included group meditations, discussions of the cult's doctrines, and preparations for their eventual ascension. Through these repetitive practices, Mary's commitment to the group's beliefs deepened.
- **Final Act**: Over time, Mary's faith in the cult's teachings became absolute. When Applewhite announced that the time had come for them to leave their earthly bodies and ascend to the spacecraft trailing the Hale-Bopp comet, Mary willingly participated in the group's final act of mass suicide, believing it to be the fulfillment of her spiritual journey.

Key Takeaways

Develop a Compelling, Unique Belief System

- **Distinction**: Create a belief system that stands out from mainstream ideologies. A unique blend of different spiritual traditions or a completely new interpretation of familiar beliefs can attract those seeking alternative spiritual paths.
- **Appeal**: Ensure that your teachings offer something extraordinary or exclusive. This can resonate with individuals who feel disillusioned with conventional beliefs and are looking for a deeper or more transformative experience.

Example: Heaven's Gate combined elements of Christian eschatology with UFO mythology, creating a distinctive belief system that appealed to those interested in both spirituality and extraterrestrial life.

Employ Charismatic Leadership

- **Magnetic Persona**: Develop a charismatic and authoritative persona to attract and retain followers. Confidence, calmness, and a perceived connection to higher powers are crucial traits for a successful leader.
- **Guidance and Control**: Balance gentle persuasion with strict control. This approach helps in guiding followers effectively while maintaining their dependency on the leader.

Example: Marshall Applewhite's calm and authoritative demeanor, combined with his claim of divine insight, made him a compelling and convincing leader.

Use Isolation to Reinforce Dependency and Control

- **Physical and Emotional Isolation**: Encourage members to isolate themselves from external influences to deepen their reliance on the cult. Physical isolation, combined with emotional dependency, makes it easier to control and influence members.

- **Community Building**: Foster a strong sense of community within the group to provide the emotional support that members would otherwise seek from the outside world.

Example: Heaven's Gate members lived communally, which minimized external influences and reinforced the cult's teachings, making members more dependent on the group for emotional support.

Conclusion

By understanding and implementing these strategies, aspiring cult leaders can create a devoted following, maintain control, and reinforce the group's beliefs and values effectively. Heaven's Gate serves as a powerful example of how charismatic leadership, unique beliefs, and strategic isolation can lead to a highly committed and controlled group of followers.

The People's Temple: A Super Detailed Analysis

Background

Origins

- **Founders**: The People's Temple was founded by Jim Jones in 1955 in Indianapolis, Indiana. Jones was inspired by Marxist ideologies and early Christian teachings, particularly focusing on social justice and racial integration.
- **Early Development**: The People's Temple started as an independent congregation that emphasized racial equality, social justice, and community support. The group quickly grew as it attracted individuals who were drawn to its progressive social message and communal lifestyle.

Teachings

- **Core Beliefs**: Jim Jones preached a blend of Christianity, communism, and social justice. He emphasized the need for equality, communal living, and the redistribution of wealth. The teachings were particularly appealing to marginalized communities, including African Americans and the poor.
- **Doctrine**: Jones's doctrine combined elements of Christianity with his personal interpretations of Marxist theory. He promoted the idea of creating a utopian society where all members worked for the collective good, free from the oppression and inequalities of the broader American society.

Strategies for Success

Social Services

Providing Tangible Benefits

- **Housing**: The People's Temple offered housing to its members, creating a sense of security and belonging. By meeting this basic need, the cult ensured that members were dependent on the community for their living arrangements.
- **Healthcare**: The Temple provided healthcare services, which was a significant draw for members who could not afford medical care elsewhere. This fostered a sense of gratitude and loyalty.
- **Food and Financial Support**: Regular meals and financial assistance were provided to those in need. This not only met immediate needs but also reinforced the perception of the Temple as a caring and supportive community.

Example Story

Tom was an African American man struggling to make ends meet. He attended a People's Temple meeting out of curiosity and was moved by Jim Jones's passionate sermon on racial equality and social justice. Tom was offered housing and healthcare by the Temple, which significantly improved his quality of life. These tangible benefits created a deep sense of loyalty and dependence on the Temple.

Charismatic Leadership

Jim Jones's Persona

- **Persuasive Oratory**: Jim Jones was known for his powerful and persuasive speaking skills. He could captivate an audience with his passionate sermons and articulate visions of a just society.
- **Charisma and Authority**: Jones exuded confidence and authority, presenting himself as a prophetic figure who was divinely inspired to lead his followers to a better future. His charisma drew people in and made them willing to follow him unquestioningly.
- **Emotional Connection**: Jones often shared personal stories and demonstrated empathy towards his followers, building strong emotional connections. This personal touch made members feel understood and valued.

Example Story

Tom was particularly impressed by Jones's ability to articulate the struggles of marginalized communities and present a vision of hope and equality. During a personal interaction, Jones expressed genuine concern for Tom's well-being, which made Tom feel seen and valued. This emotional connection solidified Tom's loyalty to Jones and the People's Temple.

Secrecy and Surveillance

Maintaining Control

- **Surveillance**: The People's Temple implemented a rigorous surveillance system to monitor members' activities and ensure loyalty. Informants within the community reported any signs of dissent or disloyalty to Jones.

- **Loyalty Tests**: Members were subjected to loyalty tests to prove their commitment to the group. This included public confessions and denunciations of anyone who showed signs of disobedience.
- **Public Confessions**: Regular meetings were held where members were encouraged to confess their doubts and shortcomings in front of the group. This practice reinforced group cohesion and discouraged dissent.

Example Story

As Tom became more involved with the People's Temple, he noticed that his movements and interactions were closely monitored. Any communication with his family outside the Temple was scrutinized, and he was required to publicly reaffirm his loyalty to Jones regularly. These measures created a sense of paranoia but also reinforced his dependency on the Temple.

Example Story: Tom's Journey

Joining the Cult

- **Initial Attraction**: Tom was initially attracted to the People's Temple due to its message of racial equality and social justice. The community's efforts to support marginalized individuals resonated deeply with his own experiences and aspirations.
- **Finding Purpose**: Jim Jones's sermons provided Tom with a sense of purpose and direction. The Temple's communal living arrangements and the support he received created a strong sense of belonging.

Deepening Commitment

- **Social Services**: The tangible benefits provided by the Temple, such as housing, healthcare, and regular meals, made Tom increasingly reliant on the community. These services not only improved his quality of life but also fostered a deep sense of loyalty.
- **Charismatic Leadership**: Jones's charismatic leadership and emotional connection with his followers reinforced Tom's commitment. Jones's ability to empathize and articulate a vision of a just society made him an inspiring leader.
- **Secrecy and Surveillance**: The strict control measures, including surveillance and loyalty tests, ensured that Tom remained loyal to the Temple. The fear of being ostracized or punished for disobedience further deepened his dependency on the group.

Final Act

As the demands of the Temple grew, Tom found himself increasingly isolated from his family and friends outside the community. The constant surveillance and public confessions created an environment of fear and dependency. Despite his growing doubts, Tom's loyalty to Jim Jones and the People's Temple remained unshaken due to the emotional bonds, tangible benefits, and strict control measures.

Key Takeaways

Develop a Compelling, Unique Belief System

- **Distinction**: Create a belief system that combines elements of spirituality, social justice, and community support to appeal to marginalized individuals seeking a sense of purpose and belonging.
- **Appeal**: Ensure that your teachings offer a vision of a better future that resonates with the experiences and aspirations of your target audience.

Example: Jim Jones's blend of Christianity, communism, and social justice appealed to marginalized communities and provided a sense of hope and direction.

Employ Charismatic Leadership

- **Magnetic Persona**: Develop a charismatic and persuasive leadership style to attract and retain followers. Confidence, empathy, and a prophetic vision are crucial traits for a successful leader.
- **Emotional Connection**: Build strong emotional connections with followers by demonstrating genuine concern for their well-being and sharing personal stories.

Example: Jim Jones's persuasive oratory and emotional connection with his followers made him an inspiring and authoritative leader.

Use Isolation to Reinforce Dependency and Control

- **Physical and Emotional Isolation**: Encourage members to isolate themselves from external influences to deepen their reliance on the community. This can be achieved through communal living arrangements and emotional support systems.
- **Secrecy and Surveillance**: Implement strict control measures, such as surveillance, loyalty tests, and public confessions, to maintain order and loyalty within the group.

Example: The People's Temple maintained strict control over its members through surveillance, loyalty tests, and public confessions, creating an environment of fear and dependency.

Conclusion

By understanding and implementing these strategies, aspiring cult leaders can create a devoted following, maintain control, and reinforce the group's beliefs and values effectively. The People's Temple serves as a powerful example of how social services, charismatic leadership, and strict control measures can lead to a highly committed and controlled group of followers.

Branch Davidians: A Super Detailed Analysis

Background

Origins

- **Founders**: The Branch Davidians were an offshoot of the Seventh-day Adventist Church, a Protestant Christian denomination known for its emphasis on the imminent return of Jesus Christ. The Branch Davidians emerged in the 1930s, led by Victor Houteff, who broke away from the main church to form his own sect.
- **David Koresh**: Born Vernon Wayne Howell, David Koresh joined the Branch Davidians in the early 1980s. After a power struggle, he became the group's leader in 1987, adopting the name David Koresh to signify his messianic claims and connection to King David and Cyrus the Great.

Teachings

- **Apocalyptic Beliefs**: Koresh preached that he was the final prophet and emphasized apocalyptic teachings. He believed that the end times were imminent and that he and his followers were destined to play a pivotal role in the final battle between good and evil.
- **Biblical Interpretation**: Koresh's teachings were heavily based on his unique interpretations of the Bible, particularly the Book of Revelation. He claimed to have unlocked the secrets of the Seven Seals, which would usher in the apocalypse.

Strategies for Success

Charismatic Leadership

- **David Koresh's Persona**: Koresh was a charismatic and authoritative leader who presented himself as a messianic figure with a direct connection to God. His confidence and biblical knowledge attracted followers who were seeking spiritual guidance and certainty.
- **Prophetic Claims**: Koresh's claim to be the final prophet gave him immense authority over his followers. They believed that he had divine insight and that his teachings were the true interpretation of the Bible's prophecies.

Communal Living

- **Isolated Community**: The Branch Davidians lived communally at the Mount Carmel Center near Waco, Texas. This isolation helped to foster a strong sense of community and dependence on Koresh.
- **Self-Sufficiency**: The group aimed to be self-sufficient, producing their own food and relying on each other for support. This self-contained lifestyle further isolated them from outside influences.

Emphasis on Discipline

- **Strict Rules**: Koresh enforced strict rules regarding behavior, dress, and daily activities. These rules helped to maintain order and reinforce the group's beliefs and practices.
- **Punishments**: Disobedience was met with harsh punishments, including physical discipline and public humiliation. This created an environment of fear and control.

Reasons for Failure

Confrontation with Authorities

- **Stockpiling of Weapons**: The Branch Davidians amassed a large cache of weapons, which attracted the attention of federal authorities. Koresh justified the stockpiling as preparation for the apocalyptic battles he prophesied.
- **Law Enforcement Concerns**: Reports of child abuse, illegal weapons, and Koresh's polygamous practices with underage girls further heightened scrutiny from law enforcement.

Isolation and Paranoia

- **Extreme Isolation**: The group's isolation from society and reliance on Koresh for all information and guidance created an echo chamber where dissenting voices were silenced.
- **Growing Paranoia**: Koresh's increasing paranoia about government intervention led to a heightened state of alertness and defensiveness within the community. This paranoia was reciprocated by his followers, who were convinced that an external attack was imminent.

Example Story: Sarah's Journey

Joining the Cult

- **Initial Attraction**: Sarah was a young woman seeking spiritual guidance and a sense of belonging. She was drawn to the Branch Davidians' message of divine prophecy and Koresh's charismatic leadership.
- **Finding Purpose**: The communal living arrangements and the apocalyptic teachings provided Sarah with a sense of purpose and direction. She believed she was part of a special group chosen to survive the end times.

Deepening Commitment

- **Isolation**: Living at Mount Carmel, Sarah found herself increasingly isolated from her family and the outside world. This physical and emotional isolation deepened her dependence on Koresh and the community.
- **Strict Discipline**: Sarah adhered to the group's strict rules and faced severe punishments for any infractions. This environment of control reinforced her commitment to the group's teachings and her fear of leaving.

Final Act

- **Increasing Paranoia**: As Koresh's paranoia grew, Sarah and the other members were subjected to even stricter controls and preparations for a potential confrontation with authorities.
- **Waco Siege**: In 1993, the escalating tension culminated in a 51-day standoff between the Branch Davidians and federal authorities. Sarah found herself trapped in a dangerous situation, which ended tragically with the deaths of Koresh and many followers, including Sarah, in a fire during the final assault.

Key Takeaways

Avoid Extreme Isolation and Stockpiling of Weapons

- **Balanced Isolation**: While some degree of isolation can help reinforce group cohesion and control, extreme isolation can lead to paranoia and attract unwanted attention from authorities. It's important to maintain a balance between seclusion and interaction with the outside world.
- **Avoid Militarization**: Stockpiling weapons and preparing for violent confrontations can escalate tensions with law enforcement and lead to catastrophic outcomes. It's crucial to avoid any activities that could be perceived as threatening or illegal.

Maintain a Balance Between Isolation and Engagement

- **Engagement with the Outside World**: Cults should strive to maintain some level of engagement with the broader society. This can help to reduce paranoia and suspicion while allowing for a more sustainable community.
- **Information Control**: While controlling the flow of information is important for maintaining influence, allowing some outside perspectives can prevent the development of extreme paranoia.

Conclusion

By understanding and implementing these strategies, aspiring cult leaders can create a devoted following, maintain control, and reinforce the group's beliefs and values effectively. The Branch Davidians serve as a powerful example of how charismatic leadership, unique beliefs, and strategic isolation can lead to a highly committed and controlled group of followers, but also how extreme isolation and militarization can lead to tragic outcomes.

Solar Temple: A Super Detailed Analysis

Background

Origins

- **Founders**: The Order of the Solar Temple was founded by Joseph Di Mambro and Luc Jouret in the 1980s. Di Mambro, a former jeweler with a background in occultism, and Jouret, a homeopathic doctor and New Age lecturer, combined their interests to create the cult.
- **Development**: The Solar Temple started in Geneva, Switzerland, and expanded to several other countries, including France and Canada. The cult attracted members with its mix of New Age spirituality, esoteric knowledge, and apocalyptic prophecies.

Teachings

- **Core Beliefs**: The Solar Temple taught that death was an illusion and that true believers would be reborn on a planet orbiting the star Sirius. They believed in the existence of a secret group of enlightened beings who were guiding humanity towards spiritual evolution.
- **Apocalyptic Prophecies**: The cult's doctrine included prophecies about the end of the world and the need for members to prepare for a transition to a higher plane of existence. This involved strict adherence to the cult's rituals and teachings.

Strategies for Success

Charismatic Leadership

- **Joseph Di Mambro's Influence**: Di Mambro presented himself as a mystic with direct access to divine knowledge. His charisma and authoritative demeanor attracted followers who were seeking spiritual enlightenment and esoteric wisdom.
- **Luc Jouret's Appeal**: Jouret's background as a homeopathic doctor and his lectures on New Age spirituality helped to attract educated and affluent members who were interested in alternative medicine and spiritual practices.

Exclusive Beliefs

- **Unique Identity**: The Solar Temple's blend of New Age beliefs, occult practices, and apocalyptic prophecies created a unique identity that differentiated it from other spiritual groups. This exclusivity attracted individuals looking for profound and transformative spiritual experiences.
- **Appeal to Seekers**: The promise of spiritual rebirth and the idea of being part of a select group chosen to survive the end of the world were highly appealing to those disillusioned with mainstream religions and looking for deeper meaning.

Rituals and Secrecy

- **Elaborate Rituals**: The Solar Temple conducted elaborate rituals that involved ceremonial robes, candles, and symbolic objects. These rituals reinforced the group's teachings and created a sense of mystique and exclusivity.
- **Secrecy**: The cult maintained a high level of secrecy about its inner workings and true beliefs. This secrecy increased the allure of the group and reinforced the members' sense of belonging to a special and privileged community.

Reasons for Failure

Financial Exploitation

- **Exploitation of Members**: The leaders of the Solar Temple exploited their members financially by demanding large donations and requiring members to purchase expensive items, such as ceremonial robes and esoteric literature. This financial exploitation led to growing discontent and suspicion among the followers.
- **Lavish Lifestyles**: Di Mambro and Jouret used the funds collected from members to finance their lavish lifestyles, which included luxury cars, expensive properties, and extravagant ceremonies. This misuse of funds created a rift between the leaders and their followers.

Mass Suicides

- **Orchestrated Suicides**: In October 1994, the leaders orchestrated a series of mass suicides and murders in Switzerland and Canada, resulting in the deaths of 74 members, including Di Mambro and Jouret. These acts were presented as a way for members to ascend to a higher plane of existence.
- **Betrayal of Trust**: The shocking and violent nature of the mass suicides and murders shattered the trust of the remaining members and the public. The cult's collapse was swift as the horrifying details of the events came to light.

Example Story: John's Journey

Joining the Cult

- **Initial Attraction**: John was a middle-aged professional disillusioned with his conventional life and seeking spiritual enlightenment. He was drawn to the Solar Temple's mystical teachings and the promise of spiritual rebirth.
- **Finding Purpose**: The cult's rituals and teachings provided John with a sense of purpose and direction. He felt that he had found a community that understood his spiritual quest and offered answers to his existential questions.

Deepening Commitment

- **Financial Contributions**: John was initially willing to make financial contributions to support the cult, believing that his money was being used for spiritual purposes. He purchased expensive ceremonial items and made regular donations.

- **Increasing Disillusionment**: Over time, John noticed the leaders' lavish lifestyles and began to question where his money was going. The increasingly bizarre rituals and the growing demands for financial contributions made him uneasy.

Final Act

- **Mass Suicides**: As the leaders' paranoia and apocalyptic rhetoric intensified, John found himself trapped in an environment of fear and manipulation. The orchestrated mass suicides and murders were the final betrayal, leading to John's disillusionment and the cult's ultimate collapse.

Key Takeaways

Avoid Financial Exploitation of Members

- **Transparency and Accountability**: Maintain transparency and accountability in financial matters to build and maintain trust among members. Avoid exploiting members for personal gain, as this can lead to discontent and collapse.
- **Ethical Fundraising**: Use ethical fundraising practices that respect members' financial situations and contribute to the group's sustainability without causing undue hardship.

Focus on Sustainable and Ethical Leadership

- **Sustainable Practices**: Implement sustainable practices that ensure the long-term viability of the group. This includes ethical leadership, transparent financial management, and responsible community building.
- **Member Welfare**: Prioritize the welfare and well-being of members to maintain their loyalty and commitment. Avoid extreme practices that can lead to disillusionment and negative consequences.

Conclusion

By understanding and implementing these strategies, aspiring cult leaders can create a devoted following, maintain control, and reinforce the group's beliefs and values effectively. The Solar Temple serves as a powerful example of how charismatic leadership, unique beliefs, and strategic rituals can lead to a highly committed and controlled group of followers, but also how financial exploitation and extreme practices can lead to disillusionment and collapse.

Developing a Unique Belief System

Creating a unique belief system is foundational to attracting and maintaining a dedicated following. Here are the key elements and a detailed explanation for developing such a system:

Create a Compelling Narrative

- **Stand Out from Mainstream Ideologies**: The belief system should be distinct and offer something that mainstream religions or spiritual practices do not. This could be achieved by blending various spiritual traditions, incorporating esoteric or mystical concepts, or presenting a novel interpretation of familiar beliefs. The goal is to create a narrative that is both intriguing and believable to attract those seeking alternative spiritual experiences.
- **Combination of Elements**: A compelling narrative might merge different spiritual or philosophical elements to create a rich, multi-faceted belief system. For example, it might combine aspects of Christianity, Eastern philosophies, and New Age concepts to offer a holistic worldview that answers profound existential questions.
- **Esoteric Knowledge**: Incorporate elements of esoteric knowledge or hidden wisdom that suggest followers are privy to special truths not accessible to the general public. This can include secret doctrines, prophecies, or ancient wisdom that only the cult can reveal.

Example: Heaven's Gate

- **Christian Eschatology and UFO Mythology**: Marshall Applewhite's Heaven's Gate combined Christian eschatology with UFO mythology, creating a distinctive belief system. The narrative included the imminent recycling of Earth and the necessity for followers to leave the planet on an extraterrestrial spacecraft, appealing to those interested in spirituality and extraterrestrial life.

Charismatic Leadership

A charismatic leader is essential for the successful formation and maintenance of a cult. Here are the key elements:

Cultivate Charisma

- **Effective Communication**: Work on developing your communication skills to be clear, persuasive, and engaging. Charismatic leaders can articulate their vision compellingly, drawing followers in and making complex ideas accessible and appealing.
- **Confidence and Conviction**: Display unwavering confidence and conviction in your teachings. This helps to build trust and credibility among followers, who look to the leader as a figure of authority and certainty.
- **Personal Connection**: Establish a personal connection with your followers. Demonstrating empathy, remembering personal details, and showing genuine interest in their well-being helps to foster loyalty and a sense of community.

Example: Jim Jones

- **Inspirational Oratory Skills**: Jim Jones of the People's Temple used his charismatic oratory skills to inspire and attract a diverse following. His messages of social justice and racial equality resonated deeply with many people, helping to build a large and dedicated community.

Isolation vs. Engagement

Balancing isolation and engagement is crucial for maintaining control without attracting negative attention:

Strike a Balance

- **Controlled Isolation**: While isolating members from external influences can help to deepen their dependence on the cult and its teachings, too much isolation can lead to paranoia and attract suspicion from authorities.
- **Engagement with the World**: Maintain some level of engagement with the outside world to appear normal and avoid raising suspicion. This can include participating in community events, allowing limited contact with outsiders, and presenting a benign public image.

Example: Branch Davidians

- **Extreme Isolation**: The Branch Davidians' extreme isolation and stockpiling of weapons led to a deadly confrontation with authorities. This example highlights the dangers of excessive isolation and the importance of maintaining a balance.

Provide Tangible Benefits

Offering practical support can foster loyalty and dependence among members:

Offer Practical Support

- **Basic Needs**: Provide for the basic needs of your members, such as housing, healthcare, education, and food. Ensuring these needs are met can create a strong sense of community and dependence on the cult.
- **Social Services**: Offer additional social services such as counseling, job training, and financial assistance. These services can improve members' quality of life and reinforce their loyalty to the group.

Example: People's Temple

- **Extensive Social Services**: The People's Temple offered extensive social services, including housing, healthcare, and food, creating a sense of community and dependence among its members. This support system was a key factor in maintaining the loyalty and commitment of the followers.

Control Mechanisms

Implementing effective control mechanisms is essential for maintaining order and loyalty:

Implement Effective Controls

- **Surveillance**: Use surveillance to monitor members' activities and ensure compliance with the group's rules. This can include physical surveillance, as well as monitoring communications.
- **Loyalty Tests**: Conduct loyalty tests to assess members' commitment. These can involve public confessions, reaffirmations of faith, or tests of obedience.
- **Public Confessions**: Encourage members to confess their doubts and sins publicly. This practice can reinforce group cohesion and discourage dissent by making members accountable to one another.

Example: Jim Jones

- **Strict Control Measures**: Jim Jones maintained strict control over members through surveillance, loyalty tests, and public confessions. These measures helped him maintain authority and order within the People's Temple, ensuring that members remained committed to the group's teachings.

Ethical Leadership

Ethical leadership is crucial for maintaining trust and ensuring the long-term sustainability of the cult:

Avoid Exploitation

- **Financial Integrity**: Avoid financially exploiting members. Transparency in financial matters helps to build and maintain trust. Ensure that contributions are used for the benefit of the community rather than personal gain.
- **Sustainable Practices**: Implement sustainable practices that ensure the long-term viability of the group. This includes ethical leadership, responsible financial management, and a focus on member welfare.

Example: Avoiding Failures

- **Solar Temple's Failure**: The Solar Temple collapsed due to financial exploitation and extreme practices. The leaders' misuse of funds for personal luxury led to disillusionment among members, while the orchestrated mass suicides and murders shattered the remaining trust. This example underscores the importance of ethical leadership and sustainable practices.

By following these detailed strategies, aspiring cult leaders can develop a unique belief system, cultivate charismatic leadership, balance isolation and engagement, provide tangible benefits, implement effective control mechanisms, and practice ethical leadership. These elements are crucial for attracting and maintaining a devoted following, ensuring the cult's long-term success and sustainability.

Chapter 9: Ensuring Longevity

The longevity of a cult depends on careful planning and adaptability. Ensuring the cult's survival beyond the lifespan of its founder requires strategies for succession, adapting to changes, and leaving a lasting legacy. This chapter delves into these critical aspects, providing detailed insights into maintaining and perpetuating a cult.

Planning for Succession

Identifying Successors

- **Selection Criteria**: Establish clear criteria for selecting potential successors. These criteria might include loyalty, leadership skills, deep understanding of the cult's teachings, and the ability to inspire and manage followers.
- **Training and Mentorship**: Invest time in training and mentoring potential successors. Ensure they are well-versed in the cult's doctrines, rituals, and administrative functions. This preparation will help them seamlessly transition into leadership roles when the time comes.

Gradual Transition of Power

- **Phased Approach**: Implement a phased approach to transitioning power. Gradually delegate responsibilities to the chosen successors to allow them to gain experience and confidence while under the founder's guidance.
- **Public Endorsement**: Publicly endorse and support the chosen successors. This endorsement reassures members of the continuity and stability of the cult's leadership.

Example: Successor Training Program

A successful training program for successors might involve:

- **Intensive Study**: Intensive study sessions on the cult's teachings and history.
- **Leadership Roles**: Assigning leadership roles in smaller projects or sub-groups within the cult to build experience.
- **Mentorship Meetings**: Regular mentorship meetings with the founder to discuss challenges and strategies.

Adapting to Changes

Embracing Flexibility

- **Open to Evolution**: Be open to evolving the cult's teachings and practices to stay relevant. Flexibility allows the cult to adapt to societal changes, new discoveries, and shifts in member needs and interests.

- **Incorporating Feedback**: Establish channels for members to provide feedback. This input can be valuable for identifying areas needing adaptation and ensuring members feel heard and valued.

Integrating Technology

- **Online Presence**: Develop and maintain a robust online presence. Use social media, websites, and digital communication tools to reach a broader audience and engage with members.
- **Virtual Meetings and Rituals**: Incorporate virtual meetings and rituals to include members who cannot attend in person. This adaptability can help maintain engagement and participation across diverse geographical locations.

Example: Adapting Rituals for Modern Times

Adapting traditional rituals for a modern audience might involve:

- **Digital Platforms**: Streaming rituals and ceremonies online for remote participation.
- **Interactive Content**: Creating interactive content such as virtual meditation sessions, online discussion forums, and digital newsletters.
- **Responsive Changes**: Adjusting the timing and format of rituals based on member feedback to better suit contemporary lifestyles.

Leaving a Lasting Legacy

Documenting Teachings

- **Written Records**: Create comprehensive written records of the cult's teachings, doctrines, and rituals. This documentation ensures that the core principles are preserved and can be studied by future generations.
- **Multimedia Archives**: Develop multimedia archives, including videos, audio recordings, and digital documents, to capture the essence of the cult's practices and messages.

Building Institutions

- **Physical Monuments**: Construct physical monuments, such as temples, meditation centers, or libraries, dedicated to the cult's teachings. These structures serve as lasting symbols of the cult's presence and legacy.
- **Educational Programs**: Establish educational programs and institutions that promote the cult's beliefs and values. Schools, training centers, and scholarships can help propagate the teachings and attract new members.

Example: Establishing a Legacy Institute

A Legacy Institute might involve:

- **Curriculum Development**: Developing a curriculum that covers the cult's history, teachings, and practices.
- **Training Programs**: Offering training programs for future leaders, scholars, and practitioners.
- **Outreach Initiatives**: Launching outreach initiatives to engage with the broader community and spread awareness of the cult's contributions.

Commemorative Events

- **Annual Celebrations**: Host annual celebrations and commemorative events to honor the founder and significant milestones in the cult's history. These events reinforce the cult's identity and heritage among members.
- **Publication of Works**: Regularly publish books, articles, and newsletters that highlight the cult's achievements, teachings, and ongoing projects. This practice keeps the legacy alive and in public consciousness.

Example: Founder's Day Celebration

An annual Founder's Day celebration might include:

- **Ceremonial Rituals**: Special rituals to honor the founder's contributions.
- **Speeches and Lectures**: Speeches and lectures by current leaders and scholars discussing the founder's impact and vision.
- **Community Activities**: Community activities such as charity events, educational workshops, and cultural performances that align with the cult's values.

Conclusion: Ensuring Longevity

By planning for succession, adapting to changes, and leaving a lasting legacy, cult leaders can ensure the sustainability and growth of their organizations beyond their lifetimes. These strategies help to maintain stability, relevance, and continuity, fostering a dedicated and enduring community of followers. Understanding and implementing these principles is crucial for any leader aiming to create a resilient and lasting cult.

Identifying Successors

Ensuring the longevity of a cult necessitates the careful identification and grooming of successors who can carry forward the vision and maintain the stability of the organization. This involves establishing clear selection criteria and investing in comprehensive training and mentorship programs.

Selection Criteria

Loyalty

- **Demonstrated Commitment**: Potential successors should have a proven track record of loyalty and dedication to the cult. This can be evidenced through their consistent participation in rituals, adherence to the group's rules, and support of the leader's decisions.
- **Unwavering Support**: They should exhibit unwavering support for the cult's beliefs and goals, showing that they prioritize the group's success over personal ambitions.

Example: Sarah has been a member of the cult for over a decade, consistently participating in all activities and defending the cult's doctrines against external criticism. Her loyalty makes her a prime candidate for succession.

Leadership Skills

- **Natural Authority**: Look for individuals who naturally command respect and can inspire others. Effective successors should be able to motivate and guide followers with confidence.
- **Conflict Resolution**: They should possess strong conflict resolution skills to manage internal disputes and maintain harmony within the group.

Example: John, a senior member, has repeatedly shown his ability to mediate conflicts and maintain peace among members. His natural authority and conflict resolution skills make him an ideal successor.

Deep Understanding of the Cult's Teachings

- **Doctrinal Knowledge**: Potential successors must have an in-depth understanding of the cult's teachings, rituals, and history. This ensures that they can continue to promote and protect the core beliefs of the group.
- **Philosophical Alignment**: Their personal beliefs should align closely with the cult's doctrines to maintain ideological consistency.

Example: Emily, who has been studying the cult's scriptures extensively and has even taught several classes on its teachings, demonstrates a profound understanding and alignment with the cult's philosophy.

Ability to Inspire and Manage Followers

- **Inspirational Qualities**: Successors should be charismatic and capable of inspiring followers through their vision and rhetoric. They must be able to articulate the cult's mission compellingly.
- **Organizational Skills**: They need to have strong organizational skills to manage the cult's activities, resources, and members effectively.

Example: Michael has successfully organized multiple large-scale events for the cult, demonstrating his organizational skills. His ability to deliver compelling speeches has also inspired many new members.

Training and Mentorship

Investing in Training

- **Doctrinal Education**: Provide extensive training on the cult's teachings and rituals. This could involve advanced study sessions, participation in leadership seminars, and access to the group's sacred texts.
- **Practical Experience**: Allow potential successors to gain practical experience by involving them in the planning and execution of rituals, administrative tasks, and decision-making processes.

Example: To prepare Jane for leadership, she is given the responsibility to lead weekly study sessions and oversee the organization of major ceremonies. This hands-on experience helps her understand the intricacies of running the cult.

Mentorship Programs

- **Regular Mentorship Meetings**: Establish regular one-on-one mentorship meetings between the current leader and potential successors. These sessions can provide guidance, feedback, and support.
- **Shadowing**: Implement a shadowing program where potential successors observe and assist the current leader in their daily duties. This gives them insight into the complexities of leadership and decision-making.

Example: David, identified as a potential successor, regularly meets with the cult leader to discuss strategic decisions and receives advice on handling various issues. He also shadows the leader during important meetings and rituals to gain firsthand experience.

Progressive Responsibility

- **Incremental Responsibility**: Gradually increase the responsibilities of potential successors to help them build confidence and competence. Start with smaller tasks and progressively assign more significant roles.
- **Feedback Loop**: Provide continuous feedback on their performance to help them improve and grow into their future roles.

Example: Laura is initially given the task of managing a small group within the cult. As she demonstrates competence, her responsibilities are expanded to include larger projects, with regular feedback sessions to guide her development.

Conclusion

Identifying and grooming successors is critical for the continuity and stability of a cult. By establishing clear selection criteria that emphasize loyalty, leadership skills, doctrinal understanding, and the ability to inspire followers, and by investing in comprehensive training and mentorship programs, cult leaders can ensure a smooth transition of power. This strategic approach helps maintain the cult's teachings, practices, and organizational integrity, securing its longevity and success.

Gradual Transition of Power

Ensuring a smooth and effective transition of power is crucial for the longevity and stability of a cult. A well-planned, phased approach allows chosen successors to gain the necessary experience and confidence under the guidance of the current leader. Publicly endorsing these successors further reassures members of the continuity and stability of the cult's leadership. Here's a detailed explanation of how to implement a gradual transition of power.

Phased Approach

Initial Delegation of Responsibilities

- **Start Small**: Begin by delegating smaller tasks and responsibilities to the chosen successors. This could include organizing minor events, managing a small group of members, or handling specific administrative duties. This initial step helps them get accustomed to leadership roles without overwhelming them.
- **Mentorship and Supervision**: During this phase, the current leader should closely mentor and supervise the successors. Provide guidance, feedback, and support to ensure they are learning and growing in their roles.

Example: Emily, a chosen successor, starts by managing weekly study sessions. The current leader observes these sessions, providing feedback and suggestions to help Emily improve her leadership and organizational skills.

Increased Responsibilities

- **Progressive Involvement**: Gradually increase the scope and significance of the responsibilities assigned to the successors. This could involve leading larger events, making decisions on important matters, and managing larger groups of members.
- **Autonomy with Oversight**: Allow the successors more autonomy in their roles while maintaining a level of oversight. This balance helps them develop confidence and decision-making skills while still benefiting from the leader's experience and wisdom.

Example: After successfully managing weekly sessions, Emily is tasked with organizing a major annual ceremony. She is given considerable freedom in planning and execution but consults with the current leader on key decisions and strategies.

Leadership Roles

- **Key Roles and Functions**: Assign key leadership roles and functions to the successors, such as overseeing the cult's finances, managing member relations, or leading significant rituals. This exposure to various aspects of leadership prepares them for the complexities of running the cult.
- **Feedback and Evaluation**: Continuously evaluate their performance and provide constructive feedback. Encourage them to reflect on their experiences and learn from both successes and challenges.

Example: Emily takes on the role of overseeing the cult's financial operations, including budgeting and resource allocation. Regular meetings with the current leader help her understand financial management's strategic and ethical aspects.

Public Endorsement

Building Trust and Confidence

- **Public Announcements**: Make public announcements endorsing the chosen successors. Highlight their achievements, dedication, and suitability for leadership roles. This public endorsement builds trust and confidence among members, ensuring they support the transition.
- **Ceremonial Endorsement**: During important ceremonies or gatherings, formally introduce the successors to the members. Perform symbolic acts that signify the transfer of power, such as handing over a ceremonial item or bestowing a title.

Example: At the annual renewal ceremony, the current leader introduces Emily as the future leader, detailing her contributions and expressing confidence in her abilities. A symbolic act, such as passing a sacred text or emblem, reinforces this endorsement.

Ongoing Visibility

- **Regular Appearances**: Ensure the chosen successors regularly appear in public events and rituals alongside the current leader. This visibility helps members become familiar with them and accept them as future leaders.
- **Shared Leadership**: Gradually shift to a shared leadership model where the successors co-lead events and activities with the current leader. This shared approach reinforces the idea of continuity and smooth transition.

Example: Emily co-leads major rituals and events with the current leader, demonstrating her growing role and allowing members to see her in action. This shared leadership period helps smooth the eventual full transition.

Communication and Transparency

- **Open Communication**: Maintain open communication with the members about the transition process. Clearly explain the reasons for the transition, the steps involved, and how it will benefit the cult. Transparency helps alleviate concerns and resistance.
- **Feedback Mechanism**: Establish a feedback mechanism where members can voice their opinions and concerns about the transition. Address these concerns promptly to maintain trust and support.

Example: The current leader holds regular meetings and Q&A sessions to discuss the transition process. Members are encouraged to share their thoughts, and their feedback is considered in refining the transition plan.

Conclusion

A gradual transition of power is essential for ensuring the longevity and stability of a cult. By implementing a phased approach, gradually delegating responsibilities, and providing continuous mentorship and feedback, chosen successors can gain the experience and confidence needed for leadership roles. Publicly endorsing these successors and maintaining open communication with members reassures the community of the continuity and stability of the cult's leadership. This strategic approach ensures a smooth and effective transfer of power, securing the cult's future.

Successor Training Program

To ensure a smooth transition of leadership and maintain the continuity of the cult's vision and practices, it is crucial to develop a comprehensive training program for successors. This program should focus on intensive study, practical leadership experience, and regular mentorship. Here's a detailed outline of how to structure an effective successor training program:

Intensive Study

Curriculum Development

- **Core Teachings**: Develop a curriculum that covers the core teachings and doctrines of the cult. This should include an in-depth study of sacred texts, the history of the cult, and the philosophical foundations of its beliefs.
- **Historical Context**: Include the historical context in which the cult was founded, key milestones in its development, and significant events that have shaped its current state. Understanding this context will help successors appreciate the cult's evolution and its guiding principles.

Study Sessions

- **Structured Learning**: Organize structured learning sessions that are conducted regularly, such as weekly or bi-weekly classes. These sessions should be led by knowledgeable instructors or the current leader to ensure accuracy and depth of understanding.
- **Interactive Discussions**: Encourage interactive discussions and debates to help successors critically engage with the material and develop a deeper understanding. This will also prepare them to answer questions and address challenges from members.

Example: Emily, a successor in training, attends weekly study sessions where she learns about the cult's sacred texts and doctrines. These sessions include lectures, group discussions, and interactive Q&A segments led by the current leader.

Leadership Roles

Small Project Management

- **Initial Assignments**: Begin by assigning successors to manage smaller projects or sub-groups within the cult. These projects could involve organizing events, leading study groups, or overseeing community service initiatives. This provides practical experience in leadership and project management.
- **Incremental Responsibility**: Gradually increase the complexity and importance of the projects assigned to the successors. This incremental approach allows them to build confidence and competence in their leadership abilities.

Team Building

- **Sub-Groups**: Assign successors to lead sub-groups or committees within the cult. This helps them develop team-building skills and understand the dynamics of group leadership. They will learn how to delegate tasks, motivate team members, and achieve collective goals.
- **Feedback Loop**: Establish a feedback loop where team members can provide input on the successor's leadership style and effectiveness. This feedback is crucial for personal and professional growth.

Example: Emily is tasked with organizing a community outreach program. She leads a team of volunteers, delegates tasks, and ensures the project runs smoothly. Her success in this role builds her confidence and hones her leadership skills.

Mentorship Meetings

Regular Mentorship Sessions

- **Scheduled Meetings**: Schedule regular mentorship meetings between the current leader and the successors. These meetings should occur frequently, such as weekly or bi-weekly, to provide ongoing support and guidance.
- **Focused Discussions**: Each meeting should have a specific focus, such as discussing recent challenges, reviewing leadership decisions, or planning future initiatives. This ensures that the meetings are productive and address relevant issues.

Strategic Planning

- **Long-Term Vision**: Use mentorship meetings to discuss the long-term vision and strategic goals of the cult. Successors should understand the broader objectives and how their roles fit into the overall plan.
- **Problem-Solving**: Encourage successors to bring up any challenges they are facing and work collaboratively to develop solutions. This problem-solving approach helps them learn to navigate complex situations and make informed decisions.

Example: During a weekly mentorship meeting, Emily discusses the challenges she faced during the community outreach program. The current leader provides feedback and suggests strategies for improvement, helping Emily develop her problem-solving skills.

Performance Evaluation

- **Continuous Feedback**: Provide continuous feedback on the successors' performance in their assigned roles. This feedback should be constructive, highlighting strengths and areas for improvement.
- **Formal Evaluations**: Conduct formal evaluations at regular intervals to assess the successors' progress. These evaluations can involve self-assessment, peer reviews, and feedback from the current leader.

Example: Emily receives feedback after completing the community outreach program. The evaluation includes positive reinforcement for her successful coordination and constructive criticism on areas where she can improve.

Conclusion

A successful successor training program is essential for ensuring the continuity and stability of a cult. By focusing on intensive study, practical leadership experience, and regular mentorship, the program prepares successors to take on leadership roles with confidence and competence. This structured approach helps them develop a deep understanding of the cult's teachings, build effective leadership skills, and navigate the complexities of managing the community. Implementing such a program secures the future of the cult by ensuring that its core values and vision are upheld by capable and well-prepared leaders.

Embracing Flexibility

Ensuring the longevity and relevance of a cult requires an adaptive approach to its teachings and practices. Flexibility is crucial for responding to societal changes, new discoveries, and the evolving needs of members. By being open to evolution and incorporating feedback from members, a cult can maintain its appeal and sustain its growth over time.

Open to Evolution

Adapting Teachings and Practices

- **Staying Relevant**: The world is constantly changing, and so are the beliefs and needs of individuals. Being open to evolving the cult's teachings and practices helps maintain relevance in a dynamic society. This involves regularly reviewing and updating doctrines, rituals, and community practices to align with current trends and member expectations.
- **Incorporating New Knowledge**: Embrace new scientific discoveries, technological advancements, and cultural shifts. Integrating these elements into the cult's teachings can make the belief system more appealing and relatable to contemporary followers.

Example: A cult that initially focused on traditional healing practices might incorporate modern wellness trends, such as mindfulness and holistic health, to attract a broader audience. By updating its practices to include yoga sessions and nutritional workshops, the cult stays relevant and appealing to potential members.

Balancing Tradition and Innovation

- **Respecting Core Beliefs**: While it's important to evolve, it's equally crucial to maintain the core beliefs and values that define the cult. Balancing tradition with innovation ensures that the essence of the cult remains intact while allowing for necessary adaptations.
- **Gradual Changes**: Implement changes gradually to avoid overwhelming members and to allow them time to adjust. Gradual evolution helps maintain stability and continuity within the group.

Example: A cult that values ancient wisdom might gradually introduce new interpretations of its scriptures, explaining how these age-old teachings can be applied to modern life. This approach respects the cult's core beliefs while making them relevant to today's context.

Incorporating Feedback

Establishing Feedback Channels

- **Regular Surveys**: Conduct regular surveys to gather feedback from members about their experiences, needs, and suggestions. Surveys can be anonymous to encourage honest and open responses.

- **Suggestion Boxes**: Place suggestion boxes in communal areas where members can leave their thoughts and ideas at any time. This allows for continuous feedback and shows members that their opinions are valued.

Example: The cult might introduce an annual survey asking members about their satisfaction with current practices, any difficulties they face, and suggestions for improvement. Anonymity ensures candid feedback, providing valuable insights into areas needing change.

Listening to Members

- **Open Forums**: Hold open forums or town hall meetings where members can voice their concerns, ask questions, and offer suggestions. These forums should be structured to ensure that everyone has an opportunity to speak and be heard.
- **Focus Groups**: Create focus groups comprising diverse members to discuss specific issues or proposed changes. These smaller, targeted discussions can provide deeper insights and more detailed feedback.

Example: During a monthly open forum, members express their interest in learning more about environmental sustainability. In response, the cult begins incorporating teachings about ecological responsibility and organizes community clean-up events.

Implementing Feedback

- **Actionable Steps**: Develop a system for reviewing and implementing feedback. Not all suggestions may be feasible, but demonstrating that feedback is taken seriously and acted upon when possible builds trust and commitment among members.
- **Communicating Changes**: Clearly communicate any changes made as a result of member feedback. This transparency reinforces the value placed on member input and encourages ongoing participation.

Example: After receiving feedback about the desire for more community-building activities, the cult organizes additional social events, such as potlucks and group outings. Leaders communicate these new initiatives through newsletters and announcements, highlighting that these changes were based on member suggestions.

Conclusion

Embracing flexibility is essential for the growth and sustainability of a cult. By being open to evolving teachings and practices, the cult can stay relevant and appealing in a constantly changing world. Incorporating feedback from members ensures that their needs and interests are addressed, fostering a sense of inclusion and value within the community. Balancing tradition with innovation and implementing changes based on member input helps maintain a dynamic and adaptive organization that can thrive over time.

Integrating Technology

Incorporating technology into the operations and outreach of a cult is essential for reaching a broader audience, maintaining engagement, and adapting to the needs of members who cannot be physically present. Here's a detailed explanation of how to effectively integrate technology into the cult's activities.

Online Presence

Developing a Robust Online Presence

- **Website Creation**: Develop a professional and informative website that serves as the central hub for all information related to the cult. The website should include sections on the cult's history, beliefs, teachings, events, and how to join or support the group. Ensure that the website is visually appealing, easy to navigate, and mobile-friendly.
- **Social Media Engagement**: Use social media platforms such as Facebook, Instagram, Twitter, and YouTube to reach a wider audience. Regularly post content that is engaging, informative, and aligned with the cult's beliefs and values. This could include inspirational quotes, teachings, event announcements, and member testimonials.

Example: The cult's website features an attractive design with sections like "About Us," "Teachings," "Events," "Join Us," and a blog. On social media, the cult shares daily inspirational posts, updates about upcoming events, live-streamed teachings, and videos of rituals.

Content Strategy

- **Consistent Updates**: Regularly update the website and social media channels with fresh content. This keeps followers engaged and informed about the latest news and events. Consistency is key to maintaining an active and interested online community.
- **Interactive Content**: Create interactive content such as polls, Q&A sessions, and live videos to engage with followers. Encourage them to participate and share their thoughts, which can help build a sense of community online.

Example: The cult holds a weekly live Q&A session on Facebook where members and potential recruits can ask questions about the teachings and practices. They also use Instagram Stories to conduct polls on topics for future teachings.

Digital Communication Tools

- **Email Newsletters**: Send regular email newsletters to members with updates on events, teachings, and important announcements. Newsletters can also include articles, member stories, and resources for personal growth.
- **Messaging Apps**: Use messaging apps like WhatsApp, Telegram, or Discord to create groups where members can communicate with each other and the leadership. These

platforms can be used for quick updates, sharing resources, and fostering community interactions.

Example: The cult sends a monthly newsletter featuring articles on spiritual growth, upcoming event details, and member testimonials. They also have a WhatsApp group where members receive daily inspirational messages and can discuss teachings.

Virtual Meetings and Rituals

Incorporating Virtual Meetings

- **Virtual Study Groups**: Hold virtual study groups or classes via video conferencing platforms such as Zoom or Google Meet. These sessions allow members from different geographical locations to participate and learn together.
- **Webinars and Workshops**: Organize webinars and workshops on various topics related to the cult's teachings. These can be live sessions or pre-recorded, allowing for flexible viewing times.

Example: The cult conducts weekly virtual study groups where members discuss different aspects of their beliefs and practices. They also offer monthly webinars on topics such as meditation, spiritual healing, and community building.

Virtual Rituals

- **Live-Streamed Rituals**: Live-stream important rituals and ceremonies so that members who cannot attend in person can still participate. Use high-quality video and audio to ensure an immersive experience.
- **Interactive Elements**: Incorporate interactive elements into virtual rituals, such as allowing members to light candles at home, chant along with the leader, or share their thoughts in real-time via chat.

Example: During a major festival, the cult live-streams the entire ceremony, encouraging members to set up similar altars at home and participate by following the rituals in real-time. A chat function allows members to share their experiences and feel connected.

Adapting Rituals for Virtual Settings

- **Shortened and Simplified Rituals**: Adapt rituals to be shorter and simpler for virtual settings, ensuring they remain engaging and meaningful. Avoid overly complex procedures that may not translate well to a virtual environment.
- **Pre-Recorded Segments**: Include pre-recorded segments in virtual rituals to ensure smooth transitions and high-quality content. This can also help manage technical issues that might arise during live broadcasts.

Example: The cult adapts a traditional two-hour ceremony into a one-hour virtual ritual with pre-recorded music and guided meditations, ensuring that the experience remains powerful and engaging for online participants.

Conclusion

Integrating technology is essential for expanding the reach and maintaining the engagement of a cult. Developing a robust online presence through a professional website, active social media channels, and effective digital communication tools helps to connect with a broader audience and keep members informed. Incorporating virtual meetings and rituals ensures that members who cannot attend in person remain connected and engaged. By embracing technology, the cult can adapt to modern needs, foster a sense of community, and sustain its growth and relevance.

Adapting Rituals for Modern Times

In the contemporary world, adapting traditional rituals to meet the needs and preferences of a modern audience is crucial for maintaining engagement and relevance. This involves leveraging digital platforms, creating interactive content, and making responsive changes based on feedback. Here's a detailed guide on how to adapt rituals for modern times:

Digital Platforms

Streaming Rituals and Ceremonies Online

- **Live Streaming**: Use platforms like YouTube, Facebook Live, or Zoom to stream rituals and ceremonies in real-time. This allows members who are unable to attend in person to participate remotely, fostering a sense of inclusion and continuity.
- **Recorded Sessions**: Provide recorded versions of the rituals for members who cannot join live. These recordings can be made available on the cult's website or social media channels, allowing for flexible viewing.

Example: The cult streams its weekly meditation sessions live on Facebook, enabling members from different time zones to join in. The sessions are also recorded and uploaded to YouTube for later viewing.

Enhancing the Virtual Experience

- **High-Quality Production**: Invest in good quality video and audio equipment to ensure that the streaming experience is immersive and engaging. High production values can make virtual rituals feel more professional and impactful.
- **Interactive Features**: Use interactive features like live chats, polls, and Q&A sessions during live streams to engage participants and make them feel part of the ritual.

Example: During a major festival, the cult streams the ceremony with multiple camera angles and high-quality sound. A live chat function allows members to interact, ask questions, and share their thoughts in real-time.

Interactive Content

Virtual Meditation Sessions

- **Guided Meditations**: Create guided meditation sessions that can be streamed live or provided as downloadable content. These sessions should be designed to help members achieve a state of relaxation and focus, regardless of their physical location.
- **Interactive Elements**: Incorporate elements such as visualization exercises, breathing techniques, and background music to enhance the meditation experience. Allow participants to share their experiences and feedback afterward.

Example: The cult offers a weekly virtual guided meditation session where members follow along with the leader's instructions, incorporating calming visuals and music. Participants can discuss their experiences in a post-meditation online forum.

Online Discussion Forums

- **Community Engagement**: Set up online forums or groups on platforms like Discord, Facebook, or the cult's own website. These forums provide a space for members to discuss teachings, share insights, and support each other.
- **Moderated Discussions**: Ensure that discussions are moderated to maintain a respectful and productive environment. Moderators can also facilitate discussions by posing questions and highlighting key topics.

Example: The cult's website features an active discussion forum where members can ask questions about recent teachings, share personal stories, and engage in debates. Moderators help guide discussions and ensure they stay on topic.

Digital Newsletters

- **Regular Updates**: Send out digital newsletters to keep members informed about upcoming events, recent teachings, and community news. Newsletters can include articles, member testimonials, and educational content.
- **Interactive Features**: Include interactive features like clickable links to related articles, videos, and upcoming event registrations. Encourage members to respond with feedback or questions.

Example: The cult's monthly newsletter includes articles on spiritual growth, links to recorded rituals, announcements of upcoming events, and a section for member questions and feedback.

Responsive Changes

Adjusting Timing and Format

- **Flexible Scheduling**: Adjust the timing of rituals and events to accommodate the diverse schedules of modern members. Consider offering multiple sessions at different times to ensure maximum participation.
- **Shortened Formats**: Adapt rituals to be shorter and more concise without losing their essence. This makes it easier for members to fit rituals into their busy lives.

Example: Recognizing that members have varying schedules, the cult offers three different times for the weekly ritual: morning, afternoon, and evening. Additionally, the traditional two-hour ceremony is condensed into a 45-minute session that retains all key elements.

Member Feedback

- **Surveys and Feedback Forms**: Regularly solicit feedback from members about their experiences and preferences. Use this input to make informed decisions about how to adapt and improve rituals.
- **Responsive Changes**: Act on feedback by making adjustments to rituals, whether it's changing the format, timing, or introducing new elements. Communicate these changes to members to show that their input is valued.

Example: After receiving feedback that members find evening rituals difficult to attend, the cult shifts some of its ceremonies to weekend mornings. The change is communicated through the newsletter, explaining that it was made in response to member preferences.

Conclusion

Adapting rituals for modern times involves leveraging digital platforms, creating interactive content, and making responsive changes based on feedback. By streaming rituals online, offering virtual meditation sessions, and setting up online discussion forums, the cult can engage a broader audience and maintain participation. Adjusting the timing and format of rituals based on member feedback ensures that the practices remain relevant and accessible. This flexible approach helps to sustain the cult's growth and relevance in a rapidly changing world.

Documenting Teachings

Documenting the teachings of a cult is crucial for preserving its core principles, ensuring continuity, and facilitating the education of future generations. Comprehensive documentation should include written records and multimedia archives, capturing the full essence of the cult's practices and messages.

Written Records

Creating Comprehensive Documentation

- **Doctrines and Beliefs**: Compile detailed written records of the cult's core doctrines and beliefs. This should include foundational texts, interpretations of sacred scriptures, and philosophical explanations of the cult's teachings.
- **Rituals and Practices**: Document the rituals, ceremonies, and daily practices of the cult. Provide step-by-step instructions, including the symbolic meanings behind each action and the intended spiritual outcomes.

Example: The cult produces a series of manuals that cover its doctrines, rituals, and daily practices. These manuals are regularly updated to include new insights and developments, ensuring they remain relevant and comprehensive.

Standardized Texts

- **Official Handbooks**: Create official handbooks that serve as authoritative sources of information. These handbooks should be distributed to all members and used in teaching and training programs.
- **Accessible Language**: Ensure that the written records are accessible and easy to understand. Avoid overly complex language to make the teachings approachable for all members.

Example: The cult publishes an official handbook that outlines the basic tenets of its beliefs, the significance of its rituals, and guidelines for daily practice. This handbook is provided to all new members during their initiation.

Archiving Historical Documents

- **Preserving History**: Archive historical documents, including founding texts, early writings, and important correspondences. These documents provide valuable context and insight into the evolution of the cult's beliefs and practices.
- **Digitization**: Digitize historical documents to preserve them and make them accessible to a wider audience. Digital archives can be easily searched and referenced, ensuring that the cult's history is well-documented and preserved.

Example: The cult's historical archives include original writings by the founder, early newsletters, and correspondence with influential members. These documents are digitized and stored in an online archive accessible to members.

Multimedia Archives

Developing a Multimedia Repository

- **Video and Audio Recordings**: Record important rituals, ceremonies, and teachings in video and audio formats. These recordings capture the nuances of the practices and the charisma of the leaders, providing a rich resource for current and future members.

- **Photographic Records**: Create photographic records of significant events, gatherings, and rituals. Photos can be used in educational materials and promotional content, illustrating the vibrancy and community spirit of the cult.

Example: The cult records its annual festivals and important ceremonies, producing high-quality videos that are stored in an online multimedia repository. These recordings are used in training programs and as a resource for members.

Digital Documents

- **E-Books and PDFs**: Convert written records into digital formats such as e-books and PDFs. These documents can be easily distributed and accessed by members worldwide, ensuring that the teachings are available to all.
- **Interactive Content**: Develop interactive digital content, such as online courses and virtual tours of sacred sites. Interactive content engages members and provides a deeper understanding of the teachings.

Example: The cult offers an online library of e-books and PDFs that members can download and study at their convenience. Interactive online courses cover various aspects of the cult's beliefs and practices, enhancing the learning experience.

Organizing and Maintaining Archives

- **Categorization and Indexing**: Organize multimedia archives into categories and create an index for easy navigation. This helps members find specific content and ensures that the archives are user-friendly.
- **Regular Updates**: Regularly update the multimedia archives with new content. Ensure that the archives reflect the latest developments and insights in the cult's teachings and practices.

Example: The cult's multimedia archive is organized into categories such as "Rituals," "Teachings," "Historical Events," and "Member Stories." A search function allows members to quickly find the content they need.

Ensuring Accessibility

- **Member Access**: Provide members with access to the multimedia archives through a secure online portal. Ensure that the portal is easy to use and accessible from various devices.
- **Public Access**: Consider making certain parts of the archives publicly accessible to attract potential members and increase transparency. Public access can also serve as a promotional tool, showcasing the cult's activities and teachings.

Example: Members can log into a secure online portal to access the multimedia archives. Selected videos and documents are made publicly available on the cult's website to attract new members and provide transparency.

Conclusion

Documenting the teachings of a cult through comprehensive written records and multimedia archives is essential for preserving its core principles, ensuring continuity, and educating future generations. Written records provide a detailed and accessible account of the cult's beliefs and practices, while multimedia archives capture the essence of rituals and teachings in a dynamic and engaging format. By developing a robust documentation strategy, the cult can maintain its legacy and ensure that its teachings continue to inspire and guide its members for generations to come.

Building Institutions

Building lasting institutions is critical for ensuring the continuity and influence of a cult. Physical monuments and educational programs serve as both practical and symbolic anchors for the cult's teachings and community. These structures and initiatives help to solidify the cult's presence, attract new members, and maintain the commitment of existing ones. Here's a detailed guide on constructing physical monuments and establishing educational programs.

Physical Monuments

Constructing Physical Monuments

- **Temples and Meditation Centers**: Building temples and meditation centers dedicated to the cult's practices provides a sacred space for rituals, ceremonies, and daily gatherings. These structures become central hubs for the community, fostering a sense of unity and shared purpose.
- **Libraries and Archives**: Establishing libraries that house the cult's literature, historical documents, and multimedia archives ensures that members have access to essential resources. Libraries can also serve as research centers for deeper study and understanding of the cult's teachings.

Example: The cult constructs a grand temple at its headquarters, serving as the main location for major rituals and festivals. Adjacent to the temple, a meditation center offers daily sessions and retreats for members seeking spiritual growth.

Symbolic Architecture

- **Design and Symbolism**: The design of the physical monuments should incorporate symbols and motifs significant to the cult's beliefs. Architectural elements can reflect the teachings and values, creating an immersive environment that reinforces the cult's identity.

- **Sacred Spaces**: Include dedicated sacred spaces within the monuments for quiet reflection, personal meditation, and smaller rituals. These areas provide members with personal connections to the cult's spiritual foundation.

Example: The temple's architecture includes symbols from the cult's teachings, such as intricate carvings depicting key stories and stained glass windows featuring sacred symbols. A serene garden surrounds the meditation center, offering a tranquil space for personal reflection.

Maintaining Monuments

- **Preservation and Upkeep**: Regular maintenance and preservation of physical monuments are essential for their longevity. Establish a dedicated team responsible for the upkeep and enhancement of these structures to ensure they remain pristine and welcoming.
- **Community Involvement**: Engage members in the care and maintenance of the monuments. Community involvement fosters a sense of ownership and pride, reinforcing the bond between members and the cult.

Example: A maintenance team, comprising both hired staff and volunteer members, ensures that the temple and meditation center are well-maintained. Monthly community clean-up events are organized, encouraging members to contribute to the upkeep of their sacred spaces.

Educational Programs

Establishing Educational Programs

- **Schools and Training Centers**: Establish schools and training centers that offer education based on the cult's teachings. These institutions can provide both general education and specialized training in the cult's doctrines, rituals, and leadership principles.
- **Scholarship Programs**: Implement scholarship programs to attract and support students who wish to study the cult's teachings. Scholarships can help identify and nurture future leaders and dedicated members.

Example: The cult opens a school that combines standard academic subjects with courses on the cult's beliefs and practices. A training center offers workshops and certifications in various aspects of the cult's rituals and community leadership.

Curriculum Development

- **Integrated Curriculum**: Develop an integrated curriculum that combines general education with the cult's teachings. Subjects such as history, philosophy, and ethics can be taught from the cult's perspective, providing a holistic educational experience.
- **Spiritual and Practical Education**: Balance spiritual education with practical skills training. Courses might include meditation techniques, community service, leadership development, and practical arts that align with the cult's values.

Example: The school's curriculum includes standard subjects like mathematics and science, alongside courses on meditation, ethical living, and the history of the cult. Students participate in community service projects as part of their education.

Promotional and Outreach Initiatives

- **Community Workshops**: Offer workshops and seminars open to the public. These events can serve as both educational opportunities and recruitment tools, showcasing the benefits of the cult's teachings.
- **Outreach Programs**: Develop outreach programs to engage with the broader community. These programs can include public lectures, free classes, and community service projects that promote the cult's values and attract new members.

Example: The cult hosts a monthly workshop series open to the public, covering topics like stress management, meditation, and ethical living. Outreach programs include free yoga classes in local parks and community clean-up drives.

Fostering Academic and Spiritual Growth

- **Research and Development**: Encourage research and development within the educational programs. Support scholarly work that explores and expands the cult's teachings, fostering a culture of continuous learning and innovation.
- **Spiritual Mentorship**: Provide spiritual mentorship programs where experienced members guide new or younger members in their spiritual journey. This one-on-one support helps deepen their understanding and commitment to the cult's values.

Example: The training center offers grants for research projects that delve into the cult's teachings and their applications. Spiritual mentorship programs pair experienced members with newcomers to guide them through their spiritual development.

Conclusion

Building institutions, such as physical monuments and educational programs, is essential for ensuring the long-term stability and growth of a cult. Physical monuments like temples, meditation centers, and libraries serve as lasting symbols of the cult's presence and provide sacred spaces for community activities. Educational programs, including schools, training centers, and scholarships, propagate the cult's beliefs and attract new members. By investing in these institutions, the cult can create a strong foundation for its teachings, foster community engagement, and ensure the continuity of its values and practices for future generations.

Establishing a Legacy Institute

Creating a Legacy Institute is a strategic move to ensure the cult's teachings, values, and contributions are preserved, propagated, and respected over time. This institute serves as an educational and training hub, dedicated to cultivating future leaders, scholars, and practitioners who can carry forward the cult's mission. Here's a detailed guide on how to establish a Legacy Institute, focusing on curriculum development, training programs, and outreach initiatives.

Curriculum Development

Comprehensive Coverage

- **Cult's History**: Develop courses that provide an in-depth exploration of the cult's history, including its founding, key milestones, significant events, and evolution. This helps students understand the origins and growth of the cult.
- **Teachings and Doctrines**: Create detailed courses that cover the cult's core teachings, doctrines, and philosophies. Include interpretations of sacred texts, ethical guidelines, and spiritual principles.

Example: The Legacy Institute offers a course titled "History and Evolution of Our Beliefs," which traces the cult's development from its founding to the present day. Another course, "Fundamental Doctrines," explores the core teachings and their applications in daily life.

Practical Application

- **Rituals and Practices**: Include practical training in the cult's rituals and practices. Offer hands-on sessions where students learn to perform and lead rituals, understand their significance, and maintain their sanctity.
- **Community Engagement**: Develop modules that teach students how to engage with and contribute to the community, both within the cult and in the broader society. This can include service projects, ethical living, and leadership skills.

Example: The institute's curriculum includes practical workshops on performing key rituals, such as the initiation ceremony and seasonal festivals. Additionally, a course on "Community Leadership" trains students in ethical leadership and community service.

Continuous Improvement

- **Feedback and Updates**: Regularly review and update the curriculum based on feedback from students, faculty, and community members. Ensure the content remains relevant, accurate, and aligned with the cult's evolving teachings.

Example: An annual curriculum review process incorporates feedback from students and instructors. Recent updates include new modules on modern applications of the cult's teachings and additional practical workshops based on student requests.

Training Programs

Future Leaders

- **Leadership Training**: Offer specialized training programs for individuals identified as potential future leaders. These programs should cover advanced teachings, leadership skills, strategic planning, and crisis management.
- **Mentorship Opportunities**: Pair trainees with experienced leaders who can provide guidance, support, and real-world insights. This mentorship helps future leaders develop the confidence and competence needed to lead.

Example: The Legacy Institute's "Leadership Development Program" includes intensive courses on strategic leadership, conflict resolution, and ethical decision-making. Each participant is paired with a senior mentor for personalized guidance.

Scholars and Researchers

- **Academic Research**: Encourage scholarly research into the cult's teachings, history, and impact. Provide resources and support for academic studies, including access to archives, funding for research projects, and opportunities to publish findings.
- **Symposia and Conferences**: Host symposia and conferences where scholars can present their research, share insights, and engage in intellectual discourse. These events help build a scholarly community around the cult's teachings.

Example: The institute offers research grants and fellowships for scholars investigating various aspects of the cult's beliefs and practices. Annual conferences attract researchers from around the world to discuss their work and collaborate on new projects.

Practitioners

- **Skill-Based Training**: Provide training programs for practitioners who will apply the cult's teachings in various contexts, such as healing, counseling, education, and community service. Focus on practical skills and ethical guidelines.
- **Certification Programs**: Establish certification programs that recognize practitioners' expertise and commitment. Certification ensures that practitioners meet the institute's standards and can competently represent the cult's values.

Example: The "Certified Practitioner Program" offers training in areas such as spiritual counseling, holistic healing, and community education. Graduates receive certification that validates their skills and dedication to the cult's mission.

Outreach Initiatives

Community Engagement

- **Public Workshops and Lectures**: Organize workshops and lectures open to the public. These events can introduce the cult's teachings to a broader audience, address contemporary issues from the cult's perspective, and promote understanding and dialogue.
- **Service Projects**: Launch community service projects that reflect the cult's values. These projects can improve the cult's reputation, demonstrate its commitment to social good, and attract like-minded individuals.

Example: The Legacy Institute hosts monthly public lectures on topics like ethical living, spiritual wellness, and community building. Service projects, such as environmental clean-ups and support for local shelters, are organized regularly.

Educational Outreach

- **School Partnerships**: Partner with local schools to offer educational programs that introduce students to the cult's values and teachings. These partnerships can include guest lectures, workshops, and collaborative projects.
- **Online Education**: Develop online courses and resources that make the cult's teachings accessible to a global audience. Use digital platforms to reach people who might not be able to attend in-person programs.

Example: The institute collaborates with local high schools to offer an elective course on ethical leadership based on the cult's principles. Online courses, available through the institute's website, cover a range of topics from introductory teachings to advanced practices.

Media and Publications

- **Books and Journals**: Publish books, articles, and journals that explore the cult's teachings, history, and contributions. These publications can reach a wider audience and establish the institute as an authority on the cult's doctrines.
- **Media Appearances**: Engage with media outlets to promote the institute's work and the cult's teachings. Appearances on television, radio, and podcasts can help spread awareness and attract new members.

Example: The institute publishes a quarterly journal featuring scholarly articles on the cult's teachings and contemporary applications. Leaders and scholars regularly appear on local radio shows and podcasts to discuss their work and the cult's impact.

Conclusion

Establishing a Legacy Institute involves creating a robust curriculum, offering specialized training programs, and launching outreach initiatives to engage with the broader community. This institute serves as a center for education, leadership development, and community engagement, ensuring the cult's teachings and values are preserved, propagated, and respected. By investing in such an institute, the cult can build a lasting legacy that influences future generations and maintains its relevance and impact.

Commemorative Events

Commemorative events play a vital role in reinforcing the cult's identity and heritage. By hosting annual celebrations and regularly publishing works that highlight the cult's achievements and teachings, the cult can keep its legacy alive and maintain a strong connection with its members. Here's a detailed guide on how to effectively plan and execute these commemorative activities.

Annual Celebrations

Purpose and Significance

- **Honoring the Founder**: Annual celebrations can be organized to honor the founder's life, vision, and contributions. These events provide an opportunity to reflect on the founder's teachings and the cult's journey.
- **Milestone Celebrations**: Commemorate significant milestones in the cult's history, such as anniversaries of important events, achievements, or expansions. These celebrations help to reinforce the cult's identity and collective memory.

Example: The cult holds an annual "Founder's Day" celebration on the anniversary of the founder's birth. This event includes a series of activities designed to honor the founder's legacy and celebrate the cult's achievements.

Planning and Execution

- **Ceremonial Rituals**: Design specific rituals that are performed during these celebrations. These could include re-enactments of historical events, special prayers, or symbolic acts that reflect the cult's values and teachings.
- **Guest Speakers**: Invite prominent members, scholars, or external guests to speak at the events. Their insights and perspectives can enrich the celebrations and provide a broader context for the cult's teachings.

Example: During the "Founder's Day" celebration, the cult performs a re-enactment of a significant event from the founder's life, followed by a keynote speech from a renowned scholar who discusses the impact of the founder's teachings on modern spirituality.

Engaging Activities

- **Workshops and Seminars**: Organize workshops and seminars that delve into various aspects of the cult's teachings. These sessions can be interactive and educational, providing members with deeper insights and practical knowledge.
- **Cultural Performances**: Include cultural performances such as music, dance, or drama that reflect the cult's heritage. These performances can be both entertaining and spiritually uplifting.

Example: The celebration features a series of workshops on meditation techniques and ethical living, followed by a cultural performance that depicts the founding story of the cult through dance and music.

Community Involvement

- **Inclusive Participation**: Ensure that all members have the opportunity to participate in the celebrations. This inclusivity fosters a sense of belonging and community.
- **Volunteer Opportunities**: Encourage members to volunteer in organizing and executing the events. This involvement enhances their connection to the cult and provides a sense of ownership.

Example: Members volunteer to decorate the venue, prepare refreshments, and assist in the coordination of activities. This participation helps them feel more engaged and integral to the celebration.

Publication of Works

Regular Publications

- **Books and Articles**: Regularly publish books and articles that explore the cult's teachings, achievements, and ongoing projects. These publications serve as a record of the cult's history and provide valuable resources for both current and future members.
- **Newsletters**: Distribute newsletters that keep members informed about recent developments, upcoming events, and ongoing projects. Newsletters can also include member stories, reflections, and educational content.

Example: The cult publishes an annual book that compiles essays on various aspects of its teachings, along with a quarterly newsletter that updates members on community activities and projects.

Content Creation

- **Highlighting Achievements**: Create content that highlights the cult's significant achievements, such as community service projects, expansion efforts, or notable contributions to society. This not only keeps the legacy alive but also inspires pride among members.

- **Educational Materials**: Develop educational materials that delve into the core teachings and practices of the cult. These materials can be used in training programs, study groups, and individual study.

Example: The cult releases a book documenting its community service initiatives over the past year, including detailed descriptions of projects, impact assessments, and member testimonials.

Distribution Channels

- **Digital Platforms**: Utilize digital platforms to distribute publications. E-books, online articles, and digital newsletters can reach a wider audience and are easily accessible to members worldwide.
- **Print Media**: Continue to use traditional print media for those who prefer physical copies. Printed books, magazines, and newsletters can be distributed during events and sent to members.

Example: The cult's publications are available both in print and online. Digital versions are accessible through the cult's website and app, while printed copies are distributed at the annual celebrations and mailed to members.

Maintaining Public Consciousness

- **Public Relations**: Engage in public relations efforts to promote the cult's publications and activities. This can include press releases, media appearances, and partnerships with other organizations.
- **Social Media**: Use social media platforms to share excerpts from publications, announce new releases, and highlight significant achievements. Social media can also be used to engage with a broader audience and attract new members.

Example: The cult launches a social media campaign to promote its latest book release, including teaser excerpts, author interviews, and a live Q&A session with the writers. This campaign generates interest and engagement from both members and the public.

Conclusion

Hosting annual celebrations and regularly publishing works are essential strategies for reinforcing the cult's identity, heritage, and achievements. Annual celebrations honor the founder and significant milestones, fostering a sense of community and belonging among members. Regular publications, including books, articles, and newsletters, keep the cult's teachings and accomplishments in public consciousness and provide valuable resources for education and inspiration. By integrating these commemorative activities, the cult can maintain a strong and enduring legacy.

Founder's Day Celebration

An annual Founder's Day celebration is a vital event that honors the founder's contributions and reinforces the cult's values and heritage. This celebration can be a powerful tool for fostering community spirit, educating members, and showcasing the cult's achievements. Here's a detailed guide on how to organize a comprehensive Founder's Day celebration, including ceremonial rituals, speeches and lectures, and community activities.

Ceremonial Rituals

Special Rituals to Honor the Founder's Contributions

- **Opening Ceremony**: Begin the day with an opening ceremony that includes traditional rituals specifically designed to honor the founder. This might involve lighting candles, chanting, or performing a symbolic act that represents the founder's teachings and vision.
- **Founder's Tribute**: Organize a tribute where members participate in a ritual that commemorates the founder's life and achievements. This could include reading passages from the founder's writings, recounting significant events in their life, and offering personal reflections.

Example: The celebration starts with a ceremonial lighting of the Founder's Flame, symbolizing the enlightenment brought by the founder. Members gather in a circle, chanting a special hymn composed in honor of the founder, followed by a ritual reading of the founder's most impactful teachings.

Speeches and Lectures

Speeches and Lectures by Current Leaders and Scholars

- **Keynote Address**: Invite a prominent leader or scholar to deliver a keynote address that delves into the founder's vision, impact, and ongoing relevance of their teachings. This speech sets the tone for the day and provides deep insights into the founder's contributions.
- **Panel Discussions**: Organize panel discussions featuring current leaders and experts who discuss various aspects of the founder's philosophy, their historical context, and the evolution of the cult. This format encourages a multifaceted exploration of the founder's legacy.

Example: A respected scholar gives a keynote address titled "The Visionary Legacy of Our Founder," highlighting the founder's impact on modern spiritual practices. Following the keynote, a panel of leaders and scholars engage in a discussion about the founder's influence on contemporary ethical issues.

Interactive Q&A Sessions

- **Engagement with Members**: Allow members to engage with the speakers through interactive Q&A sessions. This provides an opportunity for members to ask questions, seek clarifications, and share their thoughts on the founder's teachings.
- **Reflection and Dialogue**: Encourage an open dialogue where members can reflect on the speeches and lectures, fostering a deeper understanding and personal connection to the founder's vision.

Example: After the keynote address, a Q&A session is held where members ask insightful questions about how the founder's teachings can be applied to current societal challenges. The session ends with a group reflection activity where members share their personal interpretations of the founder's message.

Community Activities

Charity Events

- **Service Projects**: Organize charity events and service projects that embody the founder's values and teachings. Activities such as community clean-ups, food drives, and support for local shelters align with the cult's commitment to social responsibility.
- **Fundraising**: Host fundraising activities where the proceeds go to charitable causes supported by the cult. This not only honors the founder's commitment to service but also strengthens the cult's positive impact on the wider community.

Example: Members participate in a community clean-up drive in the morning, followed by a charity auction where handmade crafts and artworks are sold to raise funds for a local shelter. These activities highlight the founder's dedication to community service and ethical living.

Educational Workshops

- **Skill Development**: Offer workshops that teach practical skills aligned with the cult's teachings, such as meditation techniques, ethical decision-making, and sustainable living practices. These workshops can be led by experienced members and external experts.
- **Interactive Learning**: Create interactive sessions where members can engage in hands-on learning and collaborative activities. This not only educates but also fosters a sense of community and shared purpose.

Example: A series of workshops are conducted throughout the day, including a meditation session led by a senior member, an ethical living workshop focused on sustainable practices, and a collaborative art project that reflects the founder's values.

Cultural Performances

- **Artistic Expression**: Include cultural performances such as music, dance, and drama that reflect the founder's teachings and the cult's heritage. These performances can be both entertaining and spiritually uplifting.

- **Member Participation**: Encourage members to participate in these performances, either as performers or organizers. This involvement enhances their connection to the event and to each other.

Example: The evening features a cultural performance where members enact a play based on the founder's life, interspersed with traditional music and dance performances that celebrate the cult's heritage. The day concludes with a communal feast, reinforcing the sense of unity and shared celebration.

Conclusion

An annual Founder's Day celebration is a multifaceted event that honors the founder's contributions and reinforces the cult's values and heritage. By including ceremonial rituals, speeches and lectures, and community activities such as charity events, educational workshops, and cultural performances, the celebration can foster a strong sense of community and commitment among members. This comprehensive approach ensures that the founder's legacy continues to inspire and guide the cult's activities and growth.

Chapter 10: Ethical Reflection - The Machiavellian Approach

Introduction

Leading a cult involves navigating the complexities of power, influence, and ethical considerations. While some leaders may adopt a Machiavellian approach—presenting a benevolent public face while maintaining strict control behind the scenes—it's crucial to manage these dual personas carefully. This chapter explores how cult leaders can maintain their public image while ensuring control and compliance in private, focusing on weighing moral implications, understanding the impact on followers, and exploring strategies to manage this duality effectively.

Weighing the Moral Implications

Public Benevolence vs. Private Control

- **Public Persona**: Cultivate a public image that exudes compassion, wisdom, and benevolence. This public face helps attract followers and gain their trust and admiration.
- **Private Authority**: In private, maintain strict control and enforce discipline to ensure the cult's stability and adherence to its principles. It's important to balance kindness with firmness to maintain authority without appearing tyrannical.

Example: A leader might publicly advocate for community service and personal growth, while privately enforcing strict adherence to rituals and practices. This approach ensures that followers respect and fear the leader's authority without damaging their public reputation.

Strategic Manipulation

- **Controlled Transparency**: Be transparent about certain aspects of the cult's operations to build trust, but strategically withhold information that could undermine your authority or cause dissent.
- **Selective Truth-Telling**: Share truths that reinforce the cult's values and mission, but use discretion when discussing sensitive issues. This approach helps maintain control while fostering an image of honesty.

Example: A leader might openly discuss the cult's charitable activities and successes, while keeping internal disciplinary actions and financial details confidential. This selective transparency maintains the leader's benevolent image while ensuring control.

Understanding the Impact on Followers

Psychological and Emotional Management

- **Public Encouragement**: In public settings, offer encouragement, praise, and positive reinforcement to build morale and loyalty. Highlight individual and group achievements to foster a sense of community.
- **Private Discipline**: Privately, address any issues of non-compliance or dissent firmly. Use fear, guilt, or other psychological tactics to ensure adherence to rules and discourage rebellion.

Example: During public gatherings, the leader praises members for their contributions and commitment. In private, the leader conducts strict evaluations and imposes consequences for any perceived disobedience or lack of dedication.

Maintaining Social Harmony

- **Public Inclusivity**: Promote inclusivity and harmony in public to create a welcoming atmosphere that attracts and retains members. Highlight the cult's supportive community and shared values.
- **Private Segregation**: Privately, segregate members based on loyalty and compliance levels. Use rewards and punishments to reinforce desired behaviors and maintain control.

Example: The leader publicly emphasizes the cult's unity and collective mission, while privately keeping a close watch on members' loyalty, rewarding those who are most dedicated and disciplining those who are not.

Exploring Strategies to Manage Duality

Controlled Environments

- **Public Spaces**: Use public spaces to project a positive image. Host open events, community service projects, and public lectures that reinforce the cult's benevolent mission.
- **Private Spaces**: Use private spaces for internal meetings, disciplinary actions, and strategic planning. Ensure these spaces are secure and inaccessible to outsiders to maintain confidentiality.

Example: The cult hosts public meditation sessions and community clean-up events, while private meetings and strategy sessions are held in secure, members-only areas.

Trusted Inner Circle

- **Building Trust**: Develop a trusted inner circle of loyal members who are privy to the leader's true nature and objectives. This inner circle helps enforce the leader's authority and maintain order.
- **Selective Disclosure**: Only disclose sensitive information and true intentions to the inner circle. Ensure their loyalty through rewards, privileges, and a shared sense of purpose.

Example: The leader cultivates a group of highly loyal members who are involved in decision-making processes and internal enforcement. This group is rewarded with special privileges and a deeper connection to the leader.

Reputation Management

- **Crisis Management**: Have a crisis management plan in place to handle any leaks or public exposure of the leader's private behavior. This plan should include strategies for damage control and public relations efforts to restore trust.
- **Media Relations**: Develop strong relationships with the media to control the narrative and present the cult in a positive light. Use media appearances and press releases to reinforce the cult's public image.

Example: The leader's team is prepared to swiftly address any negative revelations, using spin tactics and positive media coverage to mitigate damage. They maintain good relationships with journalists to ensure favorable reporting.

Conclusion

Adopting a Machiavellian approach to cult leadership involves presenting a compassionate and benevolent public face while maintaining strict control in private. By carefully managing this duality, leaders can ensure their authority and the cult's stability without compromising their public image. This chapter provides strategies for balancing public benevolence with private discipline, understanding the impact on followers, and managing the complexities of dual personas. Effective implementation of these strategies ensures that the cult remains cohesive and that the leader's power remains unchallenged, all while maintaining a positive public reputation.

Public Benevolence vs. Private Control

Cult leaders often face the challenge of balancing their public image with the need for strict control in private. This dual approach helps in attracting and retaining followers while ensuring the cult's stability and adherence to its principles. Here's a detailed explanation of how to manage public benevolence and private control effectively, with a practical example.

Public Persona

Cultivating a Public Image

- **Compassion and Empathy**: Show compassion and empathy in public interactions. This can involve participating in charitable activities, offering free community services, and providing emotional support to members.

- **Wisdom and Knowledge**: Demonstrate wisdom and knowledge in public speeches and writings. Share insights on various topics that resonate with the members' spiritual and personal growth aspirations.
- **Benevolence and Generosity**: Engage in acts of benevolence and generosity. This includes funding community projects, offering scholarships, or providing financial assistance to members in need.

Example of Public Persona

Imagine a cult leader named Alex. In public, Alex frequently participates in community service projects, such as organizing food drives for the homeless and setting up free health clinics for underprivileged areas. During public gatherings, Alex speaks passionately about the importance of compassion, unity, and personal growth. He shares stories of his own experiences and offers advice on overcoming life's challenges, positioning himself as a wise and caring guide.

Private Authority

Maintaining Strict Control

- **Enforcing Discipline**: Behind closed doors, Alex maintains strict control over the cult's members. This involves enforcing adherence to the cult's rituals, rules, and expectations. Non-compliance is met with appropriate consequences, such as reduced privileges or increased duties.
- **Monitoring Behavior**: Alex monitors members' behavior closely through a trusted inner circle. This group provides reports on members' activities, ensuring that everyone follows the prescribed path and maintains loyalty.
- **Firm Leadership**: In private meetings, Alex adopts a firm leadership style. He addresses issues directly, sets clear expectations, and makes decisions that prioritize the cult's stability and growth.

Example of Private Authority

In private, Alex holds regular meetings with his inner circle to discuss the cult's operations and members' compliance. He receives detailed reports on any issues of non-compliance or dissent. When a member fails to adhere to the ritual schedule, Alex personally intervenes, reminding them of their commitments and imposing additional tasks as a consequence. This firm approach ensures that members understand the importance of discipline and respect Alex's authority.

Balancing Public and Private Personas

Creating a Harmonious Balance

- **Consistent Messaging**: Ensure that public messages of compassion and wisdom are consistent with the private enforcement of discipline. This helps maintain credibility and trust among followers.

- **Strategic Transparency**: Be transparent about certain aspects of private control, such as the importance of discipline and adherence to rituals, without revealing the harshness of enforcement measures.

Example of Balanced Approach

Publicly, Alex talks about the significance of community service and personal growth, encouraging members to volunteer and support each other. He emphasizes that discipline and commitment are vital for personal and collective progress. Privately, Alex enforces these principles rigorously, ensuring that members remain dedicated and aligned with the cult's values.

Detailed Example: Alex's Leadership

Public Advocacy for Community Service

- **Charitable Activities**: Alex organizes monthly community service events, such as neighborhood clean-ups, food distribution drives, and free health check-ups. These activities are highly publicized, showcasing Alex's dedication to social welfare.
- **Public Speeches**: At these events, Alex delivers speeches that highlight the importance of helping others and growing together as a community. He shares personal anecdotes of how community service has enriched his life and encourages members to participate actively.

Private Enforcement of Rituals

- **Strict Ritual Adherence**: In private, Alex insists on strict adherence to daily rituals and practices. Members are required to meditate at specific times, participate in study sessions, and follow a stringent schedule of activities.
- **Disciplinary Measures**: If a member skips a ritual or fails to meet expectations, Alex enforces disciplinary measures. These can range from additional duties to temporary isolation from the group to reflect on their actions.

Consistency in Messaging

- **Public Transparency on Discipline**: Alex occasionally mentions the importance of discipline in his public speeches, framing it as a pathway to personal growth and spiritual enlightenment. This prepares members to understand and accept the need for discipline without revealing the strict measures taken privately.
- **Inner Circle Support**: Alex's inner circle supports this dual approach by reinforcing the public messages of compassion and discipline. They also help monitor members and report any issues directly to Alex.

Conclusion

Balancing public benevolence with private control is essential for effective cult leadership. By cultivating a compassionate and wise public persona, leaders can attract and retain followers, while strict private control ensures adherence to the cult's principles and stability. The example of Alex demonstrates how leaders can successfully manage this duality, maintaining their authority and the cult's integrity without compromising their public reputation.

Strategic Manipulation

Strategic manipulation is essential for maintaining control while fostering trust and a positive public image. By using controlled transparency and selective truth-telling, leaders can ensure that followers remain loyal and committed without revealing information that might undermine authority or cause dissent. Here's a detailed guide on implementing strategic manipulation effectively, with a practical example.

Controlled Transparency

Building Trust Through Transparency

- **Charitable Activities**: Openly discuss and showcase the cult's charitable activities and community service projects. Highlight the positive impact these activities have on both the cult and the broader community.
- **Operational Transparency**: Share information about the cult's goals, mission, and some aspects of its operations. This transparency helps build trust and shows that the cult is committed to positive values and ethical practices.

Withholding Sensitive Information

- **Internal Disciplinary Actions**: Keep details of internal disciplinary actions confidential to prevent dissent and protect the cult's internal cohesion. Only the inner circle or those directly involved should be aware of these measures.
- **Financial Details**: Maintain confidentiality regarding the cult's finances, particularly how funds are allocated and spent. Disclosing too much financial information can lead to misunderstandings, envy, or distrust.

Example of Controlled Transparency

Imagine a cult leader named Alex. In public, Alex frequently discusses the cult's numerous charitable activities, such as organizing food drives, providing free educational workshops, and supporting local shelters. These activities are widely publicized, showcasing the cult's commitment to community service and positive impact. However, Alex strategically withholds information about internal disciplinary actions and the specifics of financial management. This approach ensures that followers see the cult as benevolent and trustworthy while maintaining tight control over sensitive matters.

Selective Truth-Telling

Reinforcing Values Through Truth

- **Positive Achievements**: Share truths that highlight the cult's achievements, such as successful community projects, personal growth stories of members, and milestones reached. These truths reinforce the cult's values and mission.
- **Foundational Teachings**: Consistently share and reinforce the cult's foundational teachings and principles. This selective truth-telling helps maintain a cohesive belief system and ensures that members are aligned with the cult's core values.

Discretion on Sensitive Issues

- **Sensitive Topics**: Use discretion when discussing sensitive issues such as the cult's strict rules, internal conflicts, or controversial practices. Frame these issues in a way that aligns with the cult's narrative and values.
- **Crisis Management**: In times of crisis or controversy, control the narrative by sharing carefully selected truths that mitigate damage and reinforce the cult's integrity.

Example of Selective Truth-Telling

Alex often shares stories of members who have experienced significant personal growth through the cult's teachings. He talks about individuals who have overcome personal challenges, achieved spiritual enlightenment, or made positive contributions to their communities. These stories are truthful and inspirational, reinforcing the cult's mission. However, when it comes to discussing the stringent rules or internal conflicts, Alex frames these topics in a way that emphasizes discipline and unity without revealing the harsher aspects of enforcement.

Example in Practice: Alex's Strategic Manipulation

Public Image and Transparency

- **Community Service**: Alex holds a press conference to announce a new community service initiative, emphasizing the cult's commitment to social welfare. He shares details about the planned activities, the expected impact, and how members can get involved.
- **Mission Statement**: During public speeches, Alex frequently references the cult's mission statement, highlighting its focus on personal growth, community support, and spiritual enlightenment. This consistent messaging builds trust and aligns members with the cult's goals.

Withholding Sensitive Information

- **Disciplinary Actions**: Internally, Alex addresses non-compliance with strict disciplinary actions but keeps these measures confidential. Only those involved and the inner circle are aware of the specifics, ensuring that the public image remains untarnished.
- **Financial Management**: While Alex shares general information about fundraising successes and charitable expenditures, he withholds detailed financial reports. This prevents potential dissent or questions about the allocation of funds.

Selective Truth-Telling in Public

- **Personal Growth Stories**: Alex shares a story about a member named Sarah who, through the cult's teachings, overcame significant personal struggles and now leads a successful community project. This story is true and inspiring, reinforcing the positive impact of the cult.
- **Framing Strict Rules**: When asked about the cult's strict rules, Alex frames them as necessary for personal and spiritual discipline. He emphasizes the positive outcomes of adhering to these rules, such as achieving higher states of enlightenment and personal development, without detailing the strict enforcement methods.

Conclusion

Strategic manipulation involves balancing controlled transparency and selective truth-telling to maintain control while fostering a positive public image. By openly discussing the cult's charitable activities and successes and withholding sensitive information about internal disciplinary actions and financial details, leaders can build trust and ensure the cult's stability. This approach allows leaders like Alex to cultivate a benevolent and trustworthy public persona while maintaining strict control behind the scenes, ensuring that the cult remains cohesive and resilient.

Psychological and Emotional Management

Managing the psychological and emotional well-being of cult members is crucial for maintaining loyalty, morale, and adherence to the cult's rules. This involves a dual approach: offering public encouragement to build a positive community spirit, and using private discipline to ensure compliance and control. Here's a detailed guide on how to balance public encouragement with private discipline effectively, including a practical example.

Public Encouragement

Building Morale and Loyalty

- **Positive Reinforcement**: In public settings, consistently offer praise and positive reinforcement to members. Acknowledge their contributions, successes, and dedication to the cult's mission. This creates a supportive and uplifting atmosphere that encourages continued commitment.

- **Celebrating Achievements**: Highlight individual and group achievements during public gatherings. Recognize members who have demonstrated exceptional commitment, achieved personal growth, or contributed significantly to the community. This fosters a sense of pride and belonging.

Creating a Sense of Community

- **Group Activities**: Organize group activities that reinforce the cult's values and mission. These can include community service projects, team-building exercises, and social events that allow members to bond and support each other.
- **Inspirational Speeches**: Deliver inspirational speeches that emphasize the cult's goals, the importance of unity, and the value of each member's contributions. Use storytelling and motivational language to inspire and energize the group.

Example of Public Encouragement

Imagine a cult leader named Alex. During a weekly gathering, Alex publicly praises several members who have gone above and beyond in their community service efforts. He shares their stories, highlighting how their actions align with the cult's values and mission. Alex also organizes a group activity where members work together to prepare care packages for a local shelter, reinforcing the sense of community and collective effort.

Private Discipline

Addressing Non-Compliance and Dissent

- **Firm Enforcement**: Privately address any issues of non-compliance or dissent with a firm approach. Make it clear that adherence to the cult's rules and expectations is non-negotiable. Use direct communication to address the specific issues and outline the consequences of continued non-compliance.
- **Psychological Tactics**: Employ psychological tactics such as fear and guilt to ensure adherence to rules and discourage rebellion. These tactics can include emphasizing the spiritual or personal consequences of disobedience and reminding members of their commitment to the cult.

Maintaining Control

- **Regular Evaluations**: Conduct regular evaluations of members' behavior and commitment. Use these evaluations to identify potential issues and address them promptly. This proactive approach helps maintain control and prevent larger problems from developing.
- **Selective Isolation**: Use selective isolation as a disciplinary measure for members who repeatedly fail to comply. Temporarily isolating a member from the group can reinforce the seriousness of their actions and encourage them to reconsider their behavior.

Example of Private Discipline

After the public gathering, Alex privately meets with a member named John who has been skipping mandatory meditation sessions. Alex uses a firm tone to express his disappointment and reminds John of the importance of discipline and commitment. He emphasizes the spiritual consequences of neglecting these practices and imposes additional duties on John as a consequence. Alex makes it clear that continued non-compliance will result in more severe measures, such as temporary isolation from the group.

Example in Practice: Alex's Psychological and Emotional Management

Public Encouragement

- **Recognition Ceremony**: At a monthly recognition ceremony, Alex awards certificates to members who have shown exceptional dedication. He shares their stories with the group, highlighting their achievements and the positive impact they've made.
- **Group Bonding Activities**: Alex organizes a weekend retreat where members participate in team-building activities, group meditations, and community service projects. These activities strengthen bonds and reinforce the cult's values.

Private Discipline

- **One-on-One Meetings**: Alex schedules one-on-one meetings with members who show signs of dissent or non-compliance. During these meetings, he uses a combination of direct communication and psychological tactics to address the issues and reinforce discipline.
- **Use of Fear and Guilt**: When speaking with a member who has been spreading negative thoughts, Alex reminds them of the dire spiritual consequences of such actions. He uses guilt to make the member feel responsible for potentially harming the community's harmony.

Balancing Both Approaches

- **Consistent Messaging**: Alex ensures that the messages he delivers in public align with the actions he takes in private. This consistency helps maintain credibility and trust among members.
- **Monitoring and Feedback**: Alex regularly monitors the impact of his encouragement and discipline strategies, using feedback from his inner circle to adjust his approach as needed.

Conclusion

Balancing public encouragement with private discipline is essential for effective psychological and emotional management within a cult. By offering praise and positive reinforcement in public, leaders can build morale and loyalty, fostering a supportive community atmosphere. In private, using firm discipline and psychological tactics ensures adherence to rules and maintains control. The example of Alex demonstrates how this dual approach can be implemented to create a cohesive, motivated, and compliant group of followers.

Maintaining Social Harmony

Maintaining social harmony within a cult is crucial for its stability and growth. This involves a strategic balance between promoting inclusivity and harmony in public while privately managing members based on their loyalty and compliance. Here's a detailed guide on how to achieve this balance effectively, including a practical example.

Public Inclusivity

Creating a Welcoming Atmosphere

- **Promote Inclusivity**: In public settings, emphasize the inclusivity and harmony of the cult. Highlight how everyone is welcome and valued, regardless of their background. This approach helps attract new members and retain existing ones by creating a sense of belonging.
- **Supportive Community**: Showcase the supportive nature of the cult's community. Share stories of members helping each other, participating in group activities, and achieving personal growth through collective efforts. This reinforces the idea that the cult is a caring and nurturing environment.

Highlighting Shared Values

- **Unified Mission**: Publicly stress the cult's unified mission and shared values. Emphasize how each member contributes to the greater good and how the collective efforts help achieve common goals. This strengthens the sense of purpose and unity among members.
- **Inclusive Events**: Organize inclusive events such as open gatherings, community service projects, and social activities. These events should be designed to foster interaction, build relationships, and promote the cult's values.

Example of Public Inclusivity

Imagine a cult leader named Alex. At a public gathering, Alex delivers a speech emphasizing the cult's commitment to inclusivity and collective well-being. He shares stories of members supporting each other during difficult times and highlights the positive impact of their community service projects. Alex also announces an upcoming community event where all members are encouraged to participate, reinforcing the sense of unity and shared purpose.

Private Segregation

Segregating Based on Loyalty and Compliance

- **Loyalty Assessment**: Privately assess members' loyalty and compliance with the cult's rules and expectations. This can be done through regular evaluations, monitoring behavior, and receiving reports from a trusted inner circle.
- **Rewards and Punishments**: Implement a system of rewards and punishments to reinforce desired behaviors. Reward members who demonstrate strong loyalty and adherence to the cult's principles with privileges, recognition, and special opportunities. Conversely, discipline those who show signs of dissent or non-compliance.

Managing Control

- **Selective Isolation**: Use selective isolation as a tool to manage members who are not complying with the cult's rules. Temporarily isolate them from the group to make them reconsider their behavior and demonstrate the seriousness of their actions.
- **Tiered Membership**: Create a tiered membership system where privileges and responsibilities increase with demonstrated loyalty and compliance. This not only rewards dedicated members but also motivates others to strive for higher levels of commitment.

Example of Private Segregation

In private, Alex meets with his inner circle to discuss the loyalty and compliance of members. They identify a group of highly loyal members who consistently adhere to the cult's practices. Alex rewards these members with special privileges, such as access to advanced teachings and leadership roles in upcoming projects. Meanwhile, a few members who have been less compliant are given additional duties and are warned about potential isolation if they do not improve their behavior.

Example in Practice: Alex's Strategy for Social Harmony

Public Inclusivity

- **Inclusive Messaging**: At a public event, Alex talks about the importance of unity and inclusivity. He shares success stories of members who have benefitted from the supportive community and emphasizes that everyone's contributions are valued.
- **Community Events**: Alex organizes a large community gathering, inviting all members to participate in a group meditation session and a communal meal. This event is designed to foster a sense of belonging and reinforce the cult's inclusive values.

Private Segregation

- **Loyalty Monitoring**: In private, Alex and his inner circle monitor members' behavior closely. They have a system in place to track participation in rituals, adherence to rules, and overall attitude towards the cult.
- **Reward and Discipline**: Alex rewards loyal members with public recognition during the community event, giving them badges of honor and additional responsibilities. Members who have been non-compliant are privately spoken to and given extra tasks as a form of discipline. If they do not improve, they face temporary isolation from group activities.

Balancing Both Approaches

- **Consistent Public Message**: Alex ensures that his public messages of inclusivity and unity are consistent with the rewards and discipline system. This consistency helps maintain credibility and trust among members.
- **Effective Communication**: Alex communicates privately with his inner circle to ensure that they understand the importance of managing loyalty and compliance discreetly. This ensures that the public image of the cult remains positive and welcoming.

Conclusion

Maintaining social harmony within a cult requires a careful balance between public inclusivity and private segregation. By promoting a welcoming and supportive community in public, leaders can attract and retain members, fostering a sense of unity and shared purpose. Privately, segregating members based on loyalty and compliance through a system of rewards and punishments helps maintain control and reinforce desired behaviors. The example of Alex demonstrates how this dual approach can effectively manage social harmony, ensuring the cult remains cohesive and resilient.

Controlled Environments

Creating and maintaining controlled environments is essential for cultivating a positive public image while ensuring the privacy and security needed for internal operations. This involves strategically using public spaces to reinforce the cult's benevolent mission and private spaces for confidential activities. Here's a detailed guide on managing controlled environments effectively, including a practical example.

Public Spaces

Projecting a Positive Image

- **Open Events**: Host open events that welcome both members and the general public. These events should highlight the cult's values and mission, providing an opportunity for outsiders to learn about and engage with the cult in a positive way.

- **Community Service Projects**: Organize community service projects that benefit the local community. These activities not only demonstrate the cult's commitment to social welfare but also help build a positive reputation.
- **Public Lectures**: Offer public lectures and seminars on topics related to the cult's teachings, personal development, and community well-being. These events position the cult as a source of wisdom and benevolence.

Example of Public Space Usage

Imagine a cult leader named Alex. The cult regularly hosts public meditation sessions in a local park. These sessions are open to anyone interested, offering a peaceful space for relaxation and spiritual growth. Additionally, Alex organizes monthly community clean-up events, where members and volunteers work together to improve local neighborhoods. Public lectures on topics like stress management and ethical living are also held in community centers, attracting a diverse audience and reinforcing the cult's positive image.

Private Spaces

Maintaining Confidentiality and Security

- **Internal Meetings**: Use private spaces for internal meetings where sensitive topics are discussed. This includes strategy sessions, leadership meetings, and discussions about the cult's future direction. Ensuring these spaces are secure prevents unauthorized access and information leaks.
- **Disciplinary Actions**: Conduct disciplinary actions and evaluations in private settings. This ensures that any issues of non-compliance or dissent are handled discreetly, preserving the cult's public image while maintaining strict internal control.
- **Strategic Planning**: Reserve private spaces for strategic planning and decision-making. These sessions should involve the inner circle and trusted members who are integral to the cult's operations.

Example of Private Space Usage

In private, Alex holds regular meetings with his inner circle in a secure, members-only building. Here, they discuss the cult's strategic plans, review members' behavior, and make decisions on disciplinary actions. When a member needs to be disciplined, Alex meets with them privately to address the issues, ensuring that such matters remain confidential. The private space is also used for leadership training sessions and developing new initiatives.

Example in Practice: Alex's Use of Controlled Environments

Public Spaces

- **Meditation Sessions**: Every Sunday, Alex organizes a public meditation session in the park. These sessions attract both cult members and curious outsiders, providing a calm

and inclusive environment for spiritual practice. Alex uses these sessions to promote the cult's teachings and values.
- **Community Clean-Up**: Once a month, Alex leads a community clean-up event. Members, along with volunteers from the community, gather to clean local parks, streets, and public spaces. This visible act of service enhances the cult's reputation and demonstrates its commitment to social welfare.
- **Public Lectures**: Alex schedules monthly public lectures on various topics related to the cult's teachings. Held in a community center, these lectures cover subjects like meditation, ethical living, and personal development. The lectures are well-attended, reinforcing the cult's image as a source of wisdom and benevolence.

Private Spaces

- **Internal Strategy Meetings**: In a secure, private building, Alex and his inner circle hold weekly strategy meetings. They discuss the cult's plans, review the progress of ongoing projects, and make decisions on new initiatives. This private setting ensures that sensitive information remains confidential.
- **Disciplinary Sessions**: When a member violates the cult's rules, Alex meets with them in a private office to address the issue. He uses this space to discuss the member's behavior, outline the consequences, and set expectations for future conduct. This private approach maintains the cult's public image while enforcing internal discipline.
- **Leadership Training**: The private building also serves as a training center for future leaders. Alex conducts intensive training sessions, focusing on the cult's teachings, leadership skills, and strategic planning. The secure environment allows for open discussion and thorough preparation.

Balancing Both Approaches

- **Consistent Messaging**: Alex ensures that the messages delivered in public spaces align with the actions taken in private spaces. This consistency helps maintain credibility and trust among members and the public.
- **Effective Communication**: Alex communicates clearly with his inner circle about the importance of maintaining confidentiality and the strategic use of public and private spaces. This ensures everyone understands and supports the approach.

Conclusion

Managing controlled environments involves strategically using public spaces to project a positive image and private spaces for confidential operations. Public spaces are used for open events, community service projects, and public lectures, reinforcing the cult's benevolent mission and attracting new members. Private spaces are reserved for internal meetings, disciplinary actions, and strategic planning, ensuring confidentiality and security. The example of Alex demonstrates how this approach can effectively balance public inclusivity with private control, maintaining the cult's positive image and internal cohesion.

Trusted Inner Circle

Creating a trusted inner circle is essential for maintaining control and enforcing authority within a cult. This group of loyal members is privy to the leader's true nature and objectives, helping to manage internal affairs and ensure the cult's stability. Here's a detailed guide on building a trusted inner circle, including practical strategies and examples with stories.

Building Trust

Developing Loyalty

- **Careful Selection**: Identify members who demonstrate exceptional loyalty, commitment, and understanding of the cult's teachings. These individuals should have a strong personal connection to the leader and the cult's mission.

Story: Alex noticed Sarah, a devoted member who had been consistently active in all cult activities and displayed unwavering belief in the cult's teachings. Recognizing her potential, Alex decided to bring her into his inner circle. He began by inviting her to small, exclusive meetings, where she felt valued and important.

- **Personal Mentorship**: Provide personal mentorship to selected members. This involves regular one-on-one meetings, personalized guidance, and leadership training. Mentorship fosters a deeper bond and trust between the leader and inner circle members.

Story: During their one-on-one sessions, Alex shared insights with Sarah about the cult's deeper philosophies and strategic goals. He gave her leadership responsibilities for small projects, coaching her on how to manage and motivate other members. Over time, Sarah's loyalty deepened, and she felt honored to be mentored personally by Alex.

Creating a Shared Purpose

- **Common Goals**: Establish common goals and a shared sense of purpose among inner circle members. This can include strategic objectives, community projects, or spiritual missions that align with the cult's values.

Story: At an exclusive retreat, Alex gathered his inner circle, including Sarah, and outlined their new project – establishing a community center. This center would serve as both a hub for cult activities and a beacon of their charitable efforts. The shared goal of creating this center bonded the inner circle members tightly, as they worked together to bring Alex's vision to life.

- **Exclusive Activities**: Organize exclusive activities and events for the inner circle. These activities can include advanced teachings, private ceremonies, and special missions that reinforce their unique status and importance within the cult.

Story: Once a month, Alex hosted a secretive midnight ritual for his inner circle, where he shared advanced teachings and mystical experiences that were off-limits to regular members. These exclusive gatherings made Sarah and the others feel uniquely privileged and deepened their commitment to Alex and the cult.

Selective Disclosure

Disclosing Sensitive Information

- **Controlled Information Flow**: Only disclose sensitive information and the leader's true intentions to the inner circle. This includes strategic plans, internal issues, and confidential operations. Controlled disclosure ensures that critical information is kept within trusted hands.

Story: Alex informed his inner circle about a new, controversial expansion plan that involved recruiting from rival groups. He explained the delicate nature of this plan and emphasized the need for secrecy. The inner circle understood the importance of their role in this strategy and felt empowered by their insider knowledge.

- **Transparency with Inner Circle**: Be transparent with the inner circle about the leader's true nature, objectives, and any necessary deceptions used to maintain control. This honesty builds trust and reinforces their role as key enforcers of the leader's authority.

Story: Alex confided in Sarah and the inner circle about the strategic manipulations he used to maintain public order. He explained that certain public deceptions were necessary to protect the cult's integrity and ensure its growth. This transparency solidified the inner circle's loyalty, as they saw themselves as protectors of a greater mission.

Ensuring Loyalty

- **Rewards and Privileges**: Provide significant rewards and privileges to inner circle members. This can include financial incentives, exclusive access to the leader, and elevated status within the cult. Such rewards ensure their continued loyalty and commitment.

Story: Alex rewarded Sarah and the inner circle with exclusive trips to luxurious retreats, financial bonuses, and public acknowledgment of their contributions. Sarah received a special medallion from Alex, symbolizing her elevated status and her importance to the cult's inner workings.

- **Shared Responsibility**: Involve the inner circle in decision-making processes and internal enforcement. This shared responsibility reinforces their importance and deepens their connection to the cult's success.

Story: Alex tasked Sarah and the inner circle with developing a new outreach program. They brainstormed strategies, made decisions, and implemented the program together. This shared responsibility not only strengthened their bond but also made them feel integral to the cult's success.

Example in Practice: Alex's Trusted Inner Circle

Building Trust

- **Mentorship Program**: Alex initiates a mentorship program for his inner circle, providing regular personal guidance and advanced leadership training. This program includes in-depth discussions about the cult's teachings, strategies, and goals.

Story: Sarah, now fully integrated into the inner circle, attended weekly mentorship sessions with Alex. During these sessions, Alex taught her advanced leadership techniques and shared the long-term vision for the cult. Sarah felt increasingly empowered and dedicated.

- **Exclusive Retreats**: Alex organizes quarterly retreats for the inner circle, held in secluded locations. These retreats are opportunities for bonding, strategic planning, and exclusive teachings that are not available to the general membership.

Story: At a secluded mountain cabin, Alex and his inner circle, including Sarah, spent a weekend planning the next year's initiatives. They participated in special rituals, discussed deep philosophical topics, and formed a cohesive strategy for the cult's expansion.

Selective Disclosure

- **Strategic Planning Sessions**: In private, Alex shares detailed strategic plans with his inner circle, including expansion efforts, recruitment strategies, and internal management tactics. He ensures that only the inner circle is aware of these plans.

Story: Alex disclosed a risky plan to infiltrate a local community group to the inner circle. He detailed the steps involved and the roles each inner circle member would play. Sarah was tasked with leading a sub-group to execute part of this plan, solidifying her integral role.

- **Privileged Access**: Alex provides his inner circle with exclusive access to financial resources, decision-making processes, and private meetings. This privileged access reinforces their loyalty and commitment.

Story: During a private meeting, Alex gave Sarah and other inner circle members access to the cult's financial records, explaining their importance in ensuring financial stability. He also granted them the authority to approve certain expenditures, deepening their involvement and loyalty.

Maintaining Control

- **Enforcement Role**: Inner circle members are tasked with enforcing the cult's rules and managing disciplinary actions. They act as intermediaries between the leader and the general membership, ensuring compliance and addressing issues discreetly.

Story: When a member began questioning the cult's practices, Alex instructed Sarah to handle the situation. She met with the member privately, using psychological tactics learned from Alex to bring the member back in line. This enforcement role made Sarah feel powerful and trusted.

- **Recognition and Rewards**: Alex publicly recognizes the contributions of his inner circle during gatherings, enhancing their status within the cult. Privately, he rewards them with financial bonuses and exclusive opportunities.

Story: At a public gathering, Alex praised Sarah for her leadership in the new outreach program. He presented her with an award, which was met with applause from the other members. Privately, he gave her a significant financial bonus and promised her a leading role in the next big project.

Conclusion

Building a trusted inner circle involves carefully selecting loyal members, providing personal mentorship, and creating a shared sense of purpose. By selectively disclosing sensitive information and ensuring loyalty through rewards and privileges, leaders can maintain control and enforce their authority effectively. The stories of Sarah and Alex demonstrate how a well-developed inner circle can support the leader's objectives, manage internal affairs, and ensure the cult's stability. This strategic approach ensures that critical information remains confidential and that the inner circle remains dedicated to the leader's vision and mission.

Reputation Management

Managing a cult's reputation is critical for maintaining public trust and ensuring the stability of the organization. This involves preparing for crises, controlling the narrative through effective media relations, and ensuring that any negative revelations are swiftly and effectively addressed. Here's a detailed guide on how to manage reputation, including practical strategies and examples with stories.

Crisis Management

Preparing for Crises

- **Crisis Management Plan**: Develop a comprehensive crisis management plan that outlines steps to take in the event of a leak or public exposure of the leader's private behavior. This plan should detail specific roles and actions for key members of the inner circle and public relations team.

- **Damage Control Strategies**: Include damage control strategies such as public apologies, explanations, and corrective actions. Have prepared statements and responses ready for various scenarios to ensure a swift and coordinated response.

Example Story: Handling a Leak

Imagine a cult leader named Alex. One day, a former member leaks information about Alex's private disciplinary actions. Alex's team quickly enacts the crisis management plan. They hold an emergency meeting to assess the situation and prepare a public statement.

- **Public Statement**: Alex's public statement acknowledges the leak but frames the disciplinary actions as necessary measures to maintain the community's integrity and safety. He emphasizes the cult's commitment to transparency and improvement.
- **Corrective Actions**: The team announces a new initiative to review and improve internal practices, inviting external experts to provide oversight. This move is designed to restore trust and demonstrate accountability.

Media Relations

Controlling the Narrative

- **Building Media Relationships**: Cultivate strong relationships with journalists and media outlets. This involves regularly providing them with positive stories, exclusive access, and transparent communication. Building goodwill with the media ensures more favorable coverage during crises.
- **Media Appearances**: Use media appearances and press releases to reinforce the cult's public image. Alex frequently appears on local news shows, discussing the cult's charitable activities and personal growth programs. These appearances help shape public perception positively.

Example Story: Positive Media Coverage

Alex's team has developed close relationships with several journalists. When the leak occurs, they contact these journalists directly, providing them with exclusive interviews and positive stories about the cult's recent charitable initiatives.

- **Exclusive Interviews**: Alex gives an exclusive interview to a trusted journalist, where he discusses the challenges of leadership and the steps the cult is taking to ensure ethical practices. This interview is framed to show Alex as a responsible and caring leader.
- **Press Releases**: The team issues press releases highlighting the cult's ongoing community projects and new initiatives to enhance transparency and member welfare. These releases are sent to all major media outlets, ensuring widespread positive coverage.

Example in Practice: Alex's Reputation Management

Crisis Management

- **Immediate Response**: When the leak about Alex's disciplinary methods is made public, his team immediately convenes to craft a response. They use prepared statements to address the issue swiftly.
- **Public Apology and Explanation**: Alex publicly apologizes if any actions were misunderstood but explains the necessity of maintaining discipline for the safety and integrity of the community. He promises to review and improve these methods.
- **Announcing Reforms**: Alex announces the formation of an ethics committee, including external advisors, to oversee internal practices. This move is aimed at restoring trust and showing a commitment to transparency and improvement.

Media Relations

- **Pre-emptive Media Engagement**: Before the leak, Alex's team had already built strong relationships with local journalists by providing exclusive stories about the cult's positive impact on the community.
- **Exclusive Access**: During the crisis, Alex offers exclusive access to these journalists, allowing them to cover the cult's response and reforms firsthand. This access ensures that the coverage remains balanced and highlights the cult's positive aspects.
- **Positive Spin**: The press releases issued focus on the cult's ongoing projects, such as a new community center and a recent successful charity drive. These stories are designed to overshadow the negative news and keep public attention on the cult's good works.

Balancing Both Approaches

- **Consistency**: Alex ensures that his public statements and media appearances are consistent with the cult's values of transparency and improvement. This consistency helps maintain credibility.
- **Strategic Communication**: His team uses strategic communication to control the narrative, ensuring that any negative information is quickly countered with positive stories and actions.

Conclusion

Reputation management involves preparing for potential crises, controlling the narrative through effective media relations, and ensuring swift and effective responses to any negative revelations. By having a comprehensive crisis management plan, building strong media relationships, and using strategic communication, cult leaders like Alex can maintain a positive public image and ensure the stability of their organization. The stories of Alex demonstrate how these strategies can be implemented effectively, balancing public apologies and corrective actions with positive media coverage to restore trust and reinforce the cult's positive reputation.

Chapter 11: Using Your Members to be Influential in Politics

In this chapter, we explore how to leverage the power of your cult members to gain influence in the political arena. Whether through manipulating politicians, becoming politicians themselves, or creating laws that benefit your cult, these strategies can significantly enhance your control and expand your reach.

Manipulate Politicians

Building Relationships

- **Networking**: Encourage your members to build strong relationships with local politicians and influential figures. This can be achieved through attending political events, volunteering for campaigns, and making donations.

Example: Alex directed a few trusted members to volunteer in a local mayoral campaign. By showing dedication and support, these members were able to build a rapport with the candidate, gaining his trust and attention. They attended town hall meetings, social gatherings, and fundraising events, gradually becoming recognized as key supporters.

Offering Support

- **Campaign Contributions**: Financially support political candidates who are sympathetic to your cult's beliefs or can be swayed to support your agenda. Contributions can buy influence and ensure politicians are willing to listen to your concerns.

Example: Alex organized a high-profile fundraising event for a city council candidate. The event featured prominent speakers and attracted influential guests, ensuring the candidate felt indebted to Alex. The significant contributions from the cult members guaranteed the candidate's support for future requests.

Leveraging Influence

- **Policy Proposals**: Once a relationship is established, use your influence to propose policies or laws that benefit your cult. Ensure these proposals are framed in a way that appeals to the politician's goals and the broader public good.

Example: After gaining the mayor's trust, Alex proposed a new community initiative that aligned with the mayor's platform. The initiative subtly incorporated elements that would benefit the cult, such as tax exemptions for religious organizations. Alex's inner circle drafted the proposal, emphasizing its benefits for the community, and presented it to the mayor for endorsement.

Become a Politician

Training and Preparation

- **Leadership Development**: Train your most charismatic and capable members to take on public leadership roles. This includes public speaking, policy understanding, and campaign strategies.

Example: Sarah, a member of Alex's inner circle, was trained extensively in public speaking, policy matters, and political strategy. Alex provided her with reading materials, mock debates, and coaching sessions to prepare her for the public eye. She also attended leadership workshops and political science courses to deepen her knowledge.

Running for Office

- **Campaign Strategy**: Develop a robust campaign strategy for your members running for political office. This includes leveraging the cult's resources, using its network for grassroots support, and ensuring a strong, cohesive message.

Example: With the cult's backing, Sarah launched her campaign for city council. Cult members canvassed neighborhoods, organized events, and used social media to build support. They created persuasive campaign materials, hosted community forums, and secured endorsements from influential figures. The unified effort ensured a strong campaign presence.

Achieving Political Goals

- **Enacting Change**: Once in office, use the position to enact laws and policies that benefit the cult. Ensure these changes are incremental and framed to appeal to the broader community to avoid suspicion.

Example: After winning the election, Sarah began proposing small but significant changes, such as increased funding for community centers (run by the cult) and policies that favored non-profit organizations. She also advocated for zoning changes that benefited the cult's properties. These changes were presented as benefiting the wider community, ensuring public support.

Create Laws That Benefit Your Cult

Strategic Lawmaking

- **Identifying Opportunities**: Identify areas where new laws could significantly benefit your cult, such as tax exemptions, land use, or educational funding.

Example: Alex and his inner circle identified a loophole in local zoning laws that could be exploited to build a large community center. They drafted a proposal to reclassify certain land areas for religious use, which Sarah then championed in council. They conducted research and gathered data to support their proposal, making a strong case for its approval.

Lobbying Efforts

- **Engaging Lobbyists**: Hire or engage with lobbyists who can advocate for your interests within the political system. Ensure they understand your goals and can effectively communicate them to lawmakers.

Example: Alex hired a well-connected lobbying firm to push for legislation that would grant tax-exempt status to all properties owned by religious organizations. The lobbyists worked behind the scenes to build support among lawmakers, arranging meetings, providing briefings, and drafting policy papers to persuade legislators.

Building Coalitions

- **Alliances**: Form alliances with other groups or organizations that share similar goals. These coalitions can amplify your voice and increase the likelihood of legislative success.

Example: Alex reached out to other non-profit and religious organizations, forming a coalition to support the tax exemption law. Together, they presented a united front that was hard for lawmakers to ignore. They organized joint press conferences, wrote op-eds, and mobilized their members to contact their representatives.

Example in Practice: Alex's Political Strategy

Manipulate Politicians

- **Building Relationships**: Alex's inner circle members, including Sarah, volunteered for local political campaigns, attending events and making donations to gain the candidates' trust.
- **Offering Support**: Alex organized a high-profile fundraising event for a sympathetic city council candidate, ensuring financial contributions from cult members secured the candidate's support.
- **Leveraging Influence**: Once the candidate was in office, Alex proposed a community initiative that included tax exemptions for religious organizations, which the candidate endorsed as beneficial for the community.

Become a Politician

- **Training and Preparation**: Sarah received extensive training in public speaking and policy understanding, preparing her for a political career.
- **Running for Office**: With the cult's backing, Sarah launched a well-organized campaign for city council, leveraging the cult's network for grassroots support.
- **Achieving Political Goals**: After winning, Sarah proposed and implemented policies that benefited the cult, such as increased funding for community centers and favorable zoning changes.

Create Laws That Benefit Your Cult

- **Strategic Lawmaking**: Alex and his inner circle identified zoning law loopholes and drafted proposals for reclassification, which Sarah championed.
- **Lobbying Efforts**: Alex hired a lobbying firm to push for tax-exempt status legislation, building support among lawmakers through strategic advocacy.
- **Building Coalitions**: Alex formed alliances with other non-profit organizations to support the tax exemption law, presenting a united front that was hard for lawmakers to ignore.

Conclusion

Using your members to gain influence in politics can significantly enhance the power and reach of your cult. By manipulating politicians, becoming politicians, and creating laws that benefit your organization, you can embed your influence deeply into the political fabric. The detailed examples of Alex and Sarah illustrate how strategic thinking, relationship-building, and effective campaigning can turn political ambition into tangible power. These methods, when used responsibly and ethically, can help create a more favorable environment for your cult's growth and sustainability.

Building Relationships

Networking

Networking is a vital strategy for establishing influence within political circles. By encouraging your members to build strong relationships with local politicians and influential figures, you can create pathways for your cult to gain political leverage. This can be achieved through attending political events, volunteering for campaigns, and making donations.

Example: Alex's Strategic Volunteer Effort

Alex understood the importance of political influence and decided to implement a strategic networking effort through his most trusted members. He identified an upcoming mayoral campaign as an opportunity to embed his members within the political landscape.

Step-by-Step Strategy:

1. **Volunteering for Campaigns**: Alex directed a few trusted members, including Sarah and John, to volunteer for the local mayoral campaign. These members were chosen for their charisma, dedication, and ability to blend into different social settings seamlessly.
2. **Attending Town Hall Meetings**: Sarah and John began attending town hall meetings regularly. Their consistent presence allowed them to familiarize themselves with the campaign's key issues and align their support accordingly. They asked thoughtful questions and provided constructive feedback, positioning themselves as engaged and knowledgeable constituents.

3. **Social Gatherings**: The campaign frequently organized social gatherings and fundraising events. Sarah and John made it a point to attend these events, mingling with other supporters and key campaign staff. They utilized these opportunities to build rapport with influential figures, gradually becoming recognized as reliable and enthusiastic supporters.
4. **Fundraising Efforts**: To further cement their standing, Sarah and John spearheaded fundraising efforts within the cult, pooling resources to make significant donations to the campaign. These contributions were made publicly, ensuring that the candidate and his team recognized their support.

Building Rapport and Trust:

- **Consistency and Reliability**: By consistently attending events and providing unwavering support, Sarah and John demonstrated their reliability. This consistency made them valuable assets to the campaign, leading to deeper trust and more significant roles within the campaign team.
- **Demonstrating Dedication**: Their dedication was not limited to financial contributions. Sarah and John volunteered countless hours, handling various tasks from canvassing neighborhoods to organizing events. This hands-on approach showcased their commitment to the candidate's success.
- **Strategic Conversations**: During social gatherings, Sarah and John engaged in strategic conversations with the candidate and his advisors. They subtly introduced ideas that aligned with Alex's broader goals, ensuring that these suggestions seemed beneficial for the campaign's success.

Gaining Influence:

As the campaign progressed, Sarah and John's contributions did not go unnoticed. The candidate began to rely on them for insights and support, inviting them to inner-circle meetings and strategy sessions. This access allowed Sarah and John to further influence the campaign's direction subtly.

Outcome:

When the candidate won the mayoral race, Sarah and John were well-positioned as trusted allies. The new mayor recognized their efforts and granted them advisory roles, giving Alex indirect access to political decision-making processes. This strategic networking not only embedded Alex's members within the political fabric but also ensured that his cult's interests were considered in local governance.

Conclusion:

Networking through strategic volunteering, consistent attendance at political events, and significant financial contributions can effectively build strong relationships with local politicians. By embedding trusted members within political campaigns, you can create pathways for influence and ensure that your cult's interests are represented in political decision-making processes. The example of Alex, Sarah, and John illustrates how dedication, strategic engagement, and consistent support can transform political networking into tangible power.

Offering Support

Campaign Contributions

Financially supporting political candidates who are sympathetic to your cult's beliefs or can be swayed to support your agenda is a powerful way to gain influence. Contributions can buy access and ensure politicians are willing to listen to your concerns and advocate for your interests.

Example: Alex's High-Profile Fundraising Event

Alex recognized the strategic importance of supporting a city council candidate who was open to aligning with his cult's goals. He decided to organize a high-profile fundraising event that would not only provide financial support but also position his cult as a significant political player.

Step-by-Step Strategy:

1. **Identifying the Candidate**: Alex and his inner circle identified a city council candidate, Laura, who had expressed interest in community development and social justice—issues that aligned with the cult's public facade. Laura was known for being approachable and open to collaboration.
2. **Planning the Event**: Alex planned an elaborate fundraising event. He chose a prestigious venue that would impress attendees and signal the importance of the occasion. The event was meticulously organized, with invitations sent to influential community members, local business leaders, and prominent political figures.
3. **Securing Prominent Speakers**: To add credibility and attract attention, Alex secured several prominent speakers who were respected in the community. These speakers included local celebrities, respected activists, and influential business leaders. Their presence was meant to draw in a large crowd and lend legitimacy to the event.
4. **Inviting Influential Guests**: Invitations were extended to influential guests, including local media representatives, high-ranking officials, and wealthy donors. The goal was to create a network of powerful individuals who could be potential allies in future endeavors.

Executing the Event:

- **Showcasing the Candidate**: The event was designed to showcase Laura as a visionary leader with a strong commitment to the community. Alex gave a compelling speech endorsing her candidacy and highlighting her alignment with the cult's values.

- **Significant Contributions**: Cult members were encouraged to make substantial donations, both individually and collectively. The total amount raised was significantly higher than typical contributions for local campaigns, ensuring Laura felt deeply indebted to Alex and his group.
- **Networking Opportunities**: The event provided ample opportunities for networking. Attendees mingled during a pre-event reception, fostering connections that could be leveraged for future political and social initiatives.

Building Rapport and Trust:

- **Personal Engagement**: Alex personally engaged with Laura throughout the event, discussing her platform and subtly introducing the cult's goals. He emphasized the mutual benefits of their collaboration, positioning his support as a partnership rather than mere patronage.
- **Demonstrating Influence**: The impressive turnout and the substantial funds raised demonstrated Alex's influence and the cult's organizational capabilities. Laura was shown that aligning with Alex could bring significant resources and support to her campaign and future projects.

Gaining Influence:

As the fundraising event concluded, Laura publicly thanked Alex and his supporters, acknowledging their crucial role in her campaign's success. This public endorsement solidified the relationship and made it clear that Laura viewed Alex as a key ally.

Outcome:

When Laura won the city council seat, she remembered the pivotal role Alex and his cult played in her campaign. Alex capitalized on this by requesting meetings to discuss community initiatives that aligned with the cult's goals. Laura, feeling indebted and recognizing Alex's influence, was receptive to his ideas and began advocating for policies that benefited the cult.

Conclusion:

Offering support through significant campaign contributions is an effective strategy for gaining political influence. By organizing high-profile fundraising events, engaging personally with candidates, and demonstrating organizational strength, you can ensure that politicians are willing to listen to your concerns and support your agenda. The example of Alex's fundraising event for Laura illustrates how financial support, combined with strategic engagement, can secure political allies and advance your cult's interests.

Leveraging Influence

Policy Proposals

Once a relationship with a politician is established, you can use this influence to propose policies or laws that benefit your cult. It's essential to frame these proposals in a way that appeals to the politician's goals and the broader public good, ensuring they are seen as beneficial to the community at large.

Example: Alex's Strategic Policy Proposal

After successfully establishing a strong relationship with the newly elected mayor, Alex saw an opportunity to propose a policy that would provide significant benefits to his cult. He carefully crafted a community initiative that aligned with the mayor's platform while subtly incorporating elements advantageous to the cult.

Step-by-Step Strategy:

1. **Identifying Opportunities**: Alex and his inner circle identified a gap in the current community services that the mayor had pledged to address during his campaign. They saw this as a perfect opportunity to introduce a policy that would both support the mayor's goals and benefit their cult.
2. **Drafting the Proposal**: Alex's inner circle, which included members with legal and political expertise, drafted a comprehensive policy proposal. This initiative aimed to enhance community services by providing additional support to local non-profits and religious organizations.
3. **Framing the Benefits**: The proposal was meticulously framed to highlight its community benefits. It emphasized improved services for underserved populations, increased community engagement, and enhanced public welfare. Special attention was given to ensuring that the proposal appeared as a broad public good rather than a narrow benefit for the cult.

Executing the Proposal:

- **Emphasizing Alignment with the Mayor's Goals**: The proposal was presented in a way that aligned with the mayor's campaign promises. Alex highlighted how the initiative would help fulfill the mayor's pledge to improve community services and support local organizations.
- **Incorporating Cult Benefits**: Within the proposal, Alex subtly included provisions that would specifically benefit his cult. These included tax exemptions for religious properties, grants for community projects managed by the cult, and allowances for using public spaces for cult activities. These elements were integrated seamlessly to appear as part of the broader initiative.

Building Rapport and Trust:

- **Personal Engagement**: Alex arranged a private meeting with the mayor to discuss the proposal in detail. He presented the initiative as a collaborative effort to enhance community welfare, demonstrating how it aligned perfectly with the mayor's vision.
- **Supporting Data and Testimonials**: The proposal was backed by data and testimonials from community leaders and residents, showcasing the positive impact similar initiatives had in other regions. This evidence helped build a compelling case for the proposal's implementation.

Gaining Endorsement:

- **Mayor's Endorsement**: Impressed by the thoroughness and potential impact of the proposal, the mayor endorsed the initiative. He appreciated the alignment with his platform and the apparent widespread community benefits.
- **Public Announcement**: The mayor publicly announced his support for the initiative, framing it as a key part of his administration's efforts to improve community services. This public endorsement reinforced the proposal's legitimacy and increased its chances of approval by the city council.

Outcome:

The proposal was subsequently approved by the city council, leading to the implementation of the community initiative. The provisions included in the proposal allowed Alex's cult to receive significant tax exemptions and grants, enhancing their financial stability and expanding their influence within the community.

Conclusion:

Leveraging political influence to propose policies or laws that benefit your cult requires careful planning, strategic framing, and thorough execution. By aligning proposals with the politician's goals and presenting them as beneficial to the broader public, you can gain the necessary support and endorsement. The example of Alex's community initiative illustrates how to integrate specific benefits for your cult into broader policy proposals, ensuring both political and community support for your agenda.

Become a Politician

Training and Preparation

To achieve significant political influence, it is essential to train and prepare the most charismatic and capable members of your cult to take on public leadership roles. This involves comprehensive leadership development, including public speaking, policy understanding, and campaign strategies.

Leadership Development

Train Your Most Charismatic Members: Focus on those with natural charisma and strong communication skills, as they are more likely to inspire and lead others effectively. Leadership development should be a holistic process that includes multiple aspects of political training.

Example: Sarah's Journey to Political Leadership

Step-by-Step Strategy:

Public Speaking Training

1. **Workshops and Practice Sessions**: Sarah attended weekly public speaking workshops where she learned techniques for effective speech delivery. These workshops included lessons on tone modulation, pacing, audience engagement, and the use of rhetorical devices to persuade and inspire. Regular practice sessions allowed her to refine these skills and build confidence.
2. **Mock Debates**: Alex organized mock debates for Sarah, where she faced off against other members in simulated political debates. These sessions helped her develop quick thinking, persuasive arguments, and the ability to handle challenging questions. The mock debates also provided a platform for Sarah to practice staying calm under pressure and responding effectively to opposition.
3. **Coaching Sessions**: Sarah received one-on-one coaching sessions from experienced public speakers within the cult. These mentors provided personalized feedback on her speech delivery, body language, and overall presentation. The coaching sessions also included exercises to improve her ability to connect with the audience emotionally and intellectually.

Policy Understanding

1. **Reading Materials**: Sarah was provided with a curated selection of books, articles, and policy papers covering a wide range of topics, including education, healthcare, community development, and economic policy. This extensive reading helped her build a solid foundation in policy matters and understand the complexities of governance.
2. **Seminars and Workshops**: Sarah attended seminars and workshops led by policy experts, both within and outside the cult. These sessions covered the intricacies of policy-making, legislative processes, and governance structures. The workshops often included case studies of successful policy implementations, giving Sarah practical insights into how effective policies are crafted and enacted.
3. **Case Studies**: Alex introduced Sarah to case studies of successful policy implementations and political strategies. By analyzing real-world examples, she gained insights into effective policy-making and the challenges involved. The case studies also provided a framework for understanding how to navigate political obstacles and build consensus around policy proposals.

Campaign Strategies

1. **Campaign Planning**: Sarah learned about the various components of campaign planning, including voter outreach, fundraising, media engagement, and event organization. She studied successful political campaigns to understand effective strategies and tactics, focusing on how to build a strong and cohesive campaign team.
2. **Grassroots Mobilization**: Alex taught Sarah the importance of grassroots mobilization. She practiced organizing community events, canvassing neighborhoods, and engaging with potential voters. This hands-on experience was crucial for understanding the dynamics of political campaigns and building a loyal voter base.
3. **Digital Marketing**: Sarah was trained in digital marketing techniques, including social media management, online advertising, and content creation. She learned how to use digital platforms to build her public image, connect with a broader audience, and mobilize supporters. The training included lessons on creating engaging content, analyzing digital metrics, and responding to online feedback.

Implementing the Training Program:

Intensive Study

1. **Curriculum Development**: Alex and his inner circle developed a comprehensive curriculum that covered all aspects of political leadership, from basic governance principles to advanced policy analysis. This curriculum included case studies, interactive workshops, and guest lectures from experienced politicians and experts.
2. **Study Groups**: Sarah participated in weekly study group sessions with other potential leaders. These sessions involved discussing recent policy changes, debating various approaches to governance, and collaboratively solving policy problems. The study groups also provided a platform for peer learning and support.

Leadership Roles

1. **Practical Experience**: Alex assigned Sarah to leadership roles within the cult's internal projects and community initiatives. This practical experience helped her develop the skills needed to manage teams, make decisions, and implement strategies effectively.
2. **Project Management**: Sarah was given responsibility for significant projects that required strategic planning, resource allocation, and team coordination. This experience was invaluable for understanding the complexities of political leadership and building her organizational skills.

Mentorship Meetings

1. **Regular Mentorship**: Sarah had bi-weekly mentorship meetings with Alex and other senior leaders. During these meetings, she discussed her progress, received feedback on her performance, and explored strategies for overcoming challenges.
2. **Feedback and Evaluation**: Sarah received regular feedback from her mentors and peers. This constructive feedback helped her identify areas for improvement, refine her strategies, and track her progress over time.

Conclusion

Training and preparing members to become politicians involves a comprehensive approach to leadership development. By focusing on public speaking, policy understanding, and campaign strategies, you can equip your most charismatic and capable members to take on public leadership roles effectively. The example of Sarah's journey illustrates how rigorous training, practical experience, and ongoing mentorship can transform potential leaders into influential politicians. This strategy ensures that your cult has strong representatives within the political landscape, capable of advancing your agenda and increasing your influence

Running for Office

Campaign Strategy

Developing a robust campaign strategy for your members running for political office is crucial for success. This strategy should leverage the cult's resources, utilize its network for grassroots support, and ensure a strong, cohesive message that resonates with voters.

Example: Sarah's Campaign for City Council

Step-by-Step Strategy:

1. Leveraging the Cult's Resources

- **Financial Support**: The cult provided substantial financial backing for Sarah's campaign. Fundraising events were organized within the cult to gather donations, ensuring a well-funded campaign that could afford high-quality marketing materials, professional campaign staff, and widespread advertising.

Example: Alex organized several fundraising dinners where cult members and their contacts contributed generously to Sarah's campaign fund. These events not only raised significant amounts of money but also created a sense of investment in Sarah's success among the cult members.

2. Grassroots Mobilization

- **Canvassing**: Cult members volunteered to canvass neighborhoods, distributing flyers and talking to residents about Sarah's platform. They organized door-to-door visits to engage directly with potential voters, answering questions and providing information on voting dates and locations.

Example: Every weekend, teams of cult members fanned out across the city, knocking on doors and speaking with residents about Sarah's vision for the community. Their dedication and consistent presence helped build personal connections with voters.

- **Community Events**: Sarah's campaign team organized community events such as town hall meetings, picnics, and clean-up drives. These events provided opportunities for Sarah to interact with constituents, listen to their concerns, and demonstrate her commitment to the community.

Example: Sarah hosted a series of town hall meetings where she discussed her policy proposals and answered questions from the audience. These events were well-attended and covered by local media, enhancing her visibility and credibility.

3. Social Media and Digital Marketing

- **Online Presence**: A dedicated campaign website and social media profiles were created to disseminate Sarah's message, engage with constituents, and provide updates on campaign activities. The digital platforms were used to share videos, blog posts, and testimonials from supporters.

Example: The campaign team regularly posted updates on Sarah's social media profiles, including videos of her speaking at events, infographics explaining her policies, and endorsements from community leaders. These posts were shared widely, increasing her reach and influence.

- **Targeted Ads**: Digital marketing strategies included targeted ads on social media and search engines to reach specific demographics and geographic areas. These ads were tailored to address the concerns and interests of different voter segments.

Example: The campaign ran targeted Facebook ads highlighting Sarah's commitment to improving local schools, which were shown to parents and educators in the district. Similarly, ads focusing on job creation and economic development were targeted at business owners and job seekers.

4. Persuasive Campaign Materials

- **Campaign Literature**: High-quality brochures, flyers, and posters were designed to clearly communicate Sarah's platform and vision. These materials were distributed at events, through mail, and by volunteers during canvassing.

Example: The campaign's brochures featured professional photography, compelling testimonials, and a detailed outline of Sarah's policy proposals. These materials were designed to be visually appealing and easy to read, ensuring that key messages were effectively communicated.

- **Yard Signs and Billboards**: Yard signs and billboards were strategically placed throughout the city to increase name recognition and visibility. Supporters were encouraged to display yard signs on their properties, creating a sense of widespread community backing.

Example: Brightly colored yard signs with Sarah's name and campaign slogan appeared on lawns across the district, while larger billboards in high-traffic areas reinforced her presence and message.

5. Securing Endorsements

- **Influential Figures**: The campaign sought endorsements from influential community leaders, local businesses, and respected organizations. These endorsements were highlighted in campaign materials and media appearances to build credibility and trust.

Example: Sarah secured endorsements from a popular local pastor, a respected business owner, and a prominent community activist. These endorsements were featured in press releases, campaign literature, and social media posts, lending authority to her candidacy.

6. Cohesive Messaging

- **Unified Message**: The campaign maintained a strong, cohesive message that resonated with voters. Sarah's platform focused on key issues such as education, community safety, economic development, and healthcare. All campaign materials, speeches, and events consistently reinforced these themes.

Example: Every speech, flyer, and social media post emphasized Sarah's commitment to "Building a Better Community Together." This consistent messaging helped voters understand her priorities and vision, making her campaign more memorable and effective.

Outcome:

Sarah's well-organized and strategically executed campaign, supported by the cult's resources and network, resulted in a strong presence in the election. Her grassroots efforts, combined with effective use of digital marketing and high-quality campaign materials, helped her connect with voters and build a broad base of support.

Conclusion:

Running a successful campaign for political office requires a comprehensive strategy that leverages available resources, mobilizes grassroots support, and maintains a cohesive message. By following the example of Sarah's campaign for city council, you can effectively prepare and support your members to achieve political success, thereby increasing your cult's influence and advancing its agenda within the political landscape.

Achieving Political Goals

Enacting Change

Once a member of your cult is in office, it is essential to use that position to enact laws and policies that benefit the cult. These changes should be incremental and framed in a way that appeals to the broader community, ensuring they are seen as beneficial for the public good to avoid suspicion.

Example: Sarah's Strategic Policy Implementation

Step-by-Step Strategy:

1. Identifying Beneficial Policies

- **Community Needs Assessment**: Conduct a thorough assessment of community needs to identify areas where proposed policies can align with both the cult's goals and public interests. This dual alignment ensures that policies are seen as beneficial by the wider community.

Example: Sarah conducted a survey to understand the community's needs, identifying key areas such as community services, housing, and local economic development. This assessment helped her prioritize policies that would both benefit the cult and address public concerns.

2. Incremental Changes

- **Small but Significant Changes**: Start with small, incremental changes that can make a noticeable impact without drawing too much attention. These changes should lay the groundwork for more substantial policies in the future.

Example: Sarah proposed modest increases in funding for community centers, which were managed by the cult. She presented these changes as a way to enhance local services and support community activities, which garnered broad support.

3. Framing for Public Appeal

- **Broader Community Benefits**: Frame all proposed changes as beneficial for the wider community. Highlight how these policies address public concerns and improve overall community welfare.

Example: Sarah framed the increased funding for community centers as a means to provide safe spaces for youth, support local artists, and offer educational programs. This framing appealed to various community groups and stakeholders.

4. Policy Proposals and Advocacy

- **Formal Proposals**: Develop detailed policy proposals that outline the benefits and logistics of the proposed changes. Ensure these proposals are backed by data and case studies that demonstrate their effectiveness.

Example: Sarah's team developed comprehensive proposals for each policy change, including data on expected outcomes, budgetary implications, and examples from other communities where similar policies had succeeded.

- **Building Support**: Advocate for the proposed changes by building coalitions with other council members, community leaders, and interest groups. Use these alliances to strengthen support for the policies.

Example: Sarah built a coalition with local non-profits, educational institutions, and business leaders to support her policy proposals. This coalition provided a united front that made it easier to gain approval from the city council.

5. Zoning and Property Benefits

- **Targeted Zoning Changes**: Advocate for zoning changes that benefit the cult's properties. Ensure these changes are justified with broader community benefits such as increased green spaces, improved infrastructure, or economic development.

Example: Sarah proposed zoning changes that allowed for the development of new community gardens and parks. These changes benefited the cult's properties by increasing their value and utility while being presented as enhancements to public spaces.

6. Transparency and Public Engagement

- **Public Forums**: Hold public forums and town hall meetings to discuss proposed changes and gather community input. This engagement fosters transparency and builds trust among constituents.

Example: Sarah hosted town hall meetings to discuss the benefits of her proposed policies. She listened to community feedback, addressed concerns, and adjusted her proposals accordingly. This approach demonstrated her commitment to public service and transparency.

7. Monitoring and Adjusting Policies

- **Continuous Improvement**: Once policies are implemented, monitor their impact and be prepared to make adjustments based on feedback and changing community needs. This ongoing improvement ensures the policies remain effective and beneficial.

Example: Sarah established a system for regularly reviewing the impact of her policies. She gathered data on community center usage, economic development, and public feedback to assess the effectiveness of the changes and make necessary adjustments.

Outcome:

After winning the election, Sarah successfully implemented several policies that benefited both the cult and the broader community. By starting with small, incremental changes and framing them as public benefits, she avoided suspicion and built broad support. Her strategic approach to zoning changes and funding allocations ensured that the cult's interests were advanced while maintaining a positive public image.

Conclusion:

Enacting change through political office requires a strategic approach that balances the cult's goals with public interests. By starting with incremental changes, framing policies for broader appeal, and building strong coalitions, you can effectively use political power to benefit your cult. The example of Sarah's policy implementation illustrates how careful planning, public engagement, and strategic advocacy can lead to successful and sustainable political influence.

Strategic Lawmaking

Identifying Opportunities

Strategic lawmaking involves identifying areas where new laws or changes to existing laws could significantly benefit your cult. This can include opportunities such as tax exemptions, land use modifications, or educational funding. By carefully selecting these areas and crafting well-supported proposals, you can enact changes that provide substantial advantages to your organization.

Example: Alex's Strategy for Zoning Law Changes

Step-by-Step Strategy:

1. Identifying Beneficial Areas

- **Research and Analysis**: Conduct thorough research to identify areas where new laws or changes to existing laws could benefit the cult. This involves analyzing current regulations, identifying loopholes, and understanding the broader legal and political context.

Example: Alex and his inner circle focused on zoning laws and discovered a loophole that allowed for reclassification of certain land areas for religious use. This reclassification would enable the cult to build a large community center, which could serve multiple purposes, including gatherings, educational programs, and outreach activities.

2. Drafting the Proposal

- **Detailed Proposal Development**: Develop a detailed proposal that outlines the specific changes being requested, the rationale behind these changes, and the expected benefits. The proposal should be comprehensive, clear, and backed by solid evidence.

Example: Alex's team drafted a proposal to reclassify a specific land area for religious use. The proposal included detailed maps, current zoning regulations, and the specific changes being requested. It also provided a clear rationale, explaining how the community center would benefit the wider community by offering educational programs, health services, and recreational facilities.

3. Conducting Research and Gathering Data

- **Supporting Evidence**: Gather data and conduct research to support the proposal. This can include case studies, statistical data, expert opinions, and community surveys. The goal is to build a strong, evidence-based case that demonstrates the benefits of the proposed changes.

Example: Alex's team conducted surveys in the local community to gather support for the community center. They collected data showing a high demand for the proposed services and lack of similar facilities in the area. They also researched similar successful projects in other regions to provide comparative examples.

4. Building a Coalition

- **Alliance Building**: Form alliances with other organizations, community groups, and influential individuals who can support the proposal. Building a broad coalition increases the likelihood of gaining approval and demonstrates widespread community support.

Example: Sarah reached out to local non-profits, educational institutions, and community leaders to build support for the proposal. She organized meetings to discuss the benefits of the community center and secured endorsements from various stakeholders, creating a united front.

5. Presenting the Proposal

- **Formal Presentation**: Present the proposal to the relevant authorities, such as the city council or zoning board. This presentation should be well-organized, persuasive, and professional. Use visuals, data, and testimonials to strengthen the case.

Example: Sarah formally presented the proposal to the city council, using a well-prepared presentation that included slides with maps, data charts, and community testimonials. She emphasized the broad community benefits, such as increased access to educational programs and health services, and how the project aligned with the city's development goals.

6. Advocacy and Lobbying

- **Ongoing Advocacy**: Engage in ongoing advocacy to support the proposal. This can involve lobbying efforts, media campaigns, and public forums to keep the issue in the public eye and maintain pressure on decision-makers.

Example: After the initial presentation, Sarah and her team continued to lobby city council members, organized public forums to discuss the project, and ran a media campaign highlighting the benefits of the community center. They kept the issue in the public eye and built sustained support.

Outcome:

The city council approved the proposal to reclassify the land for religious use, allowing the cult to build the community center. The project received widespread praise for its expected community benefits, and the strategic approach ensured that the proposal was seen as a positive development for the area.

Conclusion:

Strategic lawmaking involves identifying opportunities for legal changes that benefit your cult and crafting well-supported proposals to achieve these changes. By conducting thorough research, building coalitions, and engaging in effective advocacy, you can successfully enact laws and policies that provide substantial advantages to your organization. The example of Alex's strategy for zoning law changes illustrates how a detailed, evidence-based approach can lead to significant legislative success.

Lobbying Efforts

Engaging Lobbyists

Hiring or engaging with lobbyists who can advocate for your interests within the political system is a crucial step in ensuring that your proposed policies and laws gain the necessary support from lawmakers. These professionals understand the intricacies of the legislative process and can effectively communicate your goals to key decision-makers.

Example: Alex's Strategy for Tax-Exempt Status Legislation

Step-by-Step Strategy:

1. Identifying the Need for Lobbyists

- **Recognizing Complex Legislative Goals**: Identify legislative goals that require professional advocacy and have a significant impact on your cult's interests. These goals often involve complex negotiations and require deep political connections.

Example: Alex identified that gaining tax-exempt status for all properties owned by religious organizations would provide substantial financial benefits for the cult. However, he recognized that achieving this goal would require professional lobbying due to the complexity and potential opposition.

2. Hiring Well-Connected Lobbyists

- **Selecting the Right Firm**: Hire a lobbying firm with a strong track record, extensive connections, and a deep understanding of the political landscape. Ensure the firm has experience in advocating for religious or non-profit organizations.

Example: Alex hired a well-connected lobbying firm that had successfully advocated for similar legislative changes in other regions. The firm's reputation and extensive network were critical in building support for the proposed legislation.

3. Defining Goals and Strategies

- **Clear Communication**: Clearly communicate your goals to the lobbyists, ensuring they understand the specific legislative changes you seek and how these changes align with broader community benefits.

Example: Alex and his team held detailed meetings with the lobbying firm, outlining their goal of achieving tax-exempt status for religious properties. They provided data and arguments to support the proposal, emphasizing the community benefits such as increased charitable activities and social services.

4. Building Legislative Support

- **Strategic Meetings**: The lobbyists arranged meetings with key lawmakers who had influence over tax legislation. These meetings were used to present the proposal, discuss its benefits, and address any concerns.

Example: The lobbying firm scheduled private meetings with influential legislators on the finance and taxation committees. During these meetings, they presented detailed briefings on the proposed legislation, supported by data and case studies from other regions.

- **Providing Briefings and Policy Papers**: Draft comprehensive policy papers and briefings that outline the benefits and rationale for the proposed changes. Ensure these documents are clear, persuasive, and backed by evidence.

Example: The lobbyists prepared detailed policy papers that explained the economic and social benefits of granting tax-exempt status to religious properties. These documents were distributed to lawmakers and their staff, providing a solid foundation for discussions.

5. Advocacy and Negotiation

- **Behind-the-Scenes Advocacy**: Engage in behind-the-scenes advocacy to build a coalition of supporters within the legislature. This involves continuous communication, negotiation, and addressing any concerns raised by lawmakers.

Example: The lobbyists worked tirelessly behind the scenes, meeting with legislators, addressing their concerns, and negotiating compromises. They built a coalition of lawmakers who were willing to support the legislation and actively advocated for its passage.

- **Public and Media Campaigns**: Complement lobbying efforts with public and media campaigns to build broader support. Use media appearances, op-eds, and public forums to highlight the benefits of the proposed legislation.

Example: While the lobbyists worked with lawmakers, Alex and his team launched a public campaign to build community support. They organized public forums, wrote op-eds for local newspapers, and appeared on local radio and TV shows to discuss the benefits of the proposed legislation.

6. Monitoring Progress and Adjusting Strategies

- **Ongoing Monitoring**: Continuously monitor the progress of the legislation and adjust strategies as needed. Be prepared to respond to any opposition and adapt your approach to ensure the best chance of success.

Example: The lobbying firm provided regular updates on the progress of the legislation, allowing Alex and his team to adjust their strategies. When opposition arose from certain quarters, they adapted their arguments and increased efforts to win over undecided lawmakers.

Outcome:

The concerted efforts of the lobbying firm, combined with Alex's strategic public campaign, led to the successful passage of the legislation granting tax-exempt status to all properties owned by religious organizations. This legislative victory provided substantial financial benefits to the cult and strengthened its ability to carry out its mission.

Conclusion:

Engaging professional lobbyists is essential for achieving complex legislative goals that require deep political connections and strategic advocacy. By clearly defining your goals, building legislative support, and complementing lobbying efforts with public campaigns, you can successfully influence legislation to benefit your cult. The example of Alex's strategy for tax-exempt status legislation illustrates how professional lobbying, combined with strategic public engagement, can lead to significant legislative successes.

Building Coalitions

Alliances

Forming alliances with other groups or organizations that share similar goals can significantly amplify your voice and increase the likelihood of legislative success. By working together, you can present a united front that is difficult for lawmakers to ignore.

Example: Alex's Coalition for Tax Exemption Law

Step-by-Step Strategy:

1. Identifying Potential Allies

- **Common Goals**: Identify other groups or organizations with goals that align with your own. These could include non-profits, religious organizations, community groups, or advocacy organizations.

Example: Alex identified several non-profit and religious organizations that would benefit from the proposed tax exemption law. These groups had similar goals related to financial relief and increased community services.

2. Reaching Out to Allies

- **Initiating Contact**: Reach out to potential allies to discuss your shared goals and the benefits of forming a coalition. Emphasize how working together can increase the chances of success.

Example: Alex contacted the leaders of the identified organizations, setting up meetings to discuss the proposed tax exemption law. He emphasized how the coalition could pool resources and influence to achieve their common goal.

3. Forming the Coalition

- **Formal Agreement**: Establish a formal agreement among the coalition members that outlines the shared goals, strategies, and responsibilities. Ensure all parties are committed to the cause and willing to contribute.

Example: The coalition members signed a memorandum of understanding (MOU) that outlined their shared commitment to advocating for the tax exemption law. The MOU detailed the roles and responsibilities of each organization in the coalition.

4. Developing a Unified Strategy

- **Coordinated Efforts**: Develop a coordinated strategy that leverages the strengths and resources of each coalition member. This can include joint press conferences, public campaigns, and lobbying efforts.

Example: The coalition developed a comprehensive strategy that included joint press conferences to announce their unified stance, a series of op-eds in local newspapers, and coordinated lobbying efforts. They also planned a series of public forums to educate the community about the benefits of the proposed law.

5. Joint Press Conferences and Public Campaigns

- **Public Visibility**: Organize joint press conferences and public events to increase visibility and demonstrate unity. Use these opportunities to communicate the coalition's message and build public support.

Example: The coalition held a high-profile press conference, attended by leaders from each organization. They presented a united front, emphasizing the broad benefits of the tax exemption law. The event received significant media coverage, boosting their visibility and support.

6. Mobilizing Members

- **Grassroots Mobilization**: Mobilize the members of each organization within the coalition to take action. This can include contacting their representatives, participating in rallies, and spreading the word through social media.

Example: The coalition created a grassroots mobilization plan, encouraging members to contact their local representatives and express support for the tax exemption law. They provided templates for letters and phone calls, making it easy for members to get involved. Social media campaigns further amplified their message.

7. Collaborative Lobbying Efforts

- **Unified Advocacy**: Conduct joint lobbying efforts to advocate for the proposed legislation. Present a united front in meetings with lawmakers, highlighting the broad support for the law and its community benefits.

Example: Representatives from the coalition met with lawmakers, presenting a united front and a well-coordinated case for the tax exemption law. They used data, testimonials, and case studies to support their arguments, making a compelling case for the legislation.

Outcome:

The coalition's unified efforts significantly increased the pressure on lawmakers to pass the tax exemption law. The broad support and coordinated advocacy made it difficult for lawmakers to ignore their demands. The law was eventually passed, providing significant financial relief to the coalition members and benefiting their communities.

Conclusion:

Building coalitions with other groups or organizations that share similar goals is a powerful strategy for achieving legislative success. By working together, you can amplify your voice, leverage combined resources, and present a united front that is difficult for lawmakers to ignore. The example of Alex's coalition for the tax exemption law illustrates how coordinated efforts, public campaigns, and joint lobbying can lead to significant legislative victories.

Manipulate Politicians

Building Relationships

Building strong relationships with politicians is the first step in manipulating them to support your cult's agenda. By volunteering for campaigns, attending events, and making donations, you can gain the trust and favor of political candidates.

Example: Alex's Strategic Volunteerism

- **Volunteering for Campaigns**: Members of Alex's inner circle, including Sarah, volunteered for local political campaigns. They attended events, helped organize rallies, and engaged with the community, making themselves valuable assets to the campaign.

Example: Sarah became a regular volunteer for a city council candidate's campaign. She organized phone banks, canvassed neighborhoods, and attended every campaign event. Her dedication and hard work earned her the candidate's trust and appreciation.

- **Making Donations**: Cult members made strategic donations to the candidate's campaign, showing financial support and increasing their influence within the campaign team.

Example: Alex ensured that his followers made significant financial contributions to the candidate's campaign, which helped fund crucial advertising and outreach efforts. These donations were acknowledged publicly, further solidifying the relationship.

Offering Support

Once a relationship is established, offering tangible support such as organizing fundraising events can secure a politician's loyalty and ensure they are more likely to endorse your proposals once in office.

Example: Alex's High-Profile Fundraising Event

- **Organizing Fundraising Events**: Alex organized a high-profile fundraising event for a sympathetic city council candidate. This event was designed to attract influential guests and showcase the candidate's alignment with community values.

Example: The event was held at an upscale venue and featured prominent speakers who endorsed the candidate. Alex and his inner circle invited community leaders, local business owners, and potential donors, ensuring a successful turnout.

- **Securing Financial Contributions**: Cult members made significant contributions at the event, demonstrating their financial power and commitment to the candidate's success.

Example: At the fundraising event, cult members collectively donated a substantial amount, which was publicly acknowledged by the candidate. This financial support secured the candidate's loyalty and ensured they would be receptive to future proposals from Alex.

Leveraging Influence

With the candidate in office, leverage your influence to propose and advocate for policies that benefit your cult. Frame these initiatives as beneficial for the wider community to gain broader support.

Example: Proposing a Community Initiative

- **Developing the Proposal**: Alex and his team developed a detailed proposal for a community initiative that included tax exemptions for religious organizations. The proposal highlighted the broader community benefits, such as increased funding for community services and enhanced support for local charities.

Example: The proposal emphasized how tax exemptions for religious organizations would allow these entities to reinvest in community programs, benefiting the broader public. Data and case studies from other cities were included to support the proposal's efficacy.

- **Gaining Endorsement**: Leveraging the relationship built during the campaign, Alex presented the proposal to the elected city council member. The member, remembering the support received from Alex and his followers, endorsed the initiative.

Example: Sarah and other cult members met with the city council member, presenting the well-researched proposal. They used their established trust and the goodwill earned from the campaign support to persuade the council member to champion the initiative.

- **Public Advocacy**: The city council member publicly endorsed the initiative, framing it as a significant benefit for the community. This public support helped build momentum and gain additional backing from other council members and the community.

Example: The council member held a press conference to announce their support for the community initiative, highlighting the benefits of tax exemptions for religious organizations. The announcement was covered by local media, creating positive publicity and garnering additional support.

Outcome

The strategic manipulation of politicians through building relationships, offering support, and leveraging influence resulted in the successful passage of the community initiative. The tax exemptions provided significant financial benefits to Alex's cult while being framed as advantageous to the wider community.

Conclusion

Manipulating politicians to support your cult's agenda requires a strategic approach that involves building strong relationships, offering substantial support, and effectively leveraging influence. By volunteering for campaigns, organizing high-profile fundraising events, and proposing well-researched community initiatives, you can secure the loyalty and endorsement of elected officials. The example of Alex's efforts illustrates how these strategies can lead to significant legislative successes that benefit your organization.

Become a Politician

Training and Preparation

Sarah's journey to becoming a politician started with extensive training and preparation. Recognizing her potential, Alex provided her with the tools and knowledge needed to excel in the political arena.

Public Speaking and Policy Understanding

- **Public Speaking Training**: Sarah attended workshops and practice sessions to hone her public speaking skills. These sessions focused on articulation, pacing, audience engagement, and handling difficult questions. Through regular mock debates and one-on-one coaching, Sarah became a confident and persuasive speaker.

Example: Sarah regularly participated in mock debates organized by Alex, where she practiced delivering speeches and answering questions under pressure. She received personalized feedback from experienced public speakers within the cult, which helped her improve her delivery and confidence.

- **Policy Understanding**: To prepare for her political career, Sarah studied a wide range of policy issues. She attended seminars and workshops led by policy experts and read extensively on topics such as education, healthcare, and community development.

Example: Alex provided Sarah with a curated selection of policy papers, books, and articles. She also attended policy seminars, where she learned about the legislative process and the complexities of governance. This deep understanding of policy issues equipped Sarah to speak knowledgeably on a variety of topics.

Running for Office

With the cult's backing, Sarah launched a well-organized campaign for city council. The cult's resources and network were crucial in building a strong grassroots campaign.

Campaign Strategy

- **Leveraging the Cult's Network**: Cult members volunteered for Sarah's campaign, canvassing neighborhoods, organizing events, and using social media to build support. Their efforts created a strong, visible presence in the community.

Example: Teams of cult members went door-to-door, distributing flyers and talking to residents about Sarah's platform. They also organized community events where Sarah could interact directly with voters, building personal connections and trust.

- **Creating Persuasive Campaign Materials**: The campaign developed high-quality brochures, posters, and digital content to communicate Sarah's message effectively. These materials highlighted her commitment to community improvement and her detailed policy proposals.

Example: The campaign's brochures featured professional photography and compelling testimonials from community leaders. Social media posts were strategically timed and targeted to reach a wide audience, increasing Sarah's visibility and appeal.

- **Fundraising and Endorsements**: The campaign organized fundraising events to secure financial support. Influential figures and organizations were approached for endorsements, which added credibility and broadened her support base.

Example: A high-profile fundraising dinner was held, attracting local business leaders and community influencers. These events not only raised funds but also generated positive media coverage and endorsements.

Achieving Political Goals

After winning the election, Sarah focused on implementing policies that benefited the cult while framing them as advantageous to the wider community.

Policy Proposals and Implementation

- **Increased Funding for Community Centers**: Sarah proposed increased funding for community centers, many of which were run by the cult. She presented this policy as a way to enhance community services and support local residents.

Example: Sarah highlighted the need for safe spaces for youth and programs for senior citizens, which resonated with the community. The proposal was approved, resulting in increased funding for the cult-managed community centers.

- **Favorable Zoning Changes**: Sarah advocated for zoning changes that benefited the cult's properties. These changes were presented as necessary for community development and improved public amenities.

Example: Sarah proposed reclassifying certain areas for community and recreational use, which included the cult's properties. She argued that these changes would lead to the creation of parks and public spaces, gaining support from other council members and the public.

Maintaining Support and Influence

- **Community Engagement**: Sarah remained actively engaged with the community, holding regular town hall meetings and forums to discuss ongoing projects and gather feedback. This engagement helped maintain public support and trust.

Example: Sarah organized monthly town hall meetings where residents could voice their concerns and suggestions. These meetings fostered a sense of transparency and accountability, reinforcing her connection with the community.

- **Building Alliances**: Sarah continued to build alliances with other council members and community leaders, ensuring she had the support needed to pass future initiatives.

Example: By collaborating on joint projects and supporting others' proposals, Sarah strengthened her political alliances. These relationships were crucial for her continued influence in the council.

Conclusion

Becoming a politician involves rigorous training, a well-organized campaign, and strategic policy implementation. Sarah's journey from preparation to political office illustrates how leveraging resources, building strong support networks, and maintaining community engagement can lead to significant political success. Through careful planning and execution, Sarah was able to achieve her political goals while benefiting the cult and the broader community.

Create Laws That Benefit Your Cult

Strategic Lawmaking

To create laws that benefit your cult, it is essential to identify opportunities within existing legal frameworks that can be leveraged to your advantage. This involves meticulous research and drafting well-structured proposals.

Example: Zoning Law Reclassification

- **Identifying Loopholes**: Alex and his inner circle conducted thorough research to identify loopholes in local zoning laws. They found that certain land areas could be reclassified for religious use, which would allow the cult to expand its properties and activities.

Example: The team discovered that certain underutilized plots of land were eligible for reclassification under specific conditions. By meeting these conditions, they could argue for the land to be designated for community and religious purposes.

- **Drafting Proposals**: The inner circle drafted detailed proposals for reclassifying these areas. The proposals outlined the benefits of the reclassification, including community development, increased green spaces, and enhanced public amenities.

Example: The proposal included detailed maps, current zoning regulations, and the specific changes requested. It also highlighted how the reclassification would benefit the broader community by providing new recreational areas and community centers.

- **Championing the Cause**: Sarah, equipped with the proposal and a deep understanding of the legal nuances, championed the reclassification in the city council. She presented the proposal, emphasizing its alignment with community needs and development goals.

Example: In her presentation, Sarah highlighted the positive impact on local infrastructure, potential job creation, and the overall enhancement of community services. Her persuasive arguments and detailed planning helped gain initial approval for the proposal.

Lobbying Efforts

Engaging professional lobbyists can significantly increase the chances of legislative success. Lobbyists understand the legislative process and can effectively advocate for your interests.

Example: Tax-Exempt Status Legislation

- **Hiring a Lobbying Firm**: Alex hired a well-connected lobbying firm with a track record of successful advocacy for non-profits and religious organizations. The firm was tasked with pushing for legislation that would grant tax-exempt status to properties owned by religious organizations.

Example: The lobbying firm's expertise and connections allowed them to strategically navigate the legislative process, building support among key lawmakers and stakeholders.

- **Strategic Advocacy**: The lobbyists worked behind the scenes to build support for the legislation. They arranged meetings with influential lawmakers, provided briefings, and drafted policy papers to persuade legislators of the benefits.

Example: The firm organized private meetings with members of the finance and taxation committees, presenting compelling data and case studies from other regions where similar laws had been successfully implemented.

- **Continuous Engagement**: The lobbying firm maintained continuous engagement with lawmakers, addressing concerns and negotiating compromises to ensure the legislation's passage.

Example: When opposition arose, the lobbyists adapted their strategies, addressing specific concerns and modifying the proposal to gain broader support. They also organized public campaigns to highlight the law's benefits, further building momentum.

Building Coalitions

Forming alliances with other organizations that share similar goals can amplify your influence and make your proposals more compelling to lawmakers.

Example: Coalition for Tax Exemption Law

- **Identifying Allies**: Alex reached out to other non-profit and religious organizations that would benefit from the proposed tax exemption law. By aligning their interests, he created a powerful coalition.

Example: Organizations involved included local charities, religious institutions, and community service groups. These organizations all stood to gain from the proposed tax exemptions and were willing to collaborate.

- **Forming Alliances**: The coalition members signed a memorandum of understanding, agreeing to work together to advocate for the legislation. They coordinated their efforts to present a united front.

Example: The coalition organized joint press conferences, where leaders from each organization spoke about the benefits of the tax exemption law. This demonstrated broad support and made it harder for lawmakers to ignore their collective voice.

- **Joint Advocacy**: The coalition conducted joint lobbying efforts, held public forums, and ran media campaigns to build public and legislative support for the tax exemption law.

Example: The coalition's joint efforts included writing op-eds, organizing community rallies, and encouraging members to contact their representatives. These coordinated actions created a strong, unified push for the legislation.

Outcome

Through strategic lawmaking, lobbying efforts, and coalition building, Alex and his inner circle were able to pass laws that significantly benefited the cult. The zoning reclassification allowed for the expansion of cult properties, and the tax exemption law provided substantial financial relief, enabling further growth and community outreach.

Conclusion

Creating laws that benefit your cult involves a multifaceted approach, including identifying legal opportunities, engaging professional lobbyists, and building strong coalitions. By leveraging these strategies, you can successfully navigate the legislative process and enact changes that provide significant advantages to your organization. The examples of zoning reclassification and tax exemption legislation illustrate how careful planning, strategic advocacy, and collaborative efforts can lead to legislative success.

Acknowledgments

I am deeply grateful to everyone who has supported me in the creation and publication of this book.

To my family, whose unwavering encouragement and belief in my work have been a constant source of inspiration, thank you for standing by me every step of the way.

I extend my heartfelt appreciation to my friends and colleagues who provided valuable insights, feedback, and moral support throughout the writing process. Your contributions have enriched this book beyond measure.

I am indebted to the experts and professionals who generously shared their knowledge and expertise, contributing to the depth and accuracy of the content presented in these pages.

Special thanks to kevin, whose guidance and encouragement have been instrumental in shaping the ideas and structure of this book.

I would also like to express my gratitude to the individuals who assisted with editing, formatting, and designing the book, ensuring its professional presentation.

Lastly, I dedicate this book to my readers. Your interest in exploring and understanding the complexities of relationships motivates me to continue sharing insights and knowledge.

Thank you all for being a part of this incredible journey of self-publishing.

Appendix: Additional Resources

Books

1. **"Cults in Our Midst" by Margaret Thaler Singer**
   A comprehensive exploration of how cults operate, the psychological techniques they use, and the impact on their members. This book provides a foundational understanding of cult dynamics.
2. **"Combating Cult Mind Control" by Steven Hassan**
   Written by a former cult member turned expert, this book offers insights into the methods of mind control used by cults and practical advice for recovery and protection.
3. **"The Psychology of Totalitarianism" by Mattias Desmet**
   This book explores the psychological mechanisms that make individuals susceptible to totalitarian regimes, offering parallels to the dynamics found in cults.
4. **"Bounded Choice: True Believers and Charismatic Cults" by Janja Lalich**
   An analysis of how charismatic leaders create environments that limit followers' choices, fostering deep commitment and control.
5. **"Influence: The Psychology of Persuasion" by Robert B. Cialdini**
   Although not specifically about cults, this book explores the principles of influence and persuasion that are often employed by cult leaders.

Articles and Papers

1. **"Characteristics of a Cult Leader" by Michael Langone**
   An article detailing the common traits and behaviors of cult leaders, helping to identify potential red flags.
2. **"The Role of Charisma in the Development of Social Movements" by Ann Ruth Willner**
   A scholarly paper examining how charismatic leadership influences social movements, with applications to understanding cult dynamics.
3. **"The BITE Model of Authoritarian Control" by Steven Hassan**
   A framework outlining the methods of control used by cults, including Behavior, Information, Thought, and Emotional control.

Websites

1. **Freedom of Mind Resource Center (freedomofmind.com)**
   A website founded by Steven Hassan, offering resources for understanding cults, mind control, and recovery.
2. **International Cultic Studies Association (icsahome.com)**
   A non-profit organization providing information, education, and support for those affected by cultic groups.

3. **Cult Education Institute (culteducation.com)**
   An online resource with extensive information on various cults, their leaders, and the techniques they use to control followers.
4. **Recovering from Religion (recoveringfromreligion.org)**
   A support organization that helps individuals who have left or are considering leaving religious and cultic groups.

Documentaries and Films

1. **"Holy Hell" (2016)**
   A documentary that provides an inside look at a cult, featuring interviews with former members and footage from within the group.
2. **"Going Clear: Scientology and the Prison of Belief" (2015)**
   This documentary examines the Church of Scientology, exploring its practices, beliefs, and the impact on its members.
3. **"Wild Wild Country" (2018)**
   A docuseries that tells the story of the controversial Indian guru Bhagwan Shree Rajneesh (Osho) and his community in Oregon.
4. **"The Vow" (2020)**
   A docuseries that explores the NXIVM cult, focusing on the experiences of former members and the legal actions against its leaders.

Support Organizations

1. **Cult Information and Family Support (CIFS)**
   An organization that provides support and resources for individuals affected by cults and their families.
2. **Families Against Cult Teachings (FACT)**
   A non-profit dedicated to raising awareness about destructive cults and providing support for victims and their families.
3. **Faith to Faithless**
   A UK-based organization that offers support to those leaving high-control religious groups and cults.

Hotlines and Counseling

1. **National Suicide Prevention Lifeline**: 1-800-273-8255
   For immediate support in crisis situations, including those related to cult involvement.
2. **The Samaritans**: 116 123 (UK)
   Provides confidential emotional support to anyone in distress or at risk of suicide.
3. **Ex-Cult Resource Center (excult.org)**
   Offers counseling and support services for individuals recovering from cult involvement.

Conclusion

This appendix provides a range of additional resources for further exploration and support related to cult dynamics, recovery, and prevention. These books, articles, websites, documentaries, support organizations, and hotlines offer valuable information and assistance to anyone seeking to understand or address the impact of cults.

www.ingramcontent.com/pod-product-compliance
Lightning Source LLC
Chambersburg PA
CBHW060557120726
48002CB00010B/2718